Meeting the Needs of Reunited Refugee Families

RESEARCHING MULTILINGUALLY

Series Editors: Prue Holmes, *Durham University, UK*, Richard Fay, *University of Manchester, UK* and Jane Andrews, *University of the West of England, UK*

Consulting Editor: Alison Phipps, *University of Glasgow, UK*

The increasingly diverse character of many societies means that many researchers may now find themselves engaging with multilingual opportunities and complexities as they design, carry out and disseminate their research. This may be the case regardless of whether or not there is an explicit language and multilingual aspect to their research. This book series proposes to address the methodological, practical, ethical and other options and dilemmas that researchers face as they go about their research. How do they design their research methodology to account for multilingual possibilities and practices? How do they manage such linguistic complexities in the research domain? What are the implications for their research outcomes? Research methods training programmes only rarely address these questions and there is, as yet, only a limited literature available. This series proposes to establish a new track of theoretical, methodological, and ethical researcher praxis that researchers can draw upon in research(er) contexts where multiple languages are at play or might be purposefully used. In particular, the series proposes to offer critical and interpretive perspectives on research practices and endeavours in inter- and multi-disciplinary contexts and especially where languages, and the people speaking and using them, are under pressure, pain, and tension.

All books in this series are externally peer-reviewed.

Full details of all the books in this series and of all our other publications can be found on http://www.multilingual-matters.com, or by writing to Multilingual Matters, St Nicholas House, 31–34 High Street, Bristol, BS1 2AW, UK.

RESEARCHING MULTILINGUALLY: 8

Meeting the Needs of Reunited Refugee Families

An Ecological, Multilingual Approach to Language Learning

Sarah Cox

MULTILINGUAL MATTERS
Bristol • Jackson

DOI https://doi.org/10.21832/COX4600
Names: Cox, Sarah, author.
Title: Meeting the Needs of Reunited Refugee Families: An Ecological, Multilingual Approach to Language Learning/Sarah Cox.
Description: Bristol; Jackson: Multilingual Matters, 2023. | Series: Researching Multilingually: 8 | Includes bibliographical references and index. | Summary: "This book explores the gap between policy, practice and academic literature within language learning for refugees and argues that a multilingual approach, which applies translanguaging principles to use mutual language learning as linguistic hospitality, provides a more appropriate starting point than current monolingual provision"— Provided by publisher.
Identifiers: LCCN 2023017423 (print) | LCCN 2023017424 (ebook) | ISBN 9781800414600 (hardback) | ISBN 9781800414594 (paperback) | ISBN 9781800414617 (pdf) | ISBN 9781800414624 (epub)
Subjects: LCSH: Language and languages—Study and teaching. | Intercultural communication. | Multilingualism. | Translanguaging (Linguistics) | Refugees—Education—Scotland. | Refugees—Scotland—Language.
Classification: LCC P53.45 .C69 2023 (print) | LCC P53.45 (ebook) | DDC 418.0071—dc23/eng/20230525
LC record available at https://lccn.loc.gov/2023017423
LC ebook record available at https://lccn.loc.gov/2023017424

Library of Congress Cataloging in Publication Data
A catalog record for this book is available from the Library of Congress.

British Library Cataloguing in Publication Data
A catalogue entry for this book is available from the British Library.

ISBN-13: 978-1-80041-460-0 (hbk)
ISBN-13: 978-1-80041-459-4 (pbk)

Multilingual Matters
UK: St Nicholas House, 31–34 High Street, Bristol, BS1 2AW, UK.
USA: Ingram, Jackson, TN, USA.

Website: https://www.multilingual-matters.com
Twitter: Multi_Ling_Mat
Facebook: https://www.facebook.com/multilingualmatters
Blog: https://www.channelviewpublications.wordpress.com

Copyright © 2024 Sarah Cox.

All rights reserved. No part of this work may be reproduced in any form or by any means without permission in writing from the publisher.

The policy of Multilingual Matters/Channel View Publications is to use papers that are natural, renewable and recyclable products, made from wood grown in sustainable forests. In the manufacturing process of our books, and to further support our policy, preference is given to printers that have FSC and PEFC Chain of Custody certification. The FSC and/or PEFC logos will appear on those books where full certification has been granted to the printer concerned.

Typeset by SAN Publishing Services.

For all the families separated by war, natural disasters and persecution.

For the four strong women I stood with at the bus stop on Eldon Street, in Glasgow in February 2019 and for all the others who have slowly built new lives in Scotland.

For those still apart, in the hope that you will soon be with your families again.

Contents

Figures		xi
Acknowledgements		xiii
Abbreviations		xv
Foreword *Alison Phipps*		xvii
Prologue		xix
Introduction		1
Coming to the Research		2
Structure of the Book		7
Part 1: Contextualising the Research		
1	The Policy Context	13
	Introduction	13
	Global Forced Displacement	13
	The 2015/2016 Global Humanitarian Crisis	15
	UK Policy	16
	Scottish Policies for Refugee Integration and Language Learning	21
	Family Reunion	29
	Conclusions	34
2	Establishing an Ecological, Multilingual Framework	36
	Introduction	36
	Language Ecology	36
	Multilingualism, Monolingualism and Superdiversity	41
	Translanguaging	45
	Power and Identity	51
	Conclusions	54
3	Implementing a Decolonising Approach	55
	Introduction	55
	Lines of Inquiry	55
	Research Design	56

	Participating on Different Terms	57
	Carrying out the Research	64
	Conclusions	68
4	Wales and Germany	69
	Introduction	69
	Wales	69
	Visit to BRC Newport	73
	Germany	82
	Germany's 2015/2016 Response	83
	Language Learning for Refugees in Germany	85
	Conclusions: Shaping the Fieldwork in Scotland	94

Part 2: Beginning to Co-Construct a Multilingual, Ecological Praxis for Refugee Families in Scotland

5	Learning a Language is Hard Work	97
	Introduction	97
	Getting to 'Day One'	99
	Session 1	102
	Deciding the Content of the Learning Sessions	107
	Participant Profiles	108
	Session 2: *Ciao Ciao*	108
	Session 3: Another Dynamic	111
	Session 4: ዕፉን ይፈትኩ (I Like Sweetcorn)	112
	Learning from the Pilot	113
	Conclusions	119
5½	Uncovering Three Ecologies	120
	Introduction	120
	Moving into the Main Study	120
	Three 'Ecologies'	123

Part 3: Towards an 'Ecologising' of Language Learning

6	Ecology 1: Relationships	127
	Introduction	127
	Stopping and Starting, Disrupting, and Establishing	128
	Building Trust, Taking Risks and 'Investment'	130
	Finding Common Ground	137
	Emotional Labour and Ethics of Care	137
	Embedding Mutual Consideration and Wellbeing as Pedagogy	141
	The Place of Ritual and Familiarity	142
	Intergenerational Relationships	143
	Conclusions	148

7	Ecology 2: Place	150
	Introduction	150
	Defining 'Place' within an Ecological Approach	150
	Human Geography, New Scots and Making a New Home	152
	Combining Project and Place	153
	Conclusions	175
8	Ecology 3: Language and 'Languaging'	177
	Introduction	177
	An Ecological Pedagogy: The Significance of Repertoire and Collective Language Ecologies	177
	Creating an Ecological, Translanguaging Space	179
	Incorporating Translanguaging Strategies and Stances	179
	Impact Beyond Pedagogy	189
	Conclusions	200
9	Conclusions and Recommendations	201
	Introduction	201
	Synthesis of Research Findings: Returning to the Lines of Inquiry	201
	Bringing the Ecologies Together: Connecting the Interconnected	210
	Summary of Key Recommendations	212
	Future Research Directions	216
	Concluding Remarks	217
	References	218
	Index	227

Figures

Figure 2.1	'Three Worlds' Lithograph by Maurits Escher	39
Figure 4.1	The German Red Cross, Frankfurt am Main	86
Figure 5.1	Reflections on the pilot study	98
Figure 5.2	All set – the children's literature library on our first day	100
Figure 5.3	Multilingual 'welcome' sign, School of Education entrance	105
Figure 7.1	Photos and maps used to show local places of interest	155
Figure 7.2	Prompt cards for the Spring School workshop	167
Figure 7.3	The Spring School poem	168
Figure 8.1	Multilingual body poster created by the participants	184
Figure 8.2	Prompt cards from the Spring School	196

Acknowledgements

My heartfelt thanks to Professor Alison Phipps and Dr Lavinia Hirsu who supported me throughout my PhD research, which is the foundation of this book, and to the University of Glasgow College of Social Sciences who funded my PhD scholarship. I also wish to thank Professor Prue Holmes for encouraging me to develop my thesis into this book and for her guidance on earlier drafts. To the wonderful team at Multilingual Matters, a great many thanks for supporting me throughout the publishing process, and to the peer reviewers and Dr Richard Fay for taking the time to read my draft manuscript and providing such constructive feedback which helped me shape the final version.

A sincere thank you to all of the sector specialists who took part in the interviews and the Red Cross staff in Glasgow, Newport and Frankfurt who made me so welcome during my visits and enabled this research.

A special thank you to my family. To my husband, Ian, for the many hours he listened patiently to me talk about this project, particularly as a captive audience on long car journeys. And to my children, Oliver and Alfie, for sometimes giving up time with me while they were little so I could write this book.

Above all, thank you Lakmini, Semira, Rushani, Yasmine and Kamila for working with me on this project, for teaching me Tigrinya, Farsi, Tamil and Arabic and for all those things which passed between us, like all good intercultural communication, that are 'beyond – or besides words' (Thurlow, 2016: 503).

Abbreviations

BRC British Red Cross
FRIS Family Reunion Integration Service
GRC German Red Cross
ESOL English for Speakers of Other Languages
EAL English as an Additional Language
CPAR Critical Participatory Action Research
VPRS Vulnerable Persons Resettlement Scheme

Foreword

Alison Phipps

Academic debate about language pedagogy and the process of seeking asylum often takes place at arms-length, and is researched through models, laws, and technicalities. This is understandable in a field dominated by legal applications and geographical trajectories. In recent years, however, the fundamental importance of language pedagogy to the rebuilding of lives, to intimacy, to processes of multilateral integration and to care has been the focus of new language research.

At the forefront of this research is Sarah Cox's bold initiation of a language pedagogy which resolutely engages with the methodological ethics and power relations involved in the language ecologies of refugees. The bringing of languages into view as a site for critical engagement and understanding has been part of the Researching Multilingually series as the role languages play in the ways in which researchers interact with multilingual subjects and as multilingual researchers themselves. That race, gender and class might be added to be both languages as a construct and a category is becoming part of mainstream practice. To this has come the need to decolonise and to be critical of ways in which multilingualism continues with foundational assumptions about language and the normativity of educational approaches.

What much of the mainstream in language education has assumed from peace time norms, developed in Europe and North America, no longer holds as a sustaining approach to language education. Those learning may not have been formed within the context of a single education system, the movement of people across international borders has changed the understanding of where languages dwell and who speakers are. The ecologies of language pedagogy have come more and more into view as diverse and multimodal, and requiring different relational approaches.

Meeting the Needs of Reunited Refugee Families: An Ecological, Multilingual Approach to Language Learning is indeed timely as it begins where relationships, long severed, begin to heal and form again. The experience of long term separation in refugee families is an acute and painful one in the main and the joy at family reunification, and a more secure future under immigration rules, in a new country is considerable. Arrival, joyful as it is, is also disorienting and it takes a while for adjustment. In this period new language learning and requirements to become speakers of new languages also begin. From being someone competent and able to navigate life, a family member can arrive and be dispirited, disoriented, even lost with few words to describe this experience in the language of their country of arrival.

Language pedagogies of orientation, of plenty, not scarcity, of enabling, not of barriers are required at this point in time. Through her detailed research and praxis, developing a relational pedagogy of multilingual ecologies, Cox has demonstrated fresh approaches to mutuality, accompaniment, confidence building and community for newly arrived refugee families.

Her book is a breath of fresh air as well as intellectually astute and meticulously documented. The voices of the newly arrived refugee families and their experiences sing from the pages and the way in which such an approach to pedagogy might be developed and maintained is clearly articulated from page to page.

This book is a pioneering piece of research offering a relational approach to a pedagogy of mutual language learning. It is a joyful and abundant prospect to be invited into this journey.

Prologue

አውቶቡስ *Awtobus*
Visaikalam விசைக்கலம்
حافلة *Hafila*

> there is no such thing as Language, only continual languaging, an activity of human beings in the world
> Becker, 1991: 34

4 February 2019

I am standing at the bus stop on Eldon Street, opposite the School of Education with three women and four children I met for the first time this afternoon. It's early evening and we have just finished our first meeting. The biting cold wind stings my cheeks as I peer into the darkness, using my phone to light up the tiny numbers of the bus timetable. The dim streetlights are obscured by the misty rain which is slowly soaking all eight of us. I check my watch. A bus should be coming soon. I dredge my brain for how to say 'five' in Arabic, Tigrinya or Tamil. It has been a long day. I hold up my fingers and say: 'five minutes … *hamsa*?', seeking confirmation in Arabic. Kamila nods. I look to Semira, *'hamushte'* she tells me quietly in Tigrinya.

I am surrounded by chatter between the mothers and their children in three languages I do not know: Arabic, Tigrinya and Tamil. Three languages I did not know I would need to try to communicate in before today.

It is early February. We stamp our feet up and down in an effort to keep warm. We are in a city which has slowly become my home over the past 14 years. A city you have each known for only a few days (I found this out this afternoon, via the interpreters).

We stand together as a group, trying to communicate in bits and pieces of each other's languages. Each of us bringing with us our own understandings of all the other ways we have existed in language before today, in other places, with other people. Bringing our languages together from the other places we have each called home.

I peer up the hill on Gibson Street towards the library to check if the bus is coming.

Two of the boys run into the road and all four of the women, me included, instinctively reach out and shout in all four of our languages, not knowing each other's words but understanding the look of horror on each other's faces. We pull the boys back onto the pavement and look into each other's eyes, tutting and shaking our heads. This moment marks us as a group of women and as mothers.

'Ah' I say, 'the bus!' I point to the headlights turning the corner down the hill onto Gibson Street and heading towards us. *'Awtobus'* Semira tells me quietly in Tigrinya, and I repeat the word, glad of some commonality between our languages. It gives us something to grasp on to.

Although I do not know it yet, the three elements of what I will begin to understand and name as three 'ecologies' are already present in this simple act of standing at the bus stop together this cold, dark evening:

Relationships
Place
And language.

The five months that follow this evening will simply give them time and space to emerge and distil. We start this journey surrounded by these three elements, and they are present in all that follows.

This is the point at which all of these elements combine; standing in this liminal space between what has gone before and what we will construct together, joining our experiences and our languages together in a liminal ecology. Capturing this place, our relationships and our languages.

This is how our story began. With me not knowing your languages or what would unfold. This work also began with a policy review and a literature review and although those starting points will find their place in this narrative, they do not capture the reality of trying to navigate our way across an unfamiliar city in languages which were new to all of us, or the solidarity of standing together in this place, existing and being together in language.

Not one language or the other but in *all* language.

This book is an exploration of what it really means to start at 'day one'. It is an exploration of the mutuality of integration and language learning as solidarity.

I choose to start here, at this bus stop with you on this cold, dark evening waiting for the bus together.

I choose to start in Tigrinya
in Arabic
in Tamil
and in Farsi.
As much as I can.
The bus pulls up in front of us.

Introduction

In the UK, integration and language learning for refugees are often at the centre of current public and political discourses due to rising migration into Europe, the UK's shifting political climate and the intention of successive UK governments to reduce immigration figures. The increased migration into Europe, which peaked in 2015/2016, is often referred to as the 'refugee crisis', a term which reinforces the negative discourse on immigration and points to refugees as the source of a perceived problem. A more balanced view is given by framing this international humanitarian crisis as a 'reception crisis' (Phipps, 2019a) and instead questioning the way that refugees are received into their host communities.

Scotland's Refugee Integration Strategy recognises that multilingualism and linguistic diversity are important. Academic literature also highlights that there are many benefits to multilingual learning. However, most English for Speakers of Other Languages (ESOL) classes for refugees are delivered monolingually and are grounded in English-only pedagogy which leaves a gap between policy, literature and practice. Research also indicates that women arriving in the UK through family reunion may face additional challenges with language learning.

This book presents findings from a five-month teaching study which explored the development of an ecological and multilingual approach to language learning within the specific context of refugee families who had recently arrived in Glasgow through the British Red Cross Family Reunion Integration Service. The book also includes two introductory case studies in Wales and Germany to allow for comparisons with language learning support for refugees in two contexts beyond Scotland. Combining Critical Participatory Action Research (CPAR), decolonising methodology (Phipps, 2019b; Smith, 1999) and a commitment to researching multilingually (Holmes *et al.*, 2013), the research explores the participants' first tentative weeks in Glasgow and provides unique insights into the nature of the language learning support needed at the point of arrival and shortly afterwards.

The research repositions the role of the participants and their languages by drawing on academic literature on translanguaging (Blackledge & Creese, 2010; García & Li, 2014b) to explore mutual language learning as linguistic hospitality. This approach, which I term an 'ecologising' of language learning, builds on three key findings:

- The significance of decolonising, collaborative learner/teacher *relationships* during the liminal phase of refugee arrival.
- The importance of *place* and orientation.
- An increased understanding of *language and 'languaging'* as part of a multilingual approach which draws on linguistic repertoire, dialogical interaction and the impact of linguistic hospitality.

Taken together, the research findings formed an approach which participants felt 'empowered' them to learn and allowed for deeper exploration of how policy, practice and academic literature intersect within language learning for refugees, a topic which is unlikely to become any less significant in the coming years.

Coming to the Research

I came to this research having worked in English language teaching for over 20 years as a teacher and manager in ESOL contexts in the UK (14 with asylum seekers and refugees in Glasgow) and in contexts where English is a foreign language in Germany, Japan and Cambodia. I have studied, lived, worked, travelled and taught in different languages throughout my career.

Moving to Glasgow in 2006 shifted the purpose of my work beyond recognition. Teaching in Japan, where I spent four years of my twenties, was fun and rewarding. The people I taught in private language schools and companies could afford their English lessons. For some of my students, English was a hobby, for others it helped them with work, to communicate with colleagues overseas or give presentations at international conferences. Teaching refugees, asylum seekers and settled communities in Glasgow is different because it is language learning as necessity. Here ESOL learners need to learn English to survive, to buy food, to be able to earn a living, to communicate with their children's school, to build new lives, and to be able to prove a willingness and ability to 'integrate'. In simple terms, the stakes are higher.

Glasgow became my home in a way I could not have imagined and did not expect. My ESOL work connected me directly to the political context and, from working closely with ESOL learners and support organisations, I began to understand the complexities of refugee integration and language learning more deeply. I returned to the UK after a decade away and found myself in the cold Glaswegian rain, standing shoulder to shoulder with my third sector colleagues time and time again to protest the impact of the hostile environment – on the steps to the concert hall, in George Square, on Buchanan Street. My work became far more than language teaching. The cruel dawn raids when people were taken from their homes by Home Office officials and returned to their countries to exactly the circumstances they had tried to escape; their lives at risk, the constant housing issues, the Park Inn shooting during the first Covid lockdown in 2020, the Nationality and Borders Bill, Kenmure Street. In Glasgow, like other cities across the UK, the list of reasons to protest goes on and on.

I stood in the rain and felt my own cultural identity shift with each protest as the gap between the UK Government's hostile approach to immigration and Scotland's commitment to welcoming refugees became ever clearer. These matters are played out and visible in ESOL classrooms across the UK because they impact people's lives. My learners told me and my colleagues they could not afford food, or bus fares so they walked miles to their English classes. They told me they were afraid they would be sent back and that they did not feel safe. Sometimes learners did not return for their classes and no-one knew what had happened to them. Their classmates worried and tried to contact them but there was no answer. The hostile environment forces people to live in fear.

Glasgow changed the purpose of my teaching and as a result it changed me. It is impossible to do this work for as long as I have and not to want to fight for better rights for refugees and people seeking asylum. This book is born out of my desire to support this cause in the field I know best, through language, welcome and intercultural encounter.

From living interculturally (*Ichi-go ichi-e* 一期一会)...

My work with refugees in Scotland was foregrounded by my own first-hand experiences in other countries of intercultural and linguistic welcome and *unwelcome*. These experiences shaped my understanding of the profound impact of how we welcome others, and of the hospitality and hostility present within the UK and Scottish approaches to refugee integration that I explore in this book.

May 2002
I am 25 years old – a young white woman on a red bicycle cycling into a pharmaceutical company in rural Japan, built on reclaimed land by the ocean. I have just started a new job as an English language and intercultural communication trainer. I am the only white woman on a site with more than 2000 staff. I am stared at every day on my cycle from the train station. Sometimes people shout 'gaijin' (foreigner) at me. I have been living in Japan for two years now and I am used to being shouted at in the street but it is still uncomfortable.

During my first week, one of my Japanese colleagues, a senior scientist, takes the time to welcome me with a tea ceremony. He invites my two Canadian colleagues and the four of us sit closely around a small square table. Our Japanese colleague has boiled the kettle and prepared the matcha powder which he whisks into the hot water in the beautiful tea bowl for us to share. As he prepares the tea, he teaches me about the

Japanese concept of 'Ichi-go Ichi-e' *(one moment, one lifetime) and tells me how each moment in our lives is unique and cannot be repeated – we may all meet again tomorrow but we will never have the same moment again and we must savour it.*

His words and this moment will stay with me and I will be reminded of them many times. I will be reminded of them at a bus stop in Glasgow almost 20 years later as my own actions, I hope, contribute to my PhD participants' first experiences of welcome in Scotland, as newly arrived refugee women. The memory will float back to me on the icy cold Glaswegian air and remind me of the importance of these multilingual, intercultural encounters and the power they have.

He whisks the tea into a bright green froth and teaches us to acknowledge the moment together. We sit quietly and pass the bowl to each other, take a slow breath in, appreciate the bowl in front of us and savour the taste of the tea. I sip from one side, turn the bowl, lower my head in silent respect and pass the bowl to my colleague. This moment of my colleague's efforts to welcome me will remain a vivid memory for me.

Twenty years later, the same Japanese colleague contacts me out of the blue via Facebook. We have had no contact during the intervening years. I tell him I still remember the tea ceremony he welcomed me with and how he taught me about *Ichi-go Ichi-e*. He tells me remembers it well.

He is just one of the people who made me welcome in just one of the places I have lived and travelled. Now I look back and perhaps the three ecologies were there with me then too: the relationships between my colleagues and me; the place of Nagoya, my home for four years; and the languages, Japanese and English, a simpler duality than my current multilingual context. I associate such small actions with welcome and with cultural and linguistic hospitality. I believe that integration and welcome take place in such small ways. Between individuals, at local level, through such simple acts as sharing tea together.

All of my life led to the starting point for this research. This book is a deeply personal account, written in the first person and drawing on my autoethnographic fieldnotes and reflections throughout, because integration and language learning *are* personal. They are about people, their connections with each other, with place and with language.

June 2002

A few weeks after the tea ceremony I finish teaching my last class at 8pm and get ready to leave. Friday night. I unchain my red bicycle from the bicycle rack and step my foot onto the pedal. A colleague calls out to me – 'be careful Sarah-sensei, the typhoon is coming'. It's a warm night and I feel the first large, heavy drops of rain as the bicycle chain clicks into life and I begin to ride away. It's dark, the flickering light on my front wheel lights my path as I cycle out of the front gate. The gatekeeper bows 'otsukaresama deshita' *(thank you for your hard work) he calls to me*, 'otsukare' *I nod and call back in response. I am quickly out of the gate on a quiet side road. A few more heavy drops of rain fall on my face. 15-minute cycle to the train station. I'm tired and I want to be home. I can make it, I think.*

I am wrong. Spectacularly so, as I am about to find out.

I ride on, the wind picks up and the rain falls heavier. I am halfway now, too far to go back and too far to make it to the station safely. Suddenly the rain becomes torrential. I try to cross the road, a huge gust of wind hits me so hard that it blows me and my bicycle horizontal, I skid across the road to the ground, into the water, grazing both my knees. I look around me. There are no cars. No people. The town is eerily deserted. Everyone else understands about the typhoon. This is my first. The rain is now pouring down so hard that it washes my contact lens from my right eye and I can barely see.

There is nowhere to shelter. I haul my bike across the road. I can't make it to the train station I usually use but there is another one which is closer so I decide to try to reach it. I turn the corner and see the blurred lights of the station. Miraculously, a train arrives. I am so grateful to get on the train. I sit, then quickly realise no one else on the train is wet or dishevelled at all. I am surrounded by immaculately dressed Japanese women and men dressed in smart suits. I am drenched to the skin and water pours from me, creating a pool at my feet. My clothes are sticking to my body, my hair plastered against my face.

Everyone on the train stares. The staring is relentless. They point at me and say loudly 'gaijin' – foreigner. I smile but no-one smiles back. I feel the blood seeping through my trousers from my grazed knees and I sit on the train for 50 minutes to get home while everyone stares at me. There is 'welcome' and there is 'unwelcome'. I feel other. I am other. I am other because of the colour of my skin, my culture and my action of getting on the train like this which marks me as an outsider. I am hurt physically and embarrassed.

February 2003
Months later, I am trying to find the eye hospital. I am lost in a part of the city which I do not know at all. I stop to ask a man for directions. I know enough Japanese to ask for directions and I have a map, but the man sees me and crosses the road to avoid me. A woman comes along the street, 'Sumimasen' (excuse me) I say politely, I signal to the map and ask if she knows where the hospital is. Although I have asked in Japanese, she walks away quickly telling me 'Eigo wakarimasen', 'I don't understand English'. I will be late for my appointment; no-one will help me. I feel alone and frustrated.

I am not a refugee, and I do not claim that my experiences are similar to those of my participants who were forced to leave their homes due to impossible circumstances and endured family separation and trauma in their journeys to the UK. However, my experiences of intercultural and linguistic welcome and unwelcome serve an important function as they underpin my understanding of the impact of such encounters. I have felt cultural and linguistic hospitality and hostility first-hand. In the context of refugee integration, these concepts take on far deeper meaning and are far more significant. I feel a deep sense of responsibility to ensure that these first encounters are positive and welcoming because I have been in a position for the last 14 years where my actions matter in this way, in a similar way to how the actions of my colleagues mattered to me all those years ago when I lived in Japan.

...to researching multilingually

In terms of this research, I intended to provide welcome via 'linguistic hospitality' (Kearney, 2019) by learning the participants' languages and using them in the research as much as possible. The women in this study had just arrived in Glasgow and were very new to learning English. I saw it as my ethical responsibility to the participants to embed a stance of researching multilingually across the entire project as a way to shift the balance of power between us and to enable us to all share ownership of our work. I refer to the participants and me as 'we' throughout the book and to 'our' project and 'our' ways of working to reflect this shared ownership and the intention to co-create this research.

The intention to carry out the research multilingually was essential, and my approach to the study as a whole was predicated on the participants and I drawing on our full multilingual resources to co-produce the research. It was important that their ability to take part in the research was not limited by their English language level.

As Holmes *et al.* (2013) note, increased globalisation means that many researchers find they face multilingual complexities as they design, carry out and disseminate their research. The Researching Multilingually book series aims to address the methodological, practical and ethical considerations that researchers face and are rarely addressed in research methods training courses by establishing a new body of theoretical, methodological and ethical researcher praxis for researchers to draw on. This book intends to contribute to this gap by applying a researching multilingually lens within the specific context of newly arrived refugee women. It intends to shine a light on the research practices we employed by using non-dominant languages, which as Phipps (2013a) notes, can have a powerful impact in the context of seeking asylum when people may be experiencing 'pressure or pain'.

On linguistic repertoire

Since learning my first foreign language (German, from age 11), I have always incorporated words/bits from other languages into my writing. I have written journals from my travels all around the world, in all of the languages I know, in a combination that only I could ever decipher. This seemed natural. I wrote in the languages which surrounded me in each physical place as they were present in my mind at the time of writing. I did not supress them to create a monolingual account. I have always explained how these different parts of each language combine as one 'big' language or 'whole' for me. The concept of 'linguistic repertoire' on which translanguaging is based (explored in full in Chapter 2) makes sense to me from my personal understanding of how my linguistic knowledge interacts in my own mind. I name this my 'linguistic repertoire' now but I have always understood this as one system.

In terms of my own linguistic repertoire, I am a product of the British education system where French and German were privileged in the 1990s in England where I grew up. I studied French to A-level and German to degree level (with an Erasmus year in Frankfurt am Main) before moving to Japan in my early twenties. After Japan, I spent a year travelling through South/Central America, Mexico, Southeast Asia and Russia and briefly volunteered as an English teacher in Cambodia. Some of the languages I have learnt outside the UK (Japanese, Khmer, Russian) have a non-roman script and as a result I have felt my literacy skills stripped away from the point of arrival in the country. I have experienced how it feels to be unable to read or write in the language which surrounds me, and I understand the impact this had on my daily life. These experiences, like the ones I have detailed above, have shaped my understanding of language learning, teaching and intercultural work.

This research began life with ideas sketched out in a glamping pod in Fife after I saw a call for PhD research proposals for a partnership project between the University of Glasgow and the British Red Cross (BRC), the night before the start of a family camping holiday. These ideas were for a project I hoped would allow me to combine my experience in the third sector with my academic interests. I was very fortunate to be successful in my application, and my PhD enabled me to develop a project based on concepts which are dear to me: collaborative working, equality, mutual integration and language learning. My PhD ultimately led to the development of this book and allowed me to further explore multilingualism and intercultural communication, which have been a lifelong interest and focus within both my personal and professional life.

So, my journey towards writing this book began, from an afternoon in a glamping pod in Fife spent rapidly putting together my PhD application, with all of the experiences of teaching languages, learning languages and living interculturally that came with me.

Structure of the Book

This book is structured in three parts. Part 1 maps out the context for the research by introducing the policy, academic theory and methodology which underpin the project. Then I set the scene through an exploration of two brief case studies of language learning for refugees in Wales and Germany which intend to provide some broader context for the research. Part 2 introduces the first stage of the fieldwork in Scotland and explores how the participants and I began to co-construct a multilingual, ecological praxis for this research context. Part 3 frames the presentation and discussion of the research findings through the three ecologies of relationships, place and language/languaging.

Chapter 1 sets the political context for this research by exploring global forced displacement, the 2015/2016 reception crisis, the development of the UK 'hostile environment' and illustrating how UK policy contrasts with the Scottish approach to refugee integration. Here I discuss family reunion, the role of the BRC and the specific needs of women joining their partners in Scotland in this way. I question how the increased migration into Europe has been framed as the 'refugee crisis' and interrogate the way that refugees are received into their host communities.

Chapter 2 intends to show where the project sits in relation to existing scholarship by introducing the academic literature within the four key areas of language ecology, multilingualism, translanguaging, and identity within language learning. These four areas intersect to form the theoretical framework. I highlight the compatibilities between language ecology and a multilingual approach and state the relevance of Glasgow's position as a superdiverse city. I discuss the dominance of English, linguistic hierarchies and the traditional view of language separation for learning and teaching. To complete the chapter, I draw attention to the gaps between policy and practice and the unexplored opportunities for translanguaging which form the basis for the research.

Chapter 3 covers how I carried out the research (the methodological approach, research design, methodology, data analysis and my role within the research). I state the importance of the decolonising, collaborative approach both in terms of the choice of CPAR and the intention to reduce the position of English by 'decolonising multilingualism' (Phipps, 2019b) and drawing parallels with the New Scots Refugee Integration Strategy (Scottish Government, 2018). I also clarify the reasons for the fieldwork in the Red Cross branches in Newport, Wales and Frankfurt, Germany. I state the lines of inquiry and discuss the place of 'messiness' (Law, 2004) and eclecticism as method. This discussion lays the foundation for the broader interdisciplinary base which I return to in Chapters 6, 7 and 8.

Chapter 4 introduces the fieldwork in Wales and Germany which formed the first stage of the CPAR spiral and provides a comparison with language learning for refugees in Scotland. In the first part of the chapter, I discuss the work of the BRC in Newport, draw parallels between Wales and Scotland, and compare barriers to language learning for refugees in these contexts. I then highlight the absence of translanguaging and multilingual approaches for ESOL in Wales.

The second part of Chapter 4 explores the fieldwork in Germany, the findings of which have greater relevance at structural level due to a better model of funding which results in faster access to language classes. I give an overview of the nationally funded integration course with its focus on accuracy and grammar, and I discuss my visit to the GRC language school in Frankfurt am Main. I then highlight the use of monolingual teaching methods and the beliefs which underpin this.

I begin Part 2 by returning the focus to Scotland via **Chapter 5** which introduces the pilot study as the first stage of the fieldwork in Glasgow. I introduce the participants and present the 'everyday' topics which shaped the study as a whole. By detailing each of the first four learning sessions, I give an insight into 'day one' of the research and the challenges of this initial stage.

Chapter 5½ sits as a liminal half chapter framed as a bridge between the pilot and the three 'ecologies' chapters which focus on the findings from the main study. Here I introduce how I began to view the concepts of place, relationships and language as more significant, overarching themes and how I saw these brought into contact to form an 'ecologising' of language learning. By briefly introducing each of these dimensions, I illustrate how they intersect as an introduction for the three more detailed discussion chapters which follow.

Chapter 6 focuses in on the first ecology: relationships. The balance of power in our work, intergenerational relationships and the fragility of our relationships within the early weeks of the project are key themes. I discuss emotional labour and the care and nurture needed at this stage. Exploring trust and how Norton's (2013) *investment* emerged in our work emphasises the significance of our wider pedagogical interactions. I highlight the gendered dimension of our work and conclude by discussing the specific challenges the women faced in coming to Scotland to join their husbands.

I open **Chapter 7** with the concept of place and its agency within the framework of the three ecologies, and I consider how understandings of 'context' and 'environment' differ, drawing on an understanding of place and home within human geography and the sense of belonging in parallel realities. I discuss the importance of situating the learning within the physical ecology of Glasgow, bringing concepts of communitas and liminality into the discussion to illustrate the social structures which are suspended within this liminal phase of creating a new identity in a host community. I discuss the importance of our work outside the classroom as orientation to the physical ecology of superdiverse Glasgow.

I introduce the final ecology, language and 'languaging', in **Chapter 8** and explore translanguaging stances and dispositions by illustrating how the participants and I brought these into our work. The chapter explores both the practical benefits of our multilingual approach and the impact of this beyond pedagogy. I highlight the impact of my participating as learner and facilitating translanguaging in languages I do not know, and the symmetry this brought to our mutual language learning.

Chapter 9 concludes the book by drawing the three ecologies together through the synthesis of the research findings. I summarise the key findings and recommendations before making suggestions for future research directions.

Part 1
Contextualising the Research

1 The Policy Context

Introduction

This first chapter situates UK immigration and refugee integration policy within the context of forced migration across the globe. After briefly establishing the international context for the 2015/2016 reception crisis, I explore the development of the UK 'hostile environment' before discussing Scottish policies for refugee integration and language learning. These comparisons illustrate how Scotland's more welcoming approach to refugee integration contrasts with, and is constrained by, the UK 'hostile environment' policies due to Scotland's status as a devolved UK nation. I then discuss family reunion, clarify the role that the British Red Cross (BRC) plays in supporting reunited refugee families and highlight the unique challenges that face women who come to the UK in this way.

Global Forced Displacement

As I stated in the introduction, immigration and refugee integration are often at the centre of public and political discourses in the UK due to rising migration into Europe and the intention of successive UK governments to reduce net migration figures. In 2015, the number of forcibly displaced people across the world reached 65.3 million, the highest number since World War Two. Nearly 5 million of the people who make up this figure had recently been displaced from Syria due to the ongoing war (Scottish Government, 2018).

This book is written as a counter narrative to those which label this increased migration as a 'refugee crisis'; it aims to problematise what 'integration' really is and how it looks and feels at local level. The book is written from the starting point that this 'crisis' is better understood as a reception crisis and a crisis of hospitality (Phipps, 2019a) rather than a 'refugee crisis' and, as such, new ways of supporting refugees need to be found. This support must include effective ways to help refugees to build new lives in their host communities, of which language learning is a key part.

Although the high number of forcibly displaced people worldwide is widely reported, there is a common misconception that the majority of refugees come to Europe and North America. In reality, most forcibly displaced people are not able to make it to Europe or North America, and instead they seek refuge in neighbouring countries. Often these neighbouring countries are also coping with their own internal crises which result in large numbers of their own population also being displaced. Migration between countries of the Global South accounts for over a third of all international migration and in some places this may be as high as 70% (Migration for Development and Equality, 2022).

If we rely on the UK press as a source of information, it would seem that the vast majority of refugees have the sole aim of reaching the UK (with the most often cited reason for this being the UK welfare system which includes access to financial benefits, the NHS and housing). In reality, the UK is not even in the top ten refugee-receiving countries in the world. With a more efficient and humane asylum system, the UK could comfortably accommodate many more refugees that it currently does. So, if the UK press is not to be believed, where do forcibly displaced people go when they are left with no alternative but to leave their home countries for reasons including war, human rights violations, persecution and climate change?

Turkey has received more refugees than any other country since 2011, 4.3 million in total (Norwegian Refugee Council, 2023). Figures from the Norwegian Refugee Council (2023) illustrate the top 10 countries which have received the highest number of refugees relative to their population. Lebanon, with its population of just 6.8 million, is top of the list and has received refugees relative to 19.8% of its total population (1.5 million from Syria and hundreds of thousands are Palestinian). Jordan is second, having received more than 1 million refugees in the last 10 years (currently 10.4% of the total population), the majority of whom are from neighbouring Syria and some are also from Palestine. Due to its controversial agreement with Australia to receive refugees trying to reach Australia by boat, Nauru comes third and has received refugees relative to 6.8% of its population. Turkey is fourth, having received refugees relative to 5% of its population. Uganda is fifth and has received 1.8 million refugees (3.7 % of the total population) over the past 10 years from DR Congo, South Sudan, Burundi, Somalia, Rwanda and several other countries. Sudan also receives a significant number of refugees (1.2 million since 2012, 2.7 % of the total population) most of whom have fled conflict in neighbouring South Sudan. Sudan is also a transit country for refugees from Eritrea, Ethiopia and Somalia and other countries, for people who are trying to reach Europe (Norwegian Refugee Council, 2023).

In Europe, for many years, Sweden has had the most generous refugee policy and has received refugees relative to 2.6% of its total population. Due to its geographical location, near the coast of North Africa, Malta also has a high percentage of refugees which represent 2.5% of its population, many of whom are from Libya and are trying to make it to mainland Europe.

Mauritania has an open-door policy towards refugees and has received refugees relative to 2.4% of its total population. It is the largest recipient country of refugees from the civil war in neighbouring Mali and has also received refugees from the occupied Western Sahara and other countries, including Syria.

Greece has had a longstanding role as a transit country for refugees. Most of these refugees did not stay in Greece long term before the crisis in 2015/2016. This changed when the EU tightened its refugee policy and demanded that refugees should receive protection in the first European country in which they arrived. As Greece did not have the capacity to provide adequate protection to large numbers of refugees, this resulted in people being placed in overcrowded camps in very poor conditions. As a result, Greece has received refugees relative to 2.2% of its population (Norwegian Refugee Council, 2023).

In addition to these 10 countries, the following countries also received large numbers of refugees during this period:

- Germany – 1,337,000 refugees (1.6% of the total population)
- Ethiopia – 830,000 (0.7%)
- United States – 734,000 (0.2%)
- Bangladesh – 678,000 (0.4%)
- Russia – 456,000 (0.3%)
- Cameroon – 444,000 (1.6%)
- DR Congo – 403,000 (0.4%)

Figures from the Norwegian Refugee Council (2023).

To put immigration in the UK into perspective, by the end of 2018, just prior to the start of this research, there were just 126,720 refugees in the UK and 45,266 asylum claims pending, a figure which represents just 0.26% of the UK's total population (Refugee Action, 2022).

The 2015/2016 Global Humanitarian Crisis

In 2015, the war in Syria entered its fifth year and many more people were forced to leave their homes. Although many Syrians initially settled in neighbouring countries, poor conditions including a lack of employment rights and insufficient schooling for their children prompted many of these people to decide to come to Europe.

In 2015, it also became easier for Syrians to make the journey to Europe. Previously, most people reached Europe by sailing from Libya to Italy and far fewer went from Turkey to Greece, either because this route was less well known or because people were deterred by the idea of having to leave the EU again to reach Western Europe. However, in summer 2015 this changed and large numbers of Syrians began to use the Balkans route as visa restrictions in North Africa and the war in Libya made it more difficult to reach the Libyan coast. People also realised that the Balkans route was a cheaper option (Kingsley, 2015).

In September 2015, Germany announced that it would accept any Syrian asylum application even for those who had previously applied for asylum in another European country. This announcement from Germany increased migration into Europe as people no longer needed to worry about being arrested in Hungary and forced to claim asylum there. At this time, Greece, Macedonia, Serbia and Croatia made it easier for asylum seekers to travel through their countries. In the early summer, people had had to walk most of the way to Central Europe but by September the Balkan countries had all arranged transport for refugees which meant a previously difficult route became more possible (Kingsley, 2015).

As a result, the number of people arriving in Greece rose from 43,000 in 2014 to more than 750,000 in 2015 (Kingsley, 2015). Not all of the people arriving in Europe were Syrian. In Greece many people also arrived from Afghanistan and Iran as they escaped worsening conflicts. In Italy the largest number were people from Eritrea who were fleeing a dictatorship. Afghans were also leaving in large numbers from Iran.

European governments tried to avoid providing protection to the significant numbers of refugees then trying to come to Europe and tried to stop the flow of people by erecting fences in Bulgaria, Greece, Spain and Hungary, but they wrongly assumed that people would not risk their lives at sea (Kingsley, 2015). The reception crisis was exacerbated by the lack of a common European asylum policy and, as a result, asylum seekers headed for the countries where they would be most welcome or where they had existing ties. A lack of formal channels for people to claim asylum resulted in large numbers of people making the journey themselves and effectively forcing Europe's hand (Kingsley, 2015). What could have been a coordinated and hospitable process instead became chaotic due to the lack of an effective European response.

UK Policy

In the UK, immigration is often only talked only about in terms of numbers as part of a dehumanising, anti-refugee narrative. For example, the UK media and politicians frequently report on the number of refugees arriving in small boats across the channel, the number of people who die in this way, the number of people seeking asylum in the UK and net migration figures. The determination of successive UK governments to reduce the number of people seeking asylum in the UK gives the impression that the UK is consistently overwhelmed by refugees. In reality, the UK receives a very low number of refugees compared with other countries, as the figures above show. Instead of finding ways to reduce the number of people arriving and settling in the country, the UK is in desperate need of a kinder and more efficient asylum system with safe routes of passage and faster decision-making processes.

Some of the measures suggested by recent governments to improve the UK immigration system include sending people to Rwanda or deporting anyone who arrives in the UK 'illegally' (when in fact there are no alternative 'legal' routes). The UK is legally bound by international law to receive refugees under the 1951 UN Convention on Refugees (UN General Assembly, 1951) which states that anyone has the right to apply for asylum in any country that has signed the Convention. People also have the right to remain in that country until their claim is assessed by the authorities. The UK signed the Convention in 1951 and is therefore legally bound to receive refugees.

As the statistics above indicate, the UK is under no more pressure from asylum seekers and refugees than other countries. At the time of the reception crisis, of the 28 EU member states, the UK was ninth in terms of numbers of asylum applications. In 2015, the UK received just under 40,000 asylum applications. Germany received over 400,000 (Fullfact.org, 2022). As the UK receives a comparatively low number of asylum applications, it also hosts fewer refugees; less than 1% of the global total (Refugee Council, 2022).

The UK also has the highest refusal rates for asylum claims in Europe. In the UK, two in three claims are unsuccessful compared to Denmark where four in five claims are successful. The Home Office also has a very poor record of making accurate decisions on asylum cases and a large number of initial decisions are later found to be wrong. In 2016, the courts overturned Home Office decisions in 41% of asylum appeals (Care for Calais, 2022). There are also long delays in processing claims and a significant backlog of claims.

The UK media and politicians portray the UK as a country overrun by refugees and express an urgent need to prevent people coming to the UK but these narratives are completely misleading. The UK's current asylum system is not fit for purpose and, in addition to its lack of efficiency, the system is also underpinned by policies which are intentionally hostile towards refugees, creating an impression that refugees are themselves a problem which requires an urgent solution. In reality, there are comparatively low numbers of refugees in the UK and the responsibility lies with the UK Government to create a better, more welcoming asylum system and improve support for refugees as they build new lives.

The hostile environment

As Goodfellow (2019) notes, hostility towards migrants did not start with the hostile environment. The UK has a long history of racist, anti-immigration thinking (see Goodfellow, 2019) which is a product of Britain's colonial history. The hostile environment was not a deviation from the norm, but rather it was well aligned with the UK approach over previous decades. The hostile environment is relevant to this research as it provides the UK political context for immigration which constrains the Scottish approach to welcoming 'New Scots'.

In 2012, in a bid to reduce immigration figures, Theresa May, then Home Secretary, announced plans 'to create here in Britain a really hostile environment for illegal migration' (Elgot, 2018). Although it was initially suggested that the hostile environment policies aimed to target only those in the country 'illegally', the effects have been much farther reaching and deeply felt across the UK. The 'hostile environment' has evolved into a catch-all label for the UK Government's dehumanising approach to immigration which openly promotes hostility and has brought to the surface a deep-seated resentment towards migrants in the UK. Hostility towards refugees is so entrenched in the UK approach to immigration that the Government saw no need to soften the name of these new policies, instead boldly labelling them in exact accordance with their intention. The environment is indeed intended to be hostile. It is hostile by design and clearly named as such.

The negative discourse on immigration and the need to reduce immigration figures has been a key focus for successive UK governments. A leaked transcript revealed in 2013 that May intended to 'deport first and hear appeals later' (Peat, 2018). During his time as Prime Minister (2010–2016), David Cameron reinforced these ideas by publicly stating the UK needed to reduce immigration to 'tens of thousands' (Prince, 2010). This aim has been further reiterated by Priti Patel (Home Secretary at the time of writing) who launched the New Plan for Immigration in March 2021 and the controversial Nationality and Borders Bill which proposes a discriminatory two-tier asylum system to categorise refugees into two distinct groups, with different rights depending on how they arrive in the UK. This two-tier system constructs a false dichotomy between those deemed worthy of protection, the 'legitimate' or 'deserving' migrant, versus those deemed undeserving of protection (Hobbs, 2021). The rights assigned to each group also define whether their family members are granted family reunion, the length of leave given and whether a No Recourse to Public Funds (NRPF) condition is attached. At the time of writing, the Nationality and Borders Bill is being reviewed in the House of Lords and we await the outcome of its progress.

The development of the hostile environment became possible as it was established at a time when immigration dominated the political and media agendas. May began to introduce the policies of the hostile environment in 2012 and these were formalised under the Immigration Acts of 2014 (UK Government, 2014) and 2016 (UK Government, 2016). There are two key strands of the policy; firstly, employers, landlords, schools, universities, banks, doctors and local government employees are forced to act as immigration enforcement officers as they are required to check the documentation of those they believe may be in the country 'illegally', providing an 'everyday bordering' (Yuval-Davis et al., 2019). They can be charged with criminal charges if they do not report anyone unable to prove their right to be in the country. Secondly, the policies remove welfare support and access to NHS and public services, making Britain so profoundly unwelcoming that people choose to leave of their own will (Broomfield, 2017). The Home Office has been strongly criticised for its deportations under the hostile environment policies, as people have been knowingly returned to countries where their lives are at risk.

The policies of the hostile environment have been accompanied by a persistent negative discourse on immigration which has become a prominent feature of the UK media. This negative discourse was used very effectively by politicians in the 2016 EU referendum who stated that by leaving the EU the UK could 'take back control' of its borders and reduce immigration (Vote Leave, 2016), with this being seen as a necessary and desirable outcome. Misleading news reports legitimise this narrative, blaming migrants for a range of the UK's problems from long NHS waiting lists and pressure on public services to unemployment and housing shortages. The positive impact of immigration and the contribution that newcomers make to the UK economy, culture and society is absent from this narrative and the UK continues to be driven in an inward-looking direction, alongside the rise of the political far right, which dehumanises migrants and creates a discourse of othering, of 'us' and 'them'.

A 2017 article in *The London Economic* (Gelblum, 2017) illustrated the extent of this anti-immigration bias by revealing that Theresa May 'suppressed NINE reports proving immigration has little effect on employment or wages'. In fact, the reports, based on academic studies, reflected the benefits of immigration, evidencing that overseas workers had complemented rather than competed with British workers (Gelblum, 2017). The UK Government has sought to further its anti-immigration agenda and over the years this has chipped away at public opinion with many people buying into this narrative. There is no acknowledgement of the positive change that immigration brings and, as a result, the UK's immigration policies have been strongly criticised for being dehumanising, unjust and divisive (Goodfellow, 2019). In addition, this negative discourse on immigration is frequently linked to the debate on multilingualism, which extends the more general anti-immigrant sentiment into debates about language and social cohesion.

The politics of English language and social cohesion

People who have migrated to countries with dominant languages other than their own have two fundamental linguistic rights: (1) to continue speaking and maintaining their home language and (2) to acquire the language of the new country (UN General Assembly, 1948). Despite being protected under human rights legislation, the issue of learning the language of the host society remains a highly politicised issue. As Simpson (2016) notes, learning the dominant societal language of the host community is a *right* rather than an *obligation* but it is often portrayed by politicians and the UK media as the latter as part of a narrative that implies some migrants are reluctant to learn the dominant societal language at all. The crisis of hospitality is mirrored by a crisis of linguistic acceptance and a lack of tolerance of other languages; a discourse which suggests the use of languages other than English should be viewed with suspicion. It suggests that multilingualism poses a threat to national identity and that social cohesion can only be achieved if the UK shares one common language, i.e. English. In reality, the UK has never been a monolingual country and recent years have seen increased support for indigenous minority languages such as Gaelic, Scots and Welsh.

This monolingual/social cohesion bias has been reinforced through recent political discourses. In 2011, David Cameron, then Prime Minister, warned that 'immigrants unable to speak English or unwilling to integrate have created a kind of discomfort and disjointedness that has disrupted communities across Britain' (Watt & Mulholland, 2011). David Cameron also publicly linked Muslim extremism to learning English by stating that more Muslim women should learn English to help tackle extremism and that those who do not should be deported (Hughes, 2016). David Cameron is not alone in his view, the Government-commissioned *Casey Review* (2016) took this narrative even further by publicly claiming there was a need to set a date by which time everyone in the UK 'should speak English' (BBC, 2018).

In July 2019, just weeks before becoming Prime Minister, Boris Johnson stated 'there are too often parts of our country ... where English is not spoken by some people as their first language ... and that needs to be changed' (Halliday & Brooks, 2019). He stated that the most important priority for immigrants should be 'to be and to feel British ... and to learn English', claiming that 'in many parts of England you don't hear English spoken anymore' and 'this is not the kind of community we want to leave to our children and grandchildren' (Halliday & Brooks, 2019).

These views are consistently given media attention in the UK and they are relevant to this research as they place the responsibility of language learning solely with the person who is new to the country and emphasise the need for newcomers to adapt to the host community in terms of culture and language. Not being able to speak English well is seen as deficient and problematic. Viewing integration as a one-way process suggests the need for cultural and linguistic assimilation rather than a two-way process where both parties adapt and accept the other. This view contrasts sharply with the Scottish approach to refugee integration and the local context in which this research is situated.

Although part of the UK, Scotland's integration policies and language learning strategy evidence a more inclusive approach. 62% of Scotland's population voted to remain in the EU in the 2016 referendum and there is a stark contrast between the UK anti-immigrant sentiment and the way that Scotland welcomes 'New Scots'.[1] Scottish support to remain in the EU has grown further since the EU referendum and as Scotland was assured in the run-up to the 2014 Scottish independence referendum that remaining in the UK would mean remaining in the EU, many Scots feel they have been misled. People voted against Scottish independence as they were told that remaining in the UK would secure Scotland's place in the EU as part of the UK. This shift is a crucial factor in the Scottish National Party (SNP)–led campaign for a further Scottish independence referendum on the basis that Scotland could become an independent EU member state in its own right. As immigration is a reserved matter under the control of the UK Government, and the support services for refugee integration are devolved to the Scottish Government, there is tension between UK policy and organisations providing local support. This tension is particularly evident in Glasgow as it has the highest concentration of migrants in Scotland. Glasgow also has well-developed support services which have been recognised for their partnership working (Scottish Government, Convention of Scottish Local Authorities, & Scottish Refugee Council, 2017). This is partly due to Glasgow's role as a dispersal centre for asylum seekers and the need for organisations to respond to the needs of these new arrivals, the significance of which I return to in the following sections.

The difference in attitudes towards immigration and refugee integration between the UK and Scotland is further evidenced by views on the 'refugee crisis'. In September 2016, polling data on Scottish attitudes to the crisis (published by IPSOS Mori) showed that 60% of people believe that Scotland responded well to the crisis, in contrast to just 38% who felt the UK responded well (Scottish Government *et al.*, 2017). 57% agreed with the statement, 'I am confident that most refugees who come to the UK will successfully integrate into their new society' (Scottish Government *et al.*, 2017: 83). This figure was 17% higher than responses for the UK as a whole and the highest among the European countries polled (Scottish Government *et al.*, 2017).

Scottish Policies for Refugee Integration and Language Learning

Scotland has a well-established history of welcoming newcomers. This has become increasingly significant in Glasgow since it became a dispersal centre for newly arrived asylum seekers in 1999 under The Immigration and Asylum Act (UK Government, 1999). Glasgow is currently home to approximately 11% of the UK's total dispersed asylum seeker population

(Migration Scotland, 2019). It has been the only asylum dispersal area in Scotland since 2000 and the large majority of refugees in Scotland have arrived through this system rather than through resettlement programmes (Scottish Government, 2018). Scotland has also welcomed 2500 Syrian refugees in all 32 of its local authorities as part of the Syrian resettlement program and continues to welcome New Scots with a range of support services in terms of education, housing, benefits and employment.

I will focus here on two key policies which inform refugee integration and language learning in Scotland and are central to this research: the 'New Scots Refugee Integration Strategy 2018–2022' (Scottish Government, 2018) and 'Scotland's ESOL Strategy 2015–2020' (Scottish Government & Education Scotland, 2015). The New Scots Strategy takes a holistic approach to refugee integration and identifies key areas for support as: housing and welfare, education, language, health and wellbeing, communities and social connections (Scottish Government, 2018). The New Scots Strategy is also particularly significant as Scotland was the first UK nation with a refugee integration strategy (Wales became a 'Nation of Sanctuary' and introduced a Nation of Sanctuary Plan in 2019, which I return to in detail in Chapter 4).

The first New Scots Strategy was in place from 2014–2017 and put Scotland in a strong position to respond to the increased migration into Europe which coincided with the same time period. The Strategy relies on a model of partnership working, led by the Scottish Government, COSLA and the Scottish Refugee Council and is based on the 'Indicators of Integration' (Ager & Strang, 2004) commissioned by the Home Office in 2002. The Strategy has gained international recognition as a model of good practice and subsequently is looked to as the benchmark for research on refugee integration. Scotland's success with this model of refugee support is recognised in the foreword to the report on the first New Scots Strategy which highlights: 'Scotland is recognised as one of the few refugee receiving countries to make active and sustained investment in addressing the needs for integration amongst refugees and the communities in which they live' (Scottish Government *et al.*, 2017: 6).

Due to the high numbers of migrants in Glasgow, effective collaboration and partnership working has been established in the city and this is seen as a model of good practice to inform work across Scotland (Scottish Government *et al.*, 2017). Glasgow has also benefitted from increased cultural diversity and 'more stable demographics' (Scottish Government *et al.*, 2017: 26).

New Scots is grounded in human rights and acknowledges the positive contribution that refugees make to their host communities as part of mutual, 'two-way integration' from 'day one' (Scottish Government, 2018). The term 'New Scots' was intentionally chosen as part of the initial consultation to move towards official use of inclusive terminology that did not come with the stigma attached to labels such as 'refugee' or 'asylum seeker'.

The Strategy recognises refugee integration as a long-term, multi-directional process which results in positive change in individuals and their host communities. When the New Scots Strategy was refreshed for 2018–2022 following a period of consultation with New Scots and support organisations, a specific focus on language learning was added which recognises that language skills development is not limited solely to improving English (Phipps & Fassetta, 2015; Scottish Government, 2018). In contrast to the UK hostile environment policies, the Strategy emphasises the knowledge and skills refugees bring, the positive contribution they make to Scottish society and the benefits for Scotland of this diversity (Scottish Government, 2018).

The New Scots Approach is based on five key principles:

(1) *Integration From Day One*: if people are able to integrate early, particularly into education and work, they make positive contributions to communities and the economy.
(2) *A Rights-Based Approach*: the Strategy takes a holistic, human rights approach to integration that reflects both the formal international obligations the UK has and the long-standing commitment of successive Scottish Governments to address the needs of refugees and asylum seekers on the basis of principles of decency, humanity and fairness.
(3) *Refugee Involvement*: the importance of actively engaging refugees and asylum seekers. Over 700 refugees and asylum seekers engaged in the consultation process to inform the development of the strategy in 2017.
(4) *Inclusive Communities*: the Strategy supports refugees, asylum seekers to be involved in building stronger, resilient communities.
(5) *Partnership and Collaboration*: the Strategy has been developed collaboratively to coordinate the work of organisations and community groups across Scotland involved in supporting refugees and asylum seekers.

(Scottish Government, 2018: 11–13)

Until 2021, there was no funding directly linked to the implementation of New Scots which meant its success was dependent on existing support services which were funded through a range of funding streams including the Scottish Government Equality budget. Over £2.7 million was allocated from this budget for 2017–2020 to fund projects delivered by third sector organisations providing services for refugees and asylum seekers in their local communities (including employability, ESOL classes, mental health and cultural activities) (Scottish Government, 2018). In terms of language learning, ESOL classes are provided by Further Education colleges, local authorities and voluntary sector organisations. In 2021, the Asylum, Migration and Integration Fund (AMIF) allocated £5 million for projects across Scotland to support refugee integration for a 12-month period until the end of 2022 and this funding is directly linked to the implementation of the New Scots Strategy.

A challenge of the current system is that the short-term, piecemeal funding arrangements make it difficult for longer term planning for these much-needed support services. The current system also places organisations who work in partnership in direct competition for funding, which can add tension to working together. Insufficient funding also makes it difficult for organisations who provide essential services to support New Scots with language learning 'from day one' as the current system is so under-resourced. In the following section I explore the specific language focus added when the New Scots Strategy was refreshed in 2018 and how this forms the policy context for this research.

Language recommendations within New Scots

In contrast to the UK Government, the Scottish Government recognises that integration begins on the day a person arrives in Scotland rather than when a person officially gains refugee status (Marsden & Harris, 2015). The need for faster access to ESOL provision is clear, but the system remains severely under-resourced. New Scots acknowledges both the length of time needed to progress with language learning and also the lack of places to study ESOL due to inadequate funding (Scottish Government, 2018). Despite the welcome addition of AMIF funding for 2021–2022, this support is still short-term, making it difficult to ensure continuity of provision and development of services.

The theme of mutual, two-way integration is reflected in the language focus of the Strategy with the aim that refugees should have opportunities to share their languages and cultures with their host communities in positive ways (Scottish Government, 2018). In contrast to the UK monolingual/social cohesion narrative, New Scots recognises that language skills development goes beyond English and states how effective the principle of sharing languages is for English as an Additional Language (EAL) pupils in schools. These multilingual practices are underpinned by the national 'Learning in 2+ Languages' Strategy which highlights the importance of the ongoing development of the pupil's first language. New Scots recognises that the ongoing development of the home language can also support the acquisition of a second language and that bilingualism and increased linguistic diversity are beneficial for individual academic and cognitive skills (Scottish Government, 2018). There are also wider benefits of multilingualism for Scotland's economy and international reputation (Scottish Government, 2018). The growing diversity of modern languages spoken in Scotland also reflects the country's growing recognition of community and heritage languages as part of Scotland's linguistic landscape (Scottish Government, 2018).

Although EAL provision effectively supports the inclusion of home languages within language learning for children of school age, the situation for adult ESOL learners is different as there is no recognised strategy for how to incorporate learners' own languages within the learning of English. New Scots recognises the importance of promoting and valuing Scotland's linguistic diversity to enable refugees to contribute effectively to society (Scottish Government et al., 2017); however, no specific guidance on how to harness this linguistic diversity in the adult ESOL classroom is given. The peer education project 'Sharing Lives, Sharing Languages' (Hirsu & Bryson, 2017) provides a model for mutual language learning and is recognised as good practice within New Scots but this type of peer-led, multilingual learning has not yet made it into mainstream ESOL provision. Community-led organisations organise a wide variety of events to support refugees to settle into their new communities but these are not closely connected to the way in which ESOL classes themselves are delivered.

Ager and Strang (2004: 21) suggest that successful integration in terms of language learning would be a 'proportion of refugees demonstrating English language fluency at ESOL Level 2 within two years of receiving refugee status'. Although this indicator goes some way to measure progress, it is also important to recognise the 'softer' skills developed through language learning such as confidence, independence, improved social connections and increased participation in community life. These may not necessarily be evident through the results of formal testing, but they are crucial in terms of wellbeing, personal development, mental health and happiness. Much of the current system is focused on 'progression' and it is important to consider the broad range of achievements this can encompass at an individual level rather than focusing solely on progression to work, college or being assessed at a higher ESOL level. Not all progression or 'integration' is measurable in this way, nor is it appropriate or achievable for many learners, particularly those who have had limited opportunities to access education prior to coming to Scotland as they begin their learning journeys from a very different starting point. Third sector organisations, Further Education colleges and Local Authorities providing informal ESOL support in the local community recognise these softer outcomes and provide monitoring and evaluation data for funding bodies which reflect factors such as increased confidence, increased participation in community events, improved independence and less reliance on interpreters during appointments. These providers also support learners to recognise their own progression and achievements with the development of these skills.

The emphasis on employability within the current system is called into question within the recent GLIMER report (Meer et al., 2019: 32) which states concerns about a single goal 'to facilitate language training in order to build capacity and readiness to enter the labour market'. Such an approach measures success of language provision in terms of employability which contradicts the holistic approach to integration laid out in New

Scots. In the following section, I consider recommendations in Scotland's Adult ESOL Strategy and how these relate to the recommendations laid out in New Scots.

Scotland's ESOL Strategy

From 2007 to 2020, the strategic direction for ESOL in Scotland was laid out through two successive adult ESOL strategies (the first launched in 2007, the second in 2015). For the period when this research was carried out, the development and delivery of ESOL provision was informed by the second Strategy 'Welcoming Our Learners: Scotland's ESOL Strategy 2015–2020' (Scottish Government & Education Scotland, 2015). In terms of the policy area, ESOL falls between immigration and education but currently sits under the education brief, which means policy and delivery is devolved from the Westminster Government to the Welsh, Northern Irish and Scottish Governments for the devolved nations (Meer *et al.*, 2019).

The refreshed Strategy sat within the wider objectives of adult learning in Scotland and formed part of the implementation of the Adult Learning in Scotland Statement of Ambition (Scottish Government, 2014) which is built on three core principles that adult learning should be: (a) lifelong (b) life-wide and (c) learner-centred (Scottish Government & Education Scotland, 2015). The vision and principles of the ESOL Strategy also contributed to the National Outcomes and the Curriculum for Excellence which clarified the position of ESOL within the wider policy context for education in Scotland.

The Scottish ESOL Strategy was often referred to as a model of good practice as it provided a clear direction and common purpose for ESOL delivery, drawing together a diverse range of ESOL providers including Further Education colleges, local authorities, third sector organisations and small, community-led organisations. The importance of Scotland's ESOL Strategy has often been emphasised, particularly in contrast to England which still does not have an ESOL Strategy, despite one being in development for several years. Scotland's ESOL Strategy was valued by ESOL practitioners across Scotland, particularly due to the fragmented nature of the field and the patchy, short-term funding I have discussed.

Despite the positive impact of Scotland's two ESOL strategies, in 2019 the Scottish Government decided there would not be a third ESOL Strategy and instead that ESOL would become part of a broader Adult Learning Strategy when the second ESOL Strategy ended in December 2020. This decision was taken by Scottish Government without consultation with ESOL practitioners or ESOL learners. The new Adult Learning Strategy was published in 2022 and it has been met with a mixed response. Many working in ESOL are concerned that losing the ESOL Strategy is a backwards step for Scotland and that some of the specificity of ESOL is now lost as the new Strategy has a broader and more general focus on Adult Learning rather than the specific needs of ESOL learners.

I will focus this section on Scotland's second ESOL Strategy (hereafter 'the ESOL Strategy') as it provided an important part of the policy context for this research and it remains relevant for ESOL learning in Scotland in the absence of a current strategy. I aim to highlight here the importance and relevance of this ESOL Strategy in meeting the language learning needs of the reunited refugee families who are the focus this research.

In keeping with New Scots, Scotland's ESOL Strategy reflected an inclusive, collaborative approach, based on consultation with ESOL learners, taking account of the different needs of learners and detailing clear progression routes into further training, education and employment. The Strategy recognised the skills, talents, knowledge and contribution that migrants make to Scotland and that improving language skills can enable people to reach their full potential to 'contribute and integrate economically and socially' (Scottish Government & Education Scotland, 2015: 5).

The Strategy had the following vision:

> That all Scottish residents for whom English is not a first language have the opportunity to access high quality English language provision so that they can acquire the language skills to enable them to participate in Scottish life: in the workplace, through further study, within the family, the local community, Scottish society and the economy. These language skills are central to giving people a democratic voice and supporting them to contribute to the society in which they live. (Scottish Government & Education Scotland, 2015: 6)

It is important to consider the meaning of the term 'access' in this context, given the under-resourcing of the current system. The situation for ESOL in Scotland compares favourably to England which has experienced drastic funding cuts for ESOL since 2009 (Morrice et al., 2019), whereas the Scottish ESOL budget has remained consistent since 2012. Despite this, funding for ESOL in Scotland remains inadequate and demand for classes far outstrips what is actually available. Further Education colleges provide full time and part time ESOL courses for which there are lengthy waiting lists and learners typically wait a year or more for a place. This problem is exacerbated by fewer opportunities available for ESOL literacies learners and those at lower levels who begin their learning from a different starting point and who may not read or write in their own language. In addition, many learners face barriers with the practicalities of 'accessing' a class including being unable to pay for travel to class, not knowing what is available or how to apply, insufficient classes in their area, low confidence or lack of access to formal education prior to coming to Scotland. There are also specific challenges for women, particularly those arriving through family reunion (which I return to later in this chapter under 'Family Reunion', p. 29).

The ESOL Strategy was based on the five guiding principles of 'inclusion, diversity, progression, achievement and quality' (Education Scotland, 2015). In keeping with the New Scots Strategy, the ESOL Strategy recognised and valued learners' own cultures (Scottish Government & Education Scotland, 2015). The Strategy highlighted that English language skills are fundamental to participating in society and recognised ESOL learning as key to integration and to learners meeting their full potential (Scottish Government & Education Scotland, 2015). It emphasised the importance of collaboration and partnership working in line with New Scots and highlighted the breadth of ESOL provision available, which includes employability-focused ESOL, workplace delivery and support for learners with literacy needs.

The ESOL Strategy also stressed the need for 'the right kind of ESOL' to enable people to access education, improve employability and support them to progress in the workplace (Scottish Government & Education Scotland, 2015). It recognised Scotland as a diverse, complex, multicultural and multilingual nation and noted that Scotland's linguistic landscape includes Gaelic, Scots and community languages and that this diversity brings opportunities for people to learn more about their own and other cultures (Scottish Government & Education Scotland, 2015).

The Strategic Objectives state that ESOL learners should be able to access and recognise learning opportunities throughout their lives, there should be opportunities to co-design their learning experience and ESOL learners should be able to transform their lives through learning choices in personal, work, family and community settings. ESOL learners should also have opportunities to influence policy and be effectively supported in their learning journeys (Scottish Government & Education Scotland, 2015).

The approaches to integration within New Scots and the ESOL Strategy emphasise a multilingual environment and a multilateral approach to language learning (Phipps, 2018) in contrast to the policy context for ESOL in England which is viewed as 'assimilationist' (Han *et al.*, 2010) and monolingual. However, despite the recognition of the importance of linguistic diversity within New Scots and the ESOL Strategy and the growing body of academic literature which highlights the benefits of multilingual learning, most ESOL classes encourage the use of only English in the classroom, based on the premise, now outdated in the literature (which I outline in Chapter 2), that focusing solely on the 'target language' is the best way to learn. In contrast to ESOL, EAL provision for children in schools effectively includes home languages but for adults there is no recognised strategy for incorporating these into ESOL practice to support the development of new language skills. As a result, teachers have little need or motivation for integrating learners' home languages into their teaching and this results in a gap between policy and practice.

The insufficient funding for ESOL in Scotland means demand for classes far outstrips availability, making it difficult for integration from 'day one' to be supported with language learning from 'day one'. In an effort to plug the gap created by the lack of college ESOL places, local authorities and charities provide informal community ESOL classes and educational and social activities which provide a valuable lifeline but these are usually limited to a few hours per week making it difficult for learners to develop the language skills they urgently need to function in their new communities. Women arriving through family reunion, who are the focus of this study, face particular challenges.

Research indicates that asylum seekers and refugees experience distinctive barriers to ESOL education (Refugee Action, 2016; Shuttleworth, 2018). Currently, people who have arrived in Glasgow through family reunion access ESOL classes in the same way as other migrants. In the following sections, I consider how their needs may be different by exploring UK family reunion policy, the support services available and the role of the BRC.

Family Reunion

The term 'family reunion' is used to describe the process of bringing family members across international borders to be reunited. In the context of forced migration, there are many circumstances which can lead to family separation including war, persecution and natural disasters (White & Hendry, 2011). Family separation often happens unintentionally but sometimes families may choose to separate, for example to protect a family member from military recruitment or to send someone into hiding, but it is usually not intended to be permanent (Sample, 2007). As family reunion necessitates crossing international borders it is recognised as being politically sensitive (Staver, 2008) and can require collaboration between countries. Family reunion provides the most accessed safe route for family members to come to the UK and currently one in three refugees arrive in the UK in this way (British Red Cross, 2018).

In 2019, when this research took place, the UK was in political turmoil as it prepared to leave the EU and discussions continued into the eleventh hour to secure an exit deal on key legal matters between the UK and the EU. There was much uncertainty about how family reunion and immigration rules would be affected by the UK's withdrawal from the EU. The UK Government has now drafted The Nationality and Borders Bill and it is clear that it will reduce family reunion rights, leaving families who have been separated by war, violence and persecution facing impossible choices and dangerous journeys in order to be together again. These restrictions to family reunion rights through the proposed two-tier system will predominantly impact women and children, who currently account for 95% of people who receive family reunion visas.

Family reunion before Brexit

The right of the family to be united and protected by society and the state is expressed in both the United Nation's Universal Declaration of Human Rights (UN General Assembly, 1948) and the European Convention of Human Rights (Council of Europe, 1950). Living with family improves personal wellbeing and mental and physical health. It is also important for successful integration and is in the interest of the host country as it increases financially stability and improves practical and emotional support which in turn reduces the need for support from other services (Marsden & Harris, 2015).

Under the UK's immigration rules, people who have been granted refugee status or humanitarian protection can request family reunion from the UK Border Agency. Until January 2021, under EU law, the Dublin III Regulation also allowed separated family members, including unaccompanied children located in EU and EEA states, to reunite (Gower & McGuiness, 2020).

UK immigration rules are intentionally difficult to navigate as part of the 'hostile environment' and the rules for family reunion are similarly restrictive as they apply only for specified immediate family members of those who have already been granted refugee status or humanitarian protection, including those who have been resettled under the Gateway Protection Programme, Mandate Refugee Programme or the Syrian Vulnerable Persons Resettlement Scheme (VPRS) (Home Office, 2020). This narrow definition of 'family' has been strongly criticised as it applies only to pre-flight family members, specifically spouses or civil partners, unmarried or same sex partners or dependent children under the age of 18. BRC research (Marsden & Harris, 2015) highlights the inadequacy of these legal definitions of as they do not encompass the diverse, broad understandings of family in other cultures which may include elderly parents living in the same household in their country of origin. The rules also imply 'family' is a static entity and do not allow for the turbulence and upheaval of war or natural disasters which can change family circumstances, such as creating responsibility for orphaned younger siblings or children becoming separated from their parents (Marsden & Harris, 2015). Different visa rules with significant application fees and more restrictive eligibility criteria apply (including maintenance funds and knowledge of English language) for other relatives, including dependent adult relatives, adopted children, and those classed as 'post-flight' family members (House of Commons Library, 2018). Unaccompanied refugee children cannot sponsor applications from family members to bring them to the UK. The UK Government has stated this is due to concerns that if child refugees were allowed to sponsor applications this could increase risk for children and act as an incentive for parents to send children to the UK alone to seek asylum.

Home Office (2020) policy guidance states that it is also possible for family reunion to be granted 'outside the Immigration Rules' in exceptional circumstances. This may apply to a dependent child over 18, or an unaccompanied child with a close relative in the UK. However, it is also recognised that these applicants would benefit from greater certainty and improved rights 'if their cases were covered by the Immigration Rules themselves rather than policy guidance' (Gower & McGuiness, 2020: 3).

There is no charge for refugee family reunion visas and they are exempt from some of the eligibility criteria that apply to other family visa applications; however, the application process and evidence required to prove family relationships have been strongly criticised for creating 'unacceptable bureaucratic hurdles' (House of Commons Library, 2018). Further barriers have been created by the removal of legal aid for family reunion applications in England since 2013, although this was reinstated for applications involving unaccompanied children in October 2019 (Gower & McGuiness, 2020). This financial support remains in place for family reunion in Scotland.

Once a refugee has successfully gained approval to bring family members to the UK there are fresh challenges to overcome. The current system creates dependency on the refugee sponsor as the joining family members are not granted refugee status in their own right. As all financial benefits are paid to the refugee sponsor, arriving family members are financially dependent on their sponsor which places additional strain on the family unit at the crucial point of learning to live together again after what is often a significant period of separation and trauma. This dependency is even more problematic in cases of family breakdown when the newly arrived lose their visa entitlements (Marsden & Harris, 2015) and must then make an asylum application if they wish to remain in the UK.

The role of the British Red Cross and the impact of family separation

The BRC is the largest independent provider of support for refugees and asylum seekers in the UK. BRC research highlights the considerable stress that family separation causes and that separated family members often live with the goal of family reunion for years (Marsden & Harris, 2015). During the period of separation, it is not unusual for family members to lose contact for extended periods. Concern about family is linked to poor psychological health, such as depression, anxiety and somatisation (McDonald-Wilmsen & Gifford, 2009) and there may also be financial pressure to support family overseas. These factors can make it difficult for family members to settle into life in the UK as they may feel that life is 'on hold' (White & Hendry, 2011). These negative effects are exacerbated by the lengthy process of family reunion which further highlights the need for a more efficient process. Leaving a child or partner behind to make a dangerous journey is an incredibly difficult choice to make and the UK is in desperate need of a more humanitarian approach to immigration in general which enables safe routes for people to come to the UK. The current system encourages families to separate so that one person can make the dangerous journey alone with other family members joining later once the first person is granted refugee status.

Unlike people who arrive through the asylum process or resettlement programmes, those who come to the UK on a family reunion visa do not receive any formal support with accessing services. The length of separation is also a significant factor in how the family readjusts once they are reunited and research indicates that the longer the family are separated the harder the process of reunion (Marsden & Harris, 2015). Family reunion may also be partial while other family members are unable to re-join the family unit at the same time bringing further challenges.

Adjusting to living together again while adapting to a new country, a new environment and navigating a new system in a different language can be very challenging. Refugee sponsors are also at different stages of settling into the new country when their families arrive and there may be additional pressures in terms of housing, work, study, benefits and finance. Joining family members do not have to meet language requirements before coming to the UK or take the Life in the UK test and arriving family members have the same rights as the refugee sponsor in terms of access to support services including language classes. In the following section, I discuss how the BRC supports families arriving through family reunion.

British Red Cross Family Reunion Integration Service

Although more refugees arrive in the UK through family reunion than all other resettlement programmes combined, family reunion has received inadequate funding in comparison to other programs such as the Syrian Resettlement Programme (British Red Cross, 2018). This has resulted in inadequate support with health, education, housing and welfare services for family members arriving in this way. To improve support for these families, the BRC launched its Family Reunion Integration Service (FRIS) in September 2018. This was the first time UK wide funding was allocated for this specific purpose.

The FRIS aimed to support 3000 people (900 families) in 8 locations in England, Wales, Scotland and Northern Ireland between 2018 and 2021 by providing tailored support and core casework to access basic rights, register with a GP, get access to universal credit, find an appropriate place to live and register children for school. Within the UK wide project, Glasgow is twinned with Birmingham to focus on 'rebuilding the family unit' as this is recognised as a specific need.

Arriving in the UK at different times can result in significantly different integration experiences. The first family member to arrive has time to adjust, to learn the language and to begin to establish a life before the joining members (most usually wife/partner and children) arrive. Discussions with BRC staff highlighted the significant challenges faced by women arriving in the UK in this way, which includes access to support services and childcare responsibilities making it difficult to attend activities outside the home, putting them at increased risk of isolation. New Scots highlights barriers to integration for women as: 'lack of confidence; disrupted or no previous access to education; less time available, due to other caring responsibilities or lack of childcare; and family opposition to socialising, learning or working' (Scottish Government, 2018: 17). The BRC highlight that these barriers may be felt even more keenly by women whose partners have already settled in the host community. In the following section, I return to the issue of language learning for women in this situation.

The gendered nature of language learning

There is a strong network of ESOL providers in Glasgow working to support New Scots with language learning and women arriving through family reunion can access the college and community classes outlined under 'Scotland's ESOL Strategy' in the same way as other migrants. In this section, I consider how the needs of reunited families may be different to other ESOL learners particularly at the point of reunion and shortly afterwards.

Once in the host community, family dynamics often change with each member's experience with language learning; children often gain independence and confidence through school and interaction with other children and men may have more opportunities to practise their English through work outside the home. In contrast, many women experience isolation and feeling 'left behind' as they face barriers which prevent them accessing the language classes that would enable them to learn English, build confidence and integrate. Children's language skills are likely to improve through school which can mean they communicate for their mothers. The accompanying shift in family dynamics can be difficult to navigate as it creates a parent-child role reversal which can place additional strain on their relationship (Marsden & Harris, 2015).

This gendered nature of English language learning is widely acknowledged (MacKinnon, 2015; Scottish Government & Education Scotland, 2015). Two issues in particular impact women's access to ESOL provision: childcare responsibilities and cultural expectations in terms of gender roles. Adequate childcare is essential to enable women to attend ESOL classes, but provision is often insufficient (Ager & Strang, 2004; MacKinnon, 2015). Cultural differences may also inhibit women from attending classes, for example an expectation that they do not need to go out to work and therefore do not need to attend language classes. Male family members may also be reluctant to take on childcare responsibilities and some women are not comfortable taking part in language classes that include men (Meer *et al.*, 2018). As a result, the gendered nature of language learning extends into a gendered experience of integration in a more general sense. Research also shows that migrant women with low levels of education benefit from learning English with their children, as it can improve physical and mental health and provide important opportunities to meet other women in a safe environment (British Council, 2017).

The BRC report that difficulties do not end at the point of family reunification (Marsden & Harris, 2015) and many newly arrived women remain reliant on their sponsor's social networks and stronger language skills. At the time of writing, there are no language classes specifically for women in this situation other than mainstream ESOL classes which necessitate a certain level of confidence to find the class information, locate the class, travel independently and have the confidence to take part (issues I explored in my fieldwork and return to in Chapter 5). At the early stages of adjusting to life in Scotland these are significant barriers which pose a risk of isolation and impact on wellbeing and mental health. This study aims to address some of these issues by providing a language learning intervention at the critical point of family reunion and shortly afterwards.

Conclusions

In this chapter, I have discussed the political climate for immigration in the UK, and I have highlighted some of the tensions between the UK hostile environment policies and the Scottish Government's multilingual, multilateral approach to refugee integration. The New Scots Strategy and the ESOL Strategy provide a strong policy context in which to situate this research and to consider recommendations from academic literature concerning language learning for refugees. New Scots emphasises the need to support language learning from 'day one' (Scottish Government, 2018) yet insufficient funding means ESOL providers cannot meet demand for classes. I have also illustrated that women arriving through family reunion require specialist support and these needs are difficult to meet within the current under-resourced system. It is positive that the benefits of multilingualism are recognised within New Scots, but the lack of guidance on how to translate this strategy into the ESOL classroom means that Scotland's ESOL learners and practitioners are not getting the full benefit of the aims of the language recommendations which were introduced in 2018.

It is clear that family reunion is key to integration and the wellbeing of those who come to the UK under the most difficult of circumstances. Family members who arrive in the UK to join their refugee 'sponsor' face additional challenges as there is less support available to them due to the assumption that their spouse/partner is able to provide assistance, yet this is not always possible. In the following chapter, I outline the key academic literature and discuss its relevance to the policy context I have outlined in this chapter. I also consider the gap between policy and recommendations in academic literature and how these intersect with current provision for language learning for reunited families in Scotland by establishing the theoretical background for this research which aims to address some of the issues the policies have left unresolved.

Note

(1) 'New Scots' refers to refugees and asylum seekers in Scotland. The term refers to the 'New Scots Refugee Integration Strategy 2018–2022'.

2 Establishing an Ecological, Multilingual Framework

Introduction

This chapter explores how I drew together key academic literature to support the decolonising aims of the research by building a theoretical framework for an ecological, multilingual approach to language learning for newly arrived refugee women. I chose an ecological approach for this research because it afforded possibilities for closely connecting our language learning with the process of integration into the physical context of Glasgow, a need that was identified by the BRC and the participants themselves. This priority was also clear to me from my experience working with refugees and people seeking asylum in Glasgow. The study sought to combine this need with a practical application of the recommendations for multilingual approaches to refugee integration laid out in the Scottish policies in the previous chapter, which so clearly recognise the diverse communities in which most of us now live.

This chapter focuses on the four key areas on which the study is based: language ecology, multilingualism and monolingualism, translanguaging, and identity within language learning. I consider each of these themes in turn before illustrating how they intersect to form the theoretical framework for this research which is set within the political context laid out in the previous chapter. I begin by considering the term 'language ecology' as it forms the broad foundation for the research.

Language Ecology

Definitions and context

The study drew on two key elements of an ecological approach, namely: (1) the relationship between language and environment and (2) the interaction between languages in the mind (Haugen, 1972). The terms *'ecology of language'* or *'language ecology'* were brought to public attention at the beginning of the 1970s by the Norwegian American linguist Einar Haugen (1906–1994) who defined 'language ecology' as 'the study of interactions between any given language and its environment' (Haugen,

1972: 325). Haugen's definition was developed from Ernst Haeckel's original definition of 'ecology' within the life sciences which Haeckel (1866: 286) describes as 'die gesammte Wissenschaft von den Beziehungen, des Organismus zur umgebenden Aussenwelt, wohin wir im weiteren Sinne alle "Existenz-Bedingungen" rechnen können'. Kramsch and Vork Steffensen (2008: 17) translate this as 'the total science of the organism's relations to the surrounding environment, to which we can count in a wider sense all "conditions of existence". Haugen transposed this concept into the field of linguistics and is generally regarded as the founder of the term'.

Haugen's 'language ecology' relates language learning to the physical and social context and emphasises the interaction between these elements: 'language only functions in relating these users to one another and to nature i.e. their social and natural environment' (Haugen, 1972: 325). Importantly, language ecology also includes the internal interaction between languages in the minds of bi- and multilingual speakers, making it compatible with multilingual approaches such as translanguaging which is based on the idea that all linguistic knowledge is stored as one unified linguistic repertoire rather than separate compartmentalised languages (I return to this idea later in this chapter). The approach is interdisciplinary in nature and holistic as language is seen as intrinsically linked and inseparable from the physical environment and its users.

Although Haugen's 'ecology of language' essays are often referred to as the first use of the term 'language ecology', the origins of the term can be traced further back. Eliasson (2015) provides an overview of the influences in Haugen's work, noting that Voegelin and Voegelin (1964: 2) define linguistic ecology as 'as a shift of emphasis from a single language in isolation to many languages in contact'. The ideas of context and environment are noted here a decade before Haugen's work was published: 'in linguistic ecology, one begins not with a particular language but with a particular area, not with selective attention to a few languages but with comprehensive attention to all the languages in the area' (Voegelin & Voegelin, 1964: 3).

Critics of Haugen's work view the lack of methodological suggestions in his initial essays on language ecology as a weakness in terms of how these concepts might be applied; however, Haugen (1979: 247) explains he intended 'language ecology' be viewed as a metaphor, calling it 'descriptive and normative'. Haugen's ideas were significant as they prompted a notable shift into contextualised language learning and countered Chomsky's universal grammar which suggests that language is an abstract, de-contextualised and static entity (Eliasson, 2015). As Eliasson (2015: 90) points out, the most significant contribution of Haugen's pioneering paper is 'his plea for a dynamic, holistic perspective on human language' which constituted a 'valuable corrective' to linguistic approaches of the time.

Proponents of an ecological approach have built on Haugen's foundation, emphasising the centrality of context as 'the focal field of study' (Van Lier, 2002: 144). Kramsch and Vork Steffensen (2008: 18) note that 'holism' is a keyword in ecology and recognise that a holistic approach to linguistics implies that language should not be studied 'as an isolated, self-contained system, but rather in its natural surroundings, i.e. in relation to personal, situational, cultural, and societal factors'. Kramsch and Vork Steffensen (2008: 18) describe an ecological approach as a 'worldview in which everything is part of an undividable whole'. It is dialogical, reciprocal, interconnected, linguistically diverse and offers potential for 'changing ourselves and our surroundings' (Kramsch & Vork Steffensen, 2008: 19).

Haugen's understanding of languages as inseparable from their respective historical, social, political and cultural contexts is picked up again in later work by Leo van Lier (2002, 2004a, 2006, 2010) who tells us that without context 'there is no language left to be studied' (Van Lier, 2006: 20), we 'pull one string, metaphorically speaking, and all the others will move in response' (Van Lier, 2010: 4). Van Lier (2002: 144) also notes that the interrelation of these factors, although dynamic, can also be complicated and messy but the context remains central as 'it cannot be reduced, and it cannot be pushed aside or into the background'.

Van Lier (2004a) recognises how language ecology is different from other theories that decontextualise language for the purposes of studying individual linguistic features or grammatical structures. Although this can be useful, it 'obscures the dynamism of the actual teaching and learning work that goes on and cannot show the emergent and contingent nature of that work' (Van Lier, 2010: 5). Kramsch (2002) echoes that an ecological theory is needed to understand that language learning and language use is an ecosystem, a relational human activity co-constructed between people and their languages. The concepts of co-construction and language as a relational human activity are key to the discussion on translanguaging later in this chapter and became a central focus of the fieldwork. These concepts were also fundamental to the broader decolonising, multilingual aims of the research.

Layered simultaneity

In addition to the reciprocity between language and the external context, an ecological approach also refers to the layers of meaning carried within language itself which Blommaert refers to as 'layered simultaneity'. Van Lier (2010) refers to the lithograph 'Three Worlds' by Maurits Escher to illustrate this concept (see Figure 2.1). 'Layered simultaneity' (Blommaert, 2005) refers not only to the here and now, but also to the past and the future of those involved in the interaction, to the surrounding world, and to the identity projected by the speaker. Any utterance has multiple layers of meaning embedded within it, a concept illustrated by the three 'worlds'

Figure 2.1 'Three Worlds' Lithograph by Maurits Escher (M.C. Escher's "Three Worlds" © 2022 The M.C. Escher Company – The Netherlands. All rights reserved. www.mcescher.com)

in the Escher image which represent the layers of historicity, identity and presentness in every utterance (Van Lier, 2010). Blommaert (2005: 46) also recognises the fluidity and capacity for change within language as meanings adapt and become attached to language with its ongoing use: 'every utterance has a history of (ab)use, interpretation and evaluation, and this history sticks to the utterance'.

The reciprocal relationship between language use and change is particularly significant within an increasingly globalised world and given the increased number of forcibly displaced people, factors which are the context for this research. Blommaert (2005: 73) highlights that such mobility 'is not mobility across empty spaces, but mobility across spaces filled with codes, customs, rules, expectation, and so forth'. In migratory contexts, the spaces which people move through 'are always somebody's space', they are not blank and without context, culture and history (Blommaert, 2005: 73). It is natural that new meaning becomes attached to language as language is not static in nature; it is ever changing and developing. Languages are not fixed, hermetically sealed units which remain unchanged (García, 2007); they are fluid, shaped by their users, their experiences and the dynamic meaning which attaches to them over the course of time. The concept of layered simultaneity is central to this research (returned to in Chapter 7) as it recognises the experience, language and knowledge that the participants brought with them to the project and all the layers of meaning contained within their home languages.

Language ecology is not detached from other ways of teaching and learning. It complements other multilingual approaches. In the next section, I consider how the principles of language ecology, such as the connections with environment and other known languages, can be brought into the classroom as pedagogy before discussing the place of multilingualism within the theoretical framework.

Implications for research and pedagogy

Embracing an ecological approach means prioritising the context in which the speaker lives, acknowledging the interaction between languages and bringing these factors into the classroom as a strategy for teaching and learning. An ecological approach also recognises that language development is non-linear (Freeman & Cameron, 2008) rather than a progression through 'accumulated entities' (Rutherford, 1987), it is more a series of transformative experiences. Language ecology is not a separate pedagogy or a 'particular theory or model of teaching, research, or learning' (Van Lier, 2004b: 86). It can be better understood as 'a world view, a way of being and acting in the world that has an impact on how we conduct our lives, how we relate to others and to the environment, and of course also, how we conceive of teaching and learning' (Van Lier, 2004b: 86).

Communicative approaches for language learning focus on the improvement of language skills via functional skills production (Kramsch *et al.*, 2010) based on the notion that you get out what you put in (input and production). In contrast, an ecological approach is dynamic and emergent, a two-way reciprocal process where classroom learning responds to the context and vice versa (Kramsch *et al.*, 2010). Kramsch *et al.* (2010) describe the classroom as an 'ecological niche' and although this can be a safe environment, it can also be artificial, creating a 'barrier between education and the rest of living' (Little, 1991: 39). For newly arrived refugee women with care responsibilities, the context is one of profound change, disorientation and loss and this ecology cannot be separated from language learning and language use.

In practical terms, an ecological approach intentionally connects classroom learning with the real world and encourages a reciprocal relationship between the two (Levine, 2020). Learning also needs to be locally meaningful (Tudor, 2003) to respond to 'local realities' (Duff & Van Lier, 1997). Levine (2020) notes the importance of the local context for planning projects with an ecological approach and how identifying authentic aspects of the context for use within learning activities can be a useful first step (a key element of the research which I explore in Parts 2 and 3).

No 'off the shelf', fixed or prescriptive guide to a pedagogical approach for language ecology exists, and nor does it need to due to the deliberate openness which allows language and activities to emerge from the context. In Chapter 5, I introduce the real-world context of this research at the point of meeting the participants, I discuss how we brought the specific context of the project into our work, and I highlight the impact of this openness as a deliberate methodological choice which complemented the collaborative nature of CPAR.

In addition to the external context of language learning outlined here, an important feature of an ecological approach is the way that languages interact in the mind and this leads into the discussion which follows on the place of multilingualism within an ecological framework.

Multilingualism, Monolingualism and Superdiversity

Li (2013: 26) defines multilingualism as the 'coexistence, contact and interaction of different languages' at individual or societal level. This definition mirrors Haugen's ideas on the interaction of languages in the mind and underlines how multilingualism is integral to a holistic, ecological approach. Makoni and Pennycook's (2007) often-cited notion that named languages are a construct of the nation state is central to understanding multilingualism as it illustrates the contrast between this constructed notion and the way that languages interact in the mind of individuals. As Bourdieu (1991: 287) reminds us, separate languages are 'a social artefact invented at the cost of a decisive indifference to differences' based on 'the arbitrary imposition of a unique norm'. At societal level, a true language ecology redresses the position of English and represents other languages as integral and equally important to the context. This equality between languages also mirrors the decolonising and multilingual aims of this research.

As noted in Chapter 1, the UK press and successive UK governments often imply that the UK can only achieve social cohesion by sharing one common language. These views give the impression that the use of languages other than English threatens national unity and the sense of common belonging (Blackledge, 2009). In reality, far more people in the world are multilingual than monolingual but the position of monolingualism is distorted, as Skutnabb-Kangas (1995) notes, by the fact that so many monolinguals belong to 'a very powerful minority' as they are English speakers who have been able to function in all situations using their mother tongue and have never been forced to learn another language. Gramling (2016: 17) refers to this as 'monolingual privilege', noting 'what most scholarship on the topic shares is a sense that monolingualism has come at great gain to some and unspecifiable cost to others' depending on which language you speak at home. This focus on monolingualism is driven by the idea of 'one nation, one language', which Makoni and Pennycook (2007) highlight and I return to in the section 'Social justice, linguistic dominance and decolonising multilingualism'.

Simpson (2016: 181) notes that monolingualist policies resonate with the idea of a standard language as a 'unifying "glue" for a nation' but this 'imagined homogeneity', emphasised by national policy and political discourse, is challenged by mobility and diversity. Increasing globalisation disrupts the idea that the nation is a fixed entity as migration to countries where English is the dominant societal language simply outpaces the development of policies and infrastructure to meet the needs of new arrivals and the resulting increased linguistic diversity in host communities (Simpson, 2016). In short, current ways of viewing monolingualism and its relationship to the nation-state need to catch up with the increasingly multilingual communities in which most of us now live.

This increased globalisation has resulted in what Vertovec (2007) refers to as 'super-diversity', a term which he uses to describe the context of rapid demographic change in London in the early 21st century. Meissner and Vertovec (2015: 541) note than superdiversity has often been oversimplified and understood to simply mean 'more ethnic groups' rather than the term's 'fuller, original intention of recognizing multidimensional shifts in migration patterns'. The broader understanding of the term includes three components: the first element is the understanding of changing demographics arising from increased global migration; the second element is methodological and calls to 'reorient' some of the approaches to studying migration within the social sciences 'in order to address and to better understand complex and arguably new social formations' (Meissner & Vertovec, 2015: 542); the third element is practical or policy-oriented and highlights the need for policymakers and public service practitioners to recognise new conditions resulting from global migration and population change (Meissner & Vertovec, 2015).

These three interconnected aspects give the term broader meaning and make it relevant to this research as they combine to acknowledge the new social formations created by increased globalisation and the need for policy and practice to better reflect this. I brought these concepts into the research by considering the gap that exists between the policy laid out in Chapter 1, the academic literature in this chapter and the real-world delivery of the teaching study.

Vertovec (2013) notes that this superdiversity is at a level and complexity which surpasses anything the UK has previously experienced and this poses challenges for policy and research. Creese and Blackledge (2018) also recognise the increasingly superdiverse communities of major UK cities and how this creates a unique blend of cultures and languages.

Within our increasingly linguistically diverse communities it is important to consider the place of English and the implications of the current systems which privilege English above other languages. The concept of superdiversity is key to an ecological perspective as it highlights the many languages present in large cities such as Glasgow, where this research is situated. The commitment to researching multilingually by drawing on the participants' and my own full multilingual resources to co-produce the research, coupled with the decolonial research methods I outline in the next chapter, underpinned the practical application of these concepts.

Social justice, linguistic dominance and decolonising multilingualism

An ecological approach is also closely connected to issues of social justice, language hierarchies, linguistic dominance and linguistic human rights. Colonialism and globalisation have created a global hierarchy of languages within which not all languages hold equal power. Within this hierarchy, English holds a very powerful position. Phillipson and Skutnabb-Kangas (1996: 429) describe this as a 'pecking order', within which 'English has the sharpest beak'. As English is also associated with colonialism and globalisation it is also a politically fraught and distinctively powerful language (Leonard, 2014). Promoting the dominance of English contributes to linguistic inequalities and is unlikely to lead to a more stable, equitable world or to improve social justice (Phillipson & Skutnabb-Kangas, 1996). The need to reduce the dominance of English and issues of social justice are also recurrent themes within the literature on translanguaging which I discuss later in this chapter.

Phipps (2019b) notes the need for a 'decolonising' of multilingualism and 'renewed understandings' which she describes as a 'waking up' in the West, to the fact that most of the world's speakers have a variety of language repertoires. Phipps (2019b: 63) also reflects on the powerful impact of putting English last in her own multilingual research, noting how 'decentring, decolonising, giving up power as control follow easily in contexts where we do not have linguistic control'. Although English is the dominant societal language in Scotland, and is undoubtedly needed for everyday life, Scotland is officially multilingual with many languages spoken in the local community. This language ecology could be better reflected within teaching practice without reducing the importance of learning English for integration. Improving the balance between languages in the research became a central part of the pedagogical approach to the teaching study and also mirrored the broader decolonising aims of the research as a whole (explored in full in Chapter 3).

Gramling (2016: 11) notes how monolingualism renders other languages 'contextually unnecessary' as the 'national language' is promoted to the exclusion of all other languages within that context, countering an ecological perspective. Drawing on Tsuda (1994), Phillipson and Skutnabb-Kangas (1996:436) recognise there are two global contemporary language policy options; the 'diffusion of English paradigm' or an 'ecology of language' paradigm. An ecology of language builds on linguistic diversity, promotes multilingualism and the learning of other languages and improves linguistic human rights for speakers of all languages (Phillipson & Skutnabb-Kangas, 1996) rather than focusing on English as the sole priority.

In terms of how these issues translate into teaching and learning, academic literature signals that language teachers need to move towards teaching for cultural pluralism rather than for communicative competence (Kramsch & Whiteside, 2008). It is necessary and appropriate that we forge a paradigm shift towards pedagogies which counteract the dominance of English and reposition other languages to create a more balanced view of the linguistic diversity present within our local language ecologies.

Working multilingually also allows us to shift away from the idea of languages as separate, fixed entities which are compartmentalised in the brain, towards understanding language as a social construct which forms part of an integrated linguistic system (Otheguy *et al.*, 2015); a key feature of 'translanguaging' which I outline in the following section. Despite the growing body of work which recognises the benefits of multilingual learning and the increasingly globalised world in which we live, most current systems for language teaching are based on traditional views of languages as separate entities and learning is often geared towards achieving native speaker-like competence (Auer, 2007). This is particularly true in countries where monolingualism is perceived to be the norm (Prada & Turnbull, 2018) such as the UK. Recent years have seen the beginning of a gradual paradigm shift, a 'multilingual turn', towards the inclusion of more multilingual perspectives (Prada & Turnbull, 2018) which allows opportunities for critical analysis of monolingual teaching methods and consideration of alternatives.

In addition to its connections to the nation state, monolingualism is also linked to attitudes and ideologies about linguistic purity and language ownership (Prada & Turnbull, 2018). With increasing globalisation, the number of people who use English who are not 'native speakers' outstrips those who are 'native' speakers. This calls into question the appropriacy of the terminology used to refer to learners of English and the use of the term 'native', which is increasingly seen as post-colonial (see 'Power and Identity' for further detail, p. 51). The use of English as a 'lingua franca' also challenges ideas about language ownership as it contradicts the 'one nation, one language' ideology (Prada & Turnbull, 2018).

In addition to no longer being the best fit within our increasingly globalised world, teaching monolingually does not make the most of the languages which learners already know; 'the increasingly multilingual and multicultural nature of global exchanges is raising questions about the traditionally monolingual and monocultural nature of language education' (Kramsch & Whiteside, 2008: 645). In the case of the UK, many ESOL learners already know and use several languages and it simply does not make sense to teach people to be more multilingual by using monolingual methods (Simpson, 2020). Teaching monolingually also allows little scope for connecting new knowledge to what is already known which research shows can support important cognitive functions (Kroll & Bialystok, 2013).

Despite the recognition of the benefits of teaching multilingually, there is a lack of guidance on how to implement multilingual pedagogies in a meaningful way. The principles of translanguaging complement an ecological framework as they acknowledge the interaction between languages, support the disruption of socially constructed language hierarchies responsible for the suppression of the languages of minoritised peoples (Otheguy *et al.*, 2015) and encourage the development of a stronger multilingual identity (García-Mateus & Palmer, 2017). In the following section, I explore the need for a paradigm shift away from the aim of achieving monolingual competence towards an approach which valorises the full linguistic repertoire, and I explain how translanguaging may provide one way forward.

Translanguaging

'Translanguaging' refers to both the everyday practices of multilinguals to 'shuttle between languages' (Canagarajah, 2011a: 401) and it is also a recognised pedagogy based on the understanding that linguistic knowledge belongs to a 'linguistic repertoire' (García & Li, 2014a; Lewis *et al.*, 2012; MacSwan, 2017). It enables communication regardless of the socially and politically defined boundaries of named languages (Otheguy *et al.*, 2015). Translanguaging has raised awareness of a heteroglossic language ideology that values bilingualism in its own right rather than as a transition to majority language monolingualism (MacSwan, 2017).

As translanguaging contradicts teaching methods based on language separation, it firmly connects with Haugen's understanding of how languages interact in the mind. The approach is underpinned by psycholinguistic research which evidences that multilinguals activate information from all known languages even when they are only using one of their languages actively (Kroll & Bialystok, 2013). By translanguaging, learners connect new language to existing knowledge on the understanding that linguistic items do not belong to separate internal systems compartmentalised in the brain, but rather they form a unitary system on which speakers draw selectively to communicate. As my research aimed to support the participants at the very beginning of learning English, these connections were vital as they enabled participants to draw on their existing knowledge and build confidence from what they already knew.

Origins and definitions

'Translanguaging', or *'trawsieithu'* in Welsh, was developed by Welsh educationalist Cen Williams (1994) in his doctoral thesis to describe the 'deliberate and systematic use of two languages' (Lewis *et al.*, 2012: 664) for teaching and learning during the same lesson. Moving between languages in this way called into question the long-held belief of language separation in language learning, as previously held by language scholars, which was based on the idea of bilingualism being two separate languages with two separate systems. Translanguaging in the Welsh context meant alternating between Welsh and English for receptive and productive use (Baker, 2011), e.g. reading a text in Welsh and discussing it in English or listening to something in English and writing about it in Welsh. Williams (1994) recognised that this way of working supported the learning of both languages which was highly relevant in the Welsh bilingual context.

Baker (2011: 289) notes how translanguaging enabled students to engage with the language and deepen their understanding: 'to read and discuss a topic in one language, and then to write about it in another language, means that the subject matter has to be processed and "digested"'. Baker (2011) also found translanguaging enabled deeper understanding of the subject being studied as it supported the development of the weaker language, it facilitated connections between home and school, and also supported the integration of fluent speakers with early learners.

To fully understand translanguaging, we must first return to Makoni and Pennycook's (2007) notion of named languages and their relationship to the nation state to problematise the concept of 'a language'. As named languages are social, not linguistic, constructions (Otheguy *et al.*, 2015) their separation has little bearing on how languages are learnt and used. Understanding this concept is key, as it is this idea of separate named languages that has transferred into the practice of language separation within language learning and become the norm within most language classrooms: 'it is the uncritical acceptance of this foundational term that has kept us from fully grasping the implications of translanguaging' (Otheguy *et al.*, 2015: 282).

As the term has gained popularity and further developed, two theories of translanguaging have emerged and are differentiated as 'strong' and 'weak' translanguaging (Prada & Turnbull, 2018). The former maintains the idea of separate national languages (which may be closer to definitions of 'code-switching' which I discuss later in this section) but allows for a relaxing of boundaries between languages. García and Lin (2017) now define Williams' original definition as 'weak' translanguaging as, although both languages are actively used, the barriers between them continue to exist. In contrast, García and Lin (2017) propose the term 'strong' translanguaging which is based on the idea of one unitary meaning-making system (or 'linguistic repertoire'). Prada and Turnbull (2018: 13) note this as a 'conceptual expansion to complex, semiotic language practices and pedagogies of bi-/multi-lingual communities who transcend between and beyond the systems that make up their complete linguistic repertoires'.

Proponents of strong translanguaging note that language can be analysed in terms of linguistic features, such as phonemes, morphemes, words, nouns, verbs, grammatical constructions or rules, tenses etc., for both multilinguals and monolinguals but that they are essentially drawn from one unitary meaning-making system (Otheguy *et al.*, 2015). This unitary system is also described as an 'idiolect' (Otheguy *et al.*, 2015) which is a person's own unique, personal language made up of the vocabulary they know and use rather than the named language associated with each of the lexical items within their 'linguistic repertoire'. It is also the person's '*mental grammar* that emerges in interaction with other speakers and enables the person's use of language' (Otheguy *et al.*, 2015: 289).

An 'idiolect' takes the internal perspective of the individual's meaning making system in contrast to the external perspective which is defined by the named languages they use (Otheguy *et al.*, 2015). Idiolects contain lexical and grammatical features and their components (e.g. lexicon, phonology, morphosyntax) and subcomponents (nouns, tenses, case endings, pronouns) and are unique to each individual (Otheguy *et al.*, 2015). No two are idiolects are identical, even the idiolects of family members, although they share common features which enable communication (Otheguy *et al.*, 2015).

The concept of 'idiolect' also extends to monolinguals who also have a repertoire from which they select linguistic features in order to communicate. Otheguy *et al.* (2015) note that no one uses their full idiolect freely at all times as even monolinguals monitor their use of language to some extent according to the situation. Multilinguals simply have idiolects with a wider range of lexical and structural features which they must learn to suppress in order to communicate with monolinguals (Otheguy *et al.*, 2015).

Although it has a different epistemological position, translanguaging is also linked to 'code-switching' (Auer, 2007) as it also counters the way that languages are isolated for teaching and learning. Code-switching describes the practice of moving back and forth between languages to scaffold the teaching of additional languages. Although this is acknowledged as common practice within language teaching, it is 'rarely institutionally endorsed or pedagogically underpinned' (Creese & Blackledge, 2010: 105). Code-switching contrasts 'strong' translanguaging as it is based on the monoglossic view of separate linguistic systems for each language, whereas 'strong translanguaging' sees bilingual interaction as always heteroglossic (Bailey, 2012; Bakhtin, 2010) as it is based on one integrated linguistic system. As this heteroglossic and dynamic perspective flows from how speakers themselves use languages, translanguaging is seen as a more useful theory for teaching than code-switching.

This foundation of building on the dynamic bilingualism of learners and the way that language is used in real life is the reason that translanguaging has gained so much attention among educators and scholars in the 21st century (García & Lin, 2017). It is bottom-up approach centred not on languages but on the everyday practices of bilinguals (Poza, 2017) which puts the speaker at the heart of the interaction (Blackledge & Creese, 2010).

Proponents of translanguaging recognise communication as multimodal and that repertoire extends beyond language to reflect the multiplicity, fluidity, mobility, locality of the resources each speaker deploys (Moore *et al.*, 2020). From an epistemological position, translanguaging also offers new ways to understand how knowledge is produced (Moore *et al.*, 2020) which makes it compatible with the decolonising aims of this research.

The 'languaging' of 'translanguaging'

In addition to using the full linguistic repertoire, translanguaging involves shuttling between languages as speakers co-construct meaning as a creative improvisation specific to each context (Canagarajah, 2011b). Most sources cite Cen Williams' work as the origin of the term 'translanguaging'; however, Li (2017) explains his understanding of the term stems from the concept of 'languaging' rather than from the Welsh context.

Becker's (1991: 34) definition of 'languaging' as a co-constructed dialogical process was fundamental to this research: 'there is no such thing as Language, only languaging, an activity of human beings in the world'. Li (2017) reiterates the continually emerging nature of language by returning to Ortega y Gasset's (1957: 242) idea that language should not be seen as 'an accomplished fact, as a thing made and finished, but as in the process of being made'. This understanding of 'languaging' was particularly relevant within the context of this research due to our necessity to make meaning with limited shared verbal language. 'Languaging' is understood as an active, co-constructed process and it is this emphasis on dialogical interaction which gives the term its place within this ecological framework.

Further use of the term 'languaging' includes Swain (2006: 97), who explains 'languaging serves to mediate cognition' in understanding and problem-solving. 'Languaging' also connects with change and identity reconstruction through communication and context as it 'refers to the continuous process of becoming oneself through the use of language and interaction in one's linguistic and environmental surroundings' (Prada & Turnbull, 2018: 11). Prada and Turnbull also describe translingual practices as 'languaging practices that move beyond the socially constructed boundaries of languages in which a speaker holds multi-competence' (2018: 11).

Situating translanguaging within an ecological framework

Translanguaging recognises that people bring their own knowledge and experience to the learning process as it based on the 'dynamic, evolving, and negotiated nature of language' (Poza, 2017: 106). As pedagogy, it aims to make language learning more representative of the way languages are used outside the classroom where individuals move between languages for everyday communication. It places learners firmly at the centre of their own learning as it is oriented toward the user rather than a specific language (Simpson & Cooke, 2017) and promotes a sense of self-worth that is not linked solely to English language ability. Translanguaging fits particularly well with the collaborative nature of this research as it complements recommendations within New Scots (Scottish Government, 2018) to value refugees' existing skills and encourage them to share their home languages.

The benefits of implementing a translanguaging approach are well-evidenced within psycholinguistic, educational linguistic, and sociolinguistic research into language mixing (Ticheloven *et al.*, 2019). Although 'translanguaging' has gained significant support (Canagarajah, 2011b; Creese & Blackledge, 2010; García *et al.*, 2017; Otheguy *et al.*, 2015; Li, 2017; Williams, 1994), it is recognised that challenges remain about how this transfers to classroom practice in a meaningful way (García & Kleyn, 2016; Hornberger & Link, 2012). It has been criticised as pedagogically underdeveloped (Canagarajah, 2011b; García & Kleyn, 2016); Poza (2017) also notes that questions remain about translanguaging regarding implementation and outcomes. In the following section, I consider how translanguaging strategies can be brought into the classroom in a meaningful way.

Translanguaging in practice

In addition to the more general questions regarding how to implement translanguaging, much of the research to date refers to bilingual education in schools, particularly in the US within the Spanish/English context but work is also being done in the UK (see TLANG Project *et al.*, 2010 and their work in heritage schools.) The UK adult ESOL context brings additional considerations, particularly concerning the diversity of most ESOL classrooms and the variety of learners' languages (Schellekens, 2008). It is also important to consider the diverse multilingual communities which Vertovec (2007) refers to and acknowledge the differences in implementing translanguaging within such communities rather than the bilingual Spanish/English context in which García's work is based.

García and Li (2014b) identify seven ways that translanguaging can be used to leverage students' learning in the classroom:

(1) to differentiate among student levels and tailor instructional approaches;
(2) to build background knowledge;
(3) to deepen understandings, sociopolitical engagement and critical thinking;
(4) for cross-linguistic metalinguistic awareness;
(5) for cross-linguistic flexibility for competent language use;
(6) for identity investment; and
(7) to disrupt linguistic hierarchies and social structures.

Although learners may shuttle between languages for everyday communication, translanguaging does not simply just 'happen' naturally as a pedagogical practice, it still needs to be taught and supported within the classroom. One of the main issues to overcome is how teachers can use the learners' home languages when they have limited knowledge of them. García and Li (2014b) suggest that this should not be viewed as a barrier, noting that this is possible for teachers who are willing to give more power to learners and allow them to take control of their own learning to create a collaborative learning environment.

Establishing a learning environment in which learners become co-creators of knowledge requires a shift of the balance of power within the classroom which has implications for social justice, particularly in contexts where the teacher has limited knowledge of the learners' languages. The role of the teacher then shifts to 'facilitator' who guides learners (Beres, 2015; Canagarajah, 2011a). Cummins (2019: 19) describes this shift as 'the emerging role of classroom teachers as knowledge-generators' which challenges the idea that teachers need to know the learners' languages to be able to facilitate translanguaging.

García and Li (2014b: 112) suggest that learners support each other with the teacher trying to meet learners halfway: 'the teacher makes an effort to make herself understood using Spanish, and the students try to make themselves understood using English. In so doing more English is being added to the linguistic repertoire of the students, and more Spanish to that of the teacher', putting the 'two-way' process of New Scots into practice in a very real sense, taking it away from policy and into everyday life as a collaborative process. Monolingual teachers can find ways to incorporate translanguaging into their teaching; 'it shows students how to privilege interaction and collaborative dialogue over form and thus develops their voice' (García & Li, 2014b: 112).

As with an ecological approach, translanguaging can be embedded within existing approaches to language learning. Some progress towards the development of practical guides to support translanguaging activities in the classroom has been made (for example, García *et al.*, 2017; García & Kleyn, 2016). The CUNY-NYSIEB-guide (Celic & Seltzer, 2011) provides guidance and specific examples of translanguaging activities. Suggested strategies include empowering learners to use their languages through increasing visibility of other languages in the classroom, e.g. signs displayed in home languages or by learning greetings in each other's languages (García & Li, 2014b). Learners can also work together in 'language pairs' using the language of their choice with a return to Williams' (1994) methods of using one language to discuss an activity and another to produce a written or oral account. Strategies which include contrasting languages are also considered helpful to build vocabulary, improve reading comprehension and promote metalinguistic awareness (Ticheloven *et al.*, 2019), which contributes to enhanced language learning (Rauch *et al.*, 2012). Comparing languages is also described as a useful strategy for translanguaging, for example such as by searching for cognates in different languages and breaking these down into word parts, e.g. roots and affixes, to build vocabulary and enhance morphological awareness (Ticheloven *et al.*, 2019).

Poza (2017) highlights that these translanguaging strategies are flexible and can be used for activities using any of the four main skills (speaking, listening, reading, writing) to enhance learning for learners of all ages and proficiency levels. Poza (2017) also suggests that translanguaging may be most beneficial when different skills are used in combination, as it supports the transfer of skills from the more dominant language.

Translanguaging also 'helps to disrupt the socially constructed language hierarchies that are responsible for the suppression of the languages of many minoritized peoples' (Otheguy et al., 2015: 283) and it may also contribute to the development of a stronger multilingual identity (García-Mateus & Palmer, 2017). The ways in which translanguaging, multilingualism and identity intersect became particularly relevant within the liminal phase of arrival and identity reconstruction within this research, which I outline in Chapter 3 and revisit in the discussion chapters.

Power and Identity

The themes of power and identity were also key to the theoretical framework as the research sought to explore the shift in power dynamics created by taking a decolonising, collaborative approach. In this section, I turn to studies by Norton (2013), Pavlenko and Blackledge (2004), Block (2007) and illustrate how these fit with the aims of the research.

Norton's (2013) 'investment' calls into question outdated theories of language learning which see motivation as an intrinsic character trait unaffected by unequal teacher/learner power relations. Norton's construct became key to understanding the impact of shifting the balance of power within the research both in terms of the decolonising approach to the research as a whole and through the decolonising of multilingualism (Phipps, 2019b) within the teaching study. If learners 'invest' in the learning process, they recognise the benefits of improved language skills and the associated symbolic (language, education, friendship) and material resources (capital goods, money) which in turn increase social power (Norton, 2013). There is an integral relationship between 'investment' and identity within the classroom (Norton, 2013). Recognising the significance of Norton's construct draws together the key themes of context, identity and multilingualism as part of the ecological framework which underpins this research.

Identity in itself is not static; Van Lier (2004b) recognises that in a new environment people undergo a process of adaptation which requires the development of a new identity to connect their sense of self to the new culture and new language. This adaptation mirrors two-way integration as it requires 'reciprocity between the person and the host community' (Van Lier, 2004b: 96) as part of an ongoing and dynamic process; 'people do not "have" an identity, identities are constructed in practices that *produce, enact or perform* identity' (Blommaert, 2005: 205). Blommaert

(2005) also notes that identity is not static but based on semiotic potential organised within a repertoire. The concept of identity and the process of adaptation to a host community are explored in full in Chapters 3 and 7 within the discussions on liminality as they were key to the study due to the specific point at which I met the participants. The importance of the participants' own languages as integral to identity was highly visible and brought into contact with English as part of the dynamic process of settling into a host community.

Ethnolinguistic identity incorporates both linguistic and ethnic features (Blommaert, 2005); it often serves as a basis for language policies due to the connection between named languages and the nation-state outlined by Makoni and Pennycook (2007), as I discussed in the section on 'Multilingualism, Monolingualism and Superdiversity'. Embedded within this 'one nation, one language' view of identity are other beliefs about national identity, 'the ideal that the nation state should be as homogeneous – and as monolingual – as possible' (Simpson, 2016: 181), a view I highlighted in Chapter 1.

Blackledge and Pavlenko (2004: 5) also warn of the oversimplification and essentialisation of such approaches: 'a one-to-one correlation between language and identity, is criticized for its monolingual and monocultural bias', as it leaves no scope for those with multilingual or multicultural identities. It is important to recognise that at an individual level language is a key factor in our personal identity, made up of the various group identities to which each of us stakes a claim (Joseph, 2004) rather than a simple one-to-one correlation between ethnic and linguistic identity.

Norton (2013) recognises that pedagogical practices can either restrict or enable students to reimagine their future prospects as language classes form an important part of the process of 'reconstruction and repositioning' (Block, 2007: 75) within the liminal phase of refugee arrival. Pavlenko and Blackledge (2004: 8) note that this identity creation is an ongoing process as each act of speaking or silence constitutes an 'act of identity'. Norton (2013) warns how classroom practices can influence students and whether they develop subordinate or more powerful identities, which highlights the responsibility that teachers have to ensure learners' experiences are empowering.

By valorising home languages and incorporating them into the learning process in a meaningful way, translanguaging contributes to the development of a stronger multilingual identity (García-Mateus & Palmer, 2017). 'English only' classroom practices may be detrimental to fostering the 'investment' which Norton describes. As Canagarajah (2011b: 14) notes, 'ESL status is stereotypically considered developmental and deficient'. Approaches such as translanguaging are important as they can enable a reconceptualisation of identities for learners and teachers in terms of their ideologies and attitudes (Prada & Turnbull, 2018).

As Norton (2013: 44) notes, SLA theorists have not developed a theory of identity that 'integrates the language learner and the language learning context'. An ecological approach gives scope to do just this. Van Lier (2010) sees the principle of identity as central to an ecological approach alongside relationships, agency and motivation. He connects the term 'language ecology' with a sense of self and identity to include social relationships, cultural contexts, actions, activities and utterances as part of a reciprocal relationship between the individual and their world. This reciprocity is echoed by Blommaert (2005: 43): 'context and contextualisation are dialogical phenomena … it is not the speaker alone who offers context to statements and generates context, but the other parties in communication process do so as well'. This is particularly relevant when adjusting to a host community as a refugee when many of the previous support systems of culture and history have been removed and are replaced by new ones (Block, 2007). An ecological approach acknowledges this sense of identity within each specific context.

Adjusting to a host community and learning the language is dependent upon the development of a dually compatible identity, it emphasises the link between the self and the new context as part of ecology. This also requires 'having a voice in that language, and having both the right to speak and the right to be heard' (Van Lier, 2004b: 82). Genuine collaborative dialogue is needed to enable learners to develop an identity and voice in the language they are learning (Van Lier, 2004b) as part of ecological practice.

The theme of identity also extends to the terminology used to refer to learners of English and the identity projected by using these terms. García (2014b) suggests the term 'emergent bilingual' for the context of teaching bilingual children in the US. Although the term 'New Scots' has gained some traction in Scotland, it is limited to refugees/asylum seekers and does not account for other migrants and settled communities. The dominant term in the UK remains 'non-native speaker' which reinforces a notion of deficit and idealises the 'native speaker' as the target; a goal which is both unachievable and unrealistic. This terminology labels ESOL/second language learners as having a lower status to 'native' speakers, it defines people in limiting terms from a position of deficit and reaffirms a hierarchy based on English language level. In using these terms, learners are 'epistemologically construed as ever-learners whose communicative potential is summarized by their status as L2/FL speakers' (Prada & Turnbull, 2018: 10).

This terminology also does not account for learners who have more than one 'native' language and perpetuates the misconceptions discussed under 'Multilingualism, Monolingualism and Superdiversity' which no longer fit with our increasingly globalised societies and the diversity within our language learning classrooms. Further consideration of how to update this terminology is needed to move away from the deficit-oriented label of 'non-native speaker'. Supporting the participants in this study to develop a more empowering multilingual identity was an important part of the research which we aimed to explore by researching multilingually and by incorporating translanguaging pedagogy.

Conclusions

In this chapter, I have discussed the key literature which informs the theoretical framework for this project and explained how this theory underpins the research. I have highlighted the need for a paradigm shift towards incorporating multilingual approaches such as translanguaging, and I have explored the relevance for this context while working with the participants at a time of profound change as they arrive in Scotland through family reunion. The distinctiveness of ESOL in the UK as an 'interplay of life, learning and migration trajectories, of history and of government policies, and the way these come together in practice' (Simpson, 2016: 178) forms the starting point for this research.

Specifically, this study allows for further exploration of translanguaging as pedagogy within the context of family reunion. The literature shows a clear gap regarding the development of translanguaging in specific contexts and, as so many refugees arrive in the UK through family reunion, this is a useful and necessary context to explore how a multilingual, ecological approach to language learning might work for informal language learning at the point of arrival. In the following chapter, I consider how the key principles within the literature informed the research design and how I implemented an ecological and multilingual approach to language learning within the teaching study.

3 Implementing a Decolonising Approach

Introduction

In this chapter, I discuss how I carried out the research and the choices I made to apply the theories and policy recommendations in the previous two chapters within the specific research and teaching context of language learning for refugee families at the point of arrival. The chapter explains the use of critical participatory action research (CPAR), the research design, methods and data analysis. I then discuss my positionality and ethical considerations before summarising how these concepts fit together and stating the limitations of the study.

Lines of Inquiry

The policy review, literature review and initial meetings with the BRC evidenced a clear gap for language learning support for family members arriving in Glasgow through family reunion. Discussions with the BRC also highlighted that women arriving in this way face specific challenges in the early stages of adjusting to life as New Scots. In the previous chapter, I highlighted two key concepts of an ecological approach and their relevance for this research: the interrelationship between language and context, and the interaction between languages in the mind. Both of these concepts are fundamental to supporting arriving family members who have an immediate need for highly situated support and who, in many cases, are at the very beginning of learning English. The academic literature reviewed in Chapter 2 also suggests that translanguaging pedagogy may be a particularly good fit with this context due to its scope for working collaboratively with learners and improving the balance of power in the classroom. This literature also highlights the benefits of incorporating learners' home languages into the learning process in terms of identity and empowerment as part of two-way, mutual integration.

In addition, BRC and British Council research recognises that women benefit from learning language with their children and this was a research area the BRC suggested for further exploration. The combination of themes which emerged through the policy review, literature review and the input of the BRC provided the foundation for the research and shaped the methodological choices outlined in this chapter.

BRC staff suggested I consider language learning for refugees in Wales due to its status as a devolved country within the UK, bound by UK immigration rules in the same way as Scotland, and with devolved powers for support services. I was also interested to include Wales within the first stage of the research due to its bilingual status and the origins of translanguaging in Wales.

To broaden this initial stage of the research, I also decided it would be useful to compare the work of the German Red Cross (GRC) as Germany has received the highest number of refugees in Europe since 2016 and there is a well-established 600-hour introductory German language course in place. This is a very different model to the Scottish system, and I wanted to understand how Germany has supported such high numbers of refugees. The initial case studies in Wales and Germany allowed me to compare and contrast the specific language learning needs of refugees and understand how these are currently met in each of these contexts. In Chapter 4, I explore the fieldwork in Wales and Germany in full and explain how the findings shaped the teaching study in Scotland.

As I intended to create the research with the participants, fixed research questions would not have been appropriate. Instead, I used the following lines of inquiry to guide the study:

- What can we learn from language learning support for refugees in the Welsh and German contexts, and how can this learning be applied to the Scottish context?
- How can we better support reunited refugee families in Scotland through an ecological and multilingual approach to language learning?
- What significance does this approach have in terms of identity, empowerment and the dominance of English within the process of language learning?

Research Design

The fieldwork consisted of four key stages:

- Interviews with sector specialists in Wales and a two-day visit to the BRC in Newport where I interviewed staff and observed one ESOL class and one AVAIL session.
- Interviews with sector specialists in Germany and a one-day visit to the GRC in Frankfurt where I interviewed staff and observed three German as a Second Language classes.
- The pilot study in Glasgow.
- The main study in Glasgow.

The case studies in Wales and Germany (Chapter 4) were developed from literature and policy reviews for each of these contexts coupled with interviews with sector specialists and visits to the Red Cross in Wales and Germany. These case studies formed part of the initial planning stage of the CPAR spiral and informed the development of the pilot study in Glasgow. The pilot study (Chapter 5) provided a vital introductory stage of the fieldwork in Scotland as a prelude to the main study and gave participants the opportunity to learn more about the project before committing to the main study.

I took part in the teaching study as a teacher/facilitator and participant-observer within an interpretivist paradigm, using qualitative methods (three audio-recorded semi-structured interviews which the participants chose to do as group conversations, observations, fieldnotes and participant feedback) to carry out the research and gather data.

The teaching study took place from February–June 2019 (including the initial two-week pilot), engaging four families within their first weeks of arriving in Scotland. The study was based on the ideas and needs of the participants, identified by the participants themselves, set within the ecological, multilingual framework laid out in the previous chapter and shaped by the principles of engagement and collaboration within New Scots (Scottish Government, 2018). This was a practice-led, participant-centred approach, informed by ongoing dialogue and feedback to allow for participants to co-design and co-produce the research.

Participating on Different Terms

It was clear from the literature and policy reviews that the research should explore more than just the practical application of an ecological, multilingual approach. By decentring the position of English and decentring my own role in the research, I aimed to take a decolonial stance both to the teaching study and to the research in a broader sense. I drew on decolonising methodology (Phipps, 2013a, 2019b; Smith, 1999, 2013) to do this and aimed to work collaboratively with the participants to intentionally reduce my status and power as a researcher/teacher. This decision was influenced by my experiences of working with asylum seekers and refugees in Glasgow prior to starting the research and my commitment to working *with* the participants rather than carrying out research *on* them. The participants were the experts by experience, and I aimed to embed this decolonial stance in every aspect of the project.

By combining a multilingual, translanguaging approach with decolonising methodology, the research aimed to address not only the gap between policy, theory and practice but also to improve collaboration with refugee women and to empower the participants to take a more active role in their learning; a role that was not limited due to lack of knowledge of English.

Shifting the balance of power in this way, as Smith (2013) notes, can be transformative as the *researched* become the *researchers;* when 'questions are framed differently, priorities are ranked differently, problems are defined differently, people participate on different terms' (Smith, 2013: 196). I wanted to explore what participating 'on different terms' meant and the answer to this question became clearer as my relationship with the participants evolved, their confidence grew, and my linguistic incompetence further shifted the balance of power. The participants showed me what decolonising looked like in practice, in real life and in *their* lives. This shift in dynamics was so fundamental to the project that I have dedicated Chapter 6 of this book to allow full and detailed exploration of it.

This 'decolonising' extended to the pedagogy within the teaching study. I aimed to reduce the position of English and increase the status and visibility of the participants' languages by drawing on Phipps' (2019b) call to decolonise multilingualism and following the recommendations in the literature on translanguaging in Chapter 2. I participated as a learner of the participants' languages (Tigrinya, Tamil, Farsi and Arabic), operating from a position of 'linguistic incompetence' (Phipps, 2013b) as these were all new languages to me. The impact of an improved balance of power and more symmetrical teacher/learner relationships found in Norton's (2013) work on identity (Chapter 2) further complemented the decolonising methodology.

Influences from intercultural research

My approach was further informed by some of the methodological issues raised within intercultural research regarding ethical intercultural relationships. It was helpful to relate the concepts of ethics, decolonising and restorative approaches back to my own experience of working in the 'field'. Although my study is based on language learning, it is not about the 'functional quality assurance of language teaching' (Phipps, 2013a: 12) but rather it is a holistic approach where intercultural relationships are an essential part of the research.

Within this broader sense of language learning, I aimed to move beyond traditional qualitative methods of 'data collection'. We took the learning outside the classroom as much as possible to connect with the local context, a key feature of the ecological approach detailed in Chapter 2. This was particularly important to the participants as they were so new to the city and included taking the bus together to class at the start of the project, visiting the local park, a short walking tour of the University cloisters, and visits to Kelvingrove Museum and the Hunterian Museum. We also created a poem together and delivered a multilingual workshop entitled 'Bringing the Outside In' at the University UNESCO RILA (Refugee Integration through Languages and the Arts) Spring School in May 2019.

As our shared verbal language was limited, we relied on more embodied ways of communicating which resulted in what Law (2004) refers to as 'slippery' data. This included my observations of body language (touch, facial expressions, gestures, emotion) to allow for different ways of 'knowing beyond – or *beside/s* words' (Thurlow, 2016: 503).

Our learning was deliberately open and based on the dialogical interaction of 'languaging'. Woitsch (2012: 236) notes how 'language pedagogy needs emotions, wonder, awe, and magic'. These are not necessarily easily evidenced by traditional methods of 'data collection' or classroom-based learning with a rigid curriculum or fixed pedagogy. This 'colourful mixture of discovery and learning' is often forgotten and results in language pedagogy that is disconnected from 'the world out there' (Woitsch, 2012: 236). Our ecological approach aimed to harness this sense of porosity between the inside and the outside and, as such, the approach to the teaching study mirrored the methodological approach to the research in a more general sense.

Embracing 'messiness'

Creating research in this way, during this particular stage of profound change in the participants' lives, was unlikely to create data that would be easy to analyse in rigid/traditional ways. I aimed to represent the diffuse and messy reality of our work in a way that was authentic and 'broader, looser and more generous' (Law, 2004: 4), with a commitment and openness to 'other ways of knowing' (Law, 2004). Taking detailed fieldnotes helped me reflect on my work, my methods and feed my reflections into the CPAR spiral on an ongoing basis. As each learning session was delivered a week apart, this provided a window in which to reflect and plan before the next session as part of this iterative process.

Eclecticism as method

The literature reviewed in Chapter 2 provided the starting point for the research. However, as our work evolved, I learnt that I needed to consider a more interdisciplinary approach, and I began to look beyond the field of applied linguistics to consider influences from human geography, intercultural research and anthropology. Embracing a decolonising approach meant embracing this openness in method and literature, and at times I had to start again with a new body of literature to enable me to deepen my understanding. This commitment to openness meant that I could explore the emerging themes in more depth and allow the study to be genuinely guided by the participants. I consider the eclecticism this necessitated to be a justifiable method in its own right, a strength of the study and testimony to my own commitment to approaching the research with a genuinely open mind. I draw on the additional literature in Chapters

6, 7 and 8 and allow this to emerge alongside the themes in support of the discussion of findings. The need for interdisciplinary thinking is acknowledged within the literature on feminist ethics of care which I explore in full in Chapter 6.

Noddings (2012) refers to this as 'latitudinal knowledge' and explains how teachers should be able to draw on other disciplines to enrich their teaching and offer broader possibilities for their students. I do not claim to be an expert in human geography or anthropology; however, drawing on these fields added depth and breadth to the study, and I saw this as my ethical responsibility to the participants as part of the decolonising approach. In the following section, I explain how these principles complement CPAR.

Critical Participatory Action Research

The research was framed as an iterative spiral of critical participatory action research (CPAR) which Kemmis *et al.* (2014) describe as a 'practice changing practice'. Each learning session took place a week apart which allowed me to critically reflect and plan before delivering the next session.

I chose CPAR for its epistemological and ethical stance on who produces knowledge and how this knowledge is used (Stoudt & Torre, 2014) and also because CPAR is recognised for its ethical stance towards care and participation which prioritises and values relationships (Cahill *et al.*, 2007). As it also has the ability to empower participants by communicating unheard voices and acknowledges participants' power to co-construct knowledge (Gaventa & Cornwall, 2008), CPAR fitted well with the decolonising approach. It allows for exploration of the relationship between theory and practice in a direct way which complemented the aims of the research.

CPAR also acknowledges both the local and the global. In the case of this research, the local context is key but defined by broader political contexts for language learning and immigration. Also key to CPAR is the concept of 'practice architectures' (Schatzki, 2002) which enable or constrain practices without determining them. In terms of this study, the practice architectures relate to the context and structures already in place in Scotland within current support for language learning for refugee families. The study aims to examine current language classes and question what practice architectures constrain potential change.

In contrast to typical action research models which are based on a cycles of action and reflection, CPAR is based on an iterative spiral (Kemmis *et al.*, 2014, see Figure 3.1):

- planning a change;
- acting and observing the process and consequences of the change;

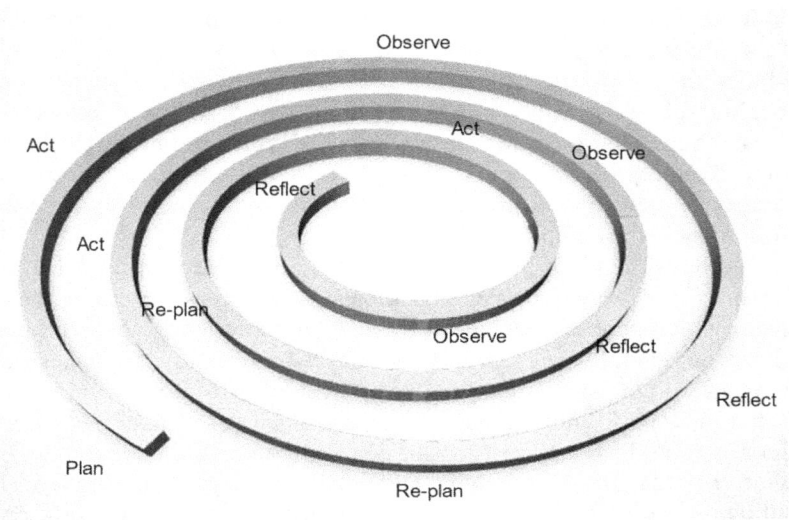

Figure 3.1 CPAR Spiral

- reflecting on these processes and consequences;
- re-planning;
- acting and observing;
- reflecting, and so on.

In the following section, I consider my own role within the CPAR framework.

An account of myself

As Phipps (2013a) notes, decolonising methodologies are not neutral or objective and CPAR also acknowledges that there are benefits of the researcher being directly involved in the research. In my case, being involved in the research meant I could draw directly on my teaching experience and the ongoing reflection on my own practice which has formed an essential part of my career. My 14 years' experience working with refugees and asylum seekers in Glasgow was fundamental to my approach, as it meant I was familiar with some of the challenges the participants faced, and I was able to provide appropriate and sensitive support.

Butler's (2005) 'giving an account of oneself' was essential to understanding my own positionality, and I draw on this in full in Chapter 7. Butler (2005) explains that individuals cannot fully clarify their positionality by themselves as it is a relational, rather than reflexive, activity dependent on multiple others and drawing on the significance of social relationships. For me, the research included elements of 'border crossing' between different roles; I was a coordinator of our project, a teacher/facilitator and a participant-observer. I was also placed in a position of vulnerability and exposure, as a learner and as my participants' student. I was a beginner, linguistically incompetent in all four of their languages, which created many 'moments of unknowingness' which Butler (2005: 20) notes 'tend to emerge in the context of relations to others'. These concepts intersect with identity reconstruction and liminality which I explore in the following section and return to in Chapters 7 and 8.

Perhaps the natural starting point for my account of myself in terms of this study is my own language biography as this seems to be the place from which people understand the teaching and learning of languages. Over the years, I have frequently been asked how many languages I speak whenever I am asked about my work. I usually answer by explaining the different ways I 'know' other languages: German from studying German language and literature as an undergraduate and an Erasmus year in Frankfurt, Japanese from living and teaching in Japan, Spanish from travelling in South/Central America and Mexico for extended periods, French from my A-levels, a bit of Khmer from volunteering in Cambodia, some Russian from travelling alone in Russia, and little bits of other languages including some basic Palestinian Arabic from the course I took in preparation for my PhD. These experiences are embedded in my way of viewing this research and my understanding of language and language learning along with the intercultural understanding of welcome and unwelcome I discussed in the introduction to this book.

Phipps (2013b) notes that linguistic incompetence can enhance ethical relationships within intercultural research as it includes opportunities for us to risk ourselves 'precisely at moments of unknowingness, when what follows us diverges from what lies before us, when our willingness to become undone to experience language as wound or lack in relation to others constitutes our chance of becoming human' (Butler, 2005: 136). Had I been linguistically competent in Tigrinya, Tamil, Farsi and Arabic, this would have been a very different piece of research. My identity and language biography continued to be shaped by this research as I became a learner of Tigrinya, Tamil, Farsi and Arabic. Our identities within the project were shaped by our shared experiences and the community we developed together.

Practicalities and considerations for researching multilingually

I made full use of my own linguistic repertoire throughout the project by operating from the heteroglossic perspective outlined in Chapter 2 and by embracing a translingual mindset (Canagarajah, 2013). The research included five new languages for me (Tigrinya, Tamil, Farsi, Arabic and, to a much lesser extent, Welsh) and also German, a language I had barely spoken for 20 years. Holmes *et al.* (2013) highlight that researchers should give full consideration of the possibilities for carrying out research in more than one language and the complexities of working in this way.

I considered how best to represent the participants' experiences and voices and how to incorporate multilingual data. During the learning sessions, much of our work was carried out orally, moving between English and the participants' languages. Each participant made notes in their language alongside English, and I noted down what I could while also ensuring activities continued to flow.

When working outside the classroom, it was impractical to make written notes. I prioritised our languaging and meaning-making as I felt writing everything down would counteract the decolonising approach. It was important that participants had ownership of their written work and could take this home with them. When appropriate, I collected examples of the participants' work but this was not always possible so the multilingual data was limited. Understanding and respecting their feelings was essential, and I prioritised their comfort and learning while balancing this with gathering data.

Instead, I wrote detailed fieldnotes after each session to capture fragments of multilingual data alongside my observations. My fieldnotes tell the narrative of the research and are autoethnographic as they draw on my role and reflections as an integral part of the fieldwork. I am written into this narrative as a participant-observer, allowing me to illustrate the nature of our multilingual interactions and the human, imperfect languaging of our work.

The place of Tigrinya, Tamil, Farsi and Arabic in the research is clearly outlined throughout this book alongside the reasons for incorporating these languages. The impact of my linguistic incompetence was so significant that I dedicate Chapter 7 to this theme to allow a full and detailed exploration.

For the case study in Germany, I read articles and websites in German and reported my findings in English. My observations and discussions with staff and learners at the GRC language school in Frankfurt took place mostly in German, and I have reported these in English. I chose to write the book in English as I wanted to focus on the use of Tigrinya, Farsi, Tamil and Arabic rather than the place of German in the research as this was not the main focus of the study.

Liminality

As the participants and I met and began working together at a time of profound change in their lives, the concept of liminality helped me better understand the significance of this period of transition and its impact on our work. Turner (1969) defines liminality as a place of 'betwixt and between' of being 'neither here nor there'. It is a stage that occurs during a process of change or development such as a rite of passage (Turner, 1969).

Beech (2011: 286) connects this middle stage with a process of identity construction and reconstruction when a person is 'neither one thing nor the other'. During this transition phase, social structures are disrupted and the usual limits of thought, self-understanding and behaviour are relaxed to accommodate this regeneration (Beech, 2011). Turner (1985) notes that liminality is essential for such regeneration and change in individuals and society, a concept I return to within the discussion on 'communitas' in Chapter 6.

This project can be viewed as a liminal space between existing identity and the new identity created through the process of learning another language and adjusting to a new life in Scotland. Meyer and Land (2005) describe a liminal space as a 'third space', a 'liquid' space, which transforms and is transformed by the person as he or she moves through it. It includes an understanding of both self-identity and social identity (Beech, 2011) and is a stage full of possibility and opportunity.

Liminality is also central to decolonising as it shifts power dynamics from control and dependency into more equal ones that were not previously possible (Phipps, 2019b). These liminal shifts were framed within the ecology of our relationship, as our own identities adapted, as I explore in Chapter 7. In the following section, I discuss how these principles were reflected in the research methods.

Carrying Out the Research

In this section, I outline the four main stages of the research and the methods used to carry out the project.

Understanding the work of the Red Cross in Glasgow, Wales and Germany

To gain an understanding of the work of the BRC in Glasgow, I spent two half days shadowing drop-in sessions for refugee clients to learn about BRC services, client needs and their referral system. I also observed two ESOL classes to help me understand how these language learning needs are currently being met. These discussions and observations informed the development of the teaching study.

I carried out 10 interviews with sector specialists in Wales and Germany (five in each country) to enable insight from experts supporting refugees with language learning in these contexts. I also visited the Red Cross branches in Newport and Frankfurt, met with staff and observed language classes in each setting. Findings from Wales and Germany were recorded in fieldnotes and observations and are explored in Chapter 4.

Fieldwork in Scotland

Participants self-selected for the teaching study which meant I had very little information about them before we met. An initial information session formed the first session of the two-week pilot (4 two-hour sessions).

The pilot study (Chapter 5) enabled the participants and me to evaluate the teaching methods and materials before the main study and gave participants the opportunity to try the learning sessions before deciding if they wanted to continue. The content of the learning sessions was decided in collaboration with the research participants, allowing participants to co-design the project as much as possible.

As I did not meet the participants until the first day of the pilot, I was restricted in terms of how much I could plan in advance. This openness was critical to CPAR and the decolonising approach. I gathered ideas and suggestions as preparation, guided by conversations with BRC staff in Glasgow and the findings from Wales and Germany. My initial ideas included using picture books to develop intergenerational activities; however, at the first meeting the participants requested that we focus on 'everyday' topics to support them with settling into life in Glasgow such as using the bus, shopping, healthcare and things to do in the local area. Content was informed by ongoing feedback from participants.

I initially intended for the main study to consist of 7 two-hour sessions, but this was extended twice at the participants' request to 14 two-hour learning sessions. I observed every learning session and wrote detailed fieldnotes which included informal dialogue and feedback from participants as well as my own reflections. I draw on these fieldnotes in Chapters 6, 7, 8 and 9.

The teaching study incorporated translanguaging methodology with learners working together using their full linguistic repertoire to complete tasks. The characteristics of a co-learning relationship (García & Li, 2014b) were embedded in the study, and I discuss these in full in Chapter 6 alongside the principles of translanguaging which were fundamental to our work.

Intergenerational learning

As my research included family members of different age groups, I needed to consider the intergenerational aspect of the project and to ensure that all age groups were engaged in the learning sessions. This included family members working together to complete tasks in their own languages but also consideration of how unrelated participants might interact during the sessions. Again, this was something I could not be sure of until the first day of the pilot as it depended on the ages of the children.

In Scotland, 'Generations Working Together' define good practice for intergenerational work as reciprocal, participatory, culturally grounded, mutual respectful and inter-disciplinary to broaden and enable inclusive thinking (Generations Working Together, 2015). I ensured I had planned specific outcomes for each age group by tailoring activities for parents and children based on the focus on family relationships and how we could support these through learning language together. An example of such an intergenerational activity with different tasks and different outcomes is given in Chapter 9 through our activity to create a multilingual body poster. The principles of good practice suggested here are compatible with CPAR and an ecological approach.

Interviews with teaching study participants

I facilitated three 'semi-structured' audio-recorded interviews during the teaching study (the end of the pilot, halfway through the main study and at the end of the main study). Participants opted to do these as group conversations. Each interview was supported by interpreters. Transcripts and a 'key findings' document were returned to participants for approval.

Ethics of care

Ethical intercultural relationships were essential to the project due to the circumstances through which the women had arrived in the UK. Yuval-Davis (2011) notes how feminist ethics of care transcends cultures as respect and trust must be mutual, rather than one person in a more dominant position caring for someone needy; concepts reflected in the collaborative nature of our work.

I had an ethical responsibility towards the participants and their welfare that went far beyond the formal process of applying for ethical approval to carry out the research. As I met the participants so soon after their arrival in Scotland, it was important that I worked sensitively to create a positive and welcoming experience to support them to look towards their futures as New Scots rather than focusing on the circumstances which had resulted in their need to leave their countries. I reminded participants that they did not have to refer to their individual circumstances unless they wanted to. I did not ask personal questions regarding their circumstances and assured them participation in all activities was optional.

I also made sure the participants understood the significance of their role within the research by reiterating the importance of their views and thanking them for being part of the project. The BRC provided interpreters to support me to explain the research aims and ensure informed consent in the first session, for the interviews, and to check the key findings and transcripts.

I knew that participants might require additional support which fell outside the remit of this project. The partnership with the BRC meant I could refer participants to relevant support services if necessary. Pseudonyms are used throughout this book to protect identity, which was agreed at the point of informed consent.

The role of interpreters

The BRC provided interpreters for the interviews, the information session and to check the key findings and transcripts. Interpreters were not present for any of the other learning activities. During the initial planning stage, I considered if it would be possible for participants to support each other informally rather than working with interpreters, but as the adults did not share a language and were at the very beginning of learning English, this was not possible. I took guidance from the BRC and we agreed interpreters were the best option.

Working with interpreters allowed me to ask participants about their views in their own language, which I felt underpinned the multilingual approach and enabled more detailed discussion. However, it also brought additional considerations as I questioned how I could authentically capture the participants' voices if their words were interpreted by a third party. Having interpreters present only for the interviews also altered the dynamics during our interactions, as I explore in detail in Chapter 6.

Data analysis

The data (fieldnotes, interview transcripts, observations, participant feedback) were analysed using thematic analysis (Braun & Clarke, 2006) coupled with bricolage (Denzin & Lincoln, 2008). Denzin and Lincoln (2008) describe the role of the interpretive bricoleur as a 'quilt maker' who draws together different materials to create a patchwork quilt. I operated as bricoleur by piecing the data together in this way, which allowed me to apply the interpretative framework at a theoretical and methodological level and respond to the research as it emerged.

I also compared data sources using crystallisation (Richardson & St Pierre, 2018) which refers to the crystal as a metaphor for comparing different types of data, as it is multidimensional. Ellingson (2009) stresses the importance of encountering and making sense of data through more than one way of knowing and compares this to viewing an object through a crystal.

As crystallisation also allows writing as a part of the data analysis, I found it to be a good fit with the reflexive nature of CPAR as my texts included findings from the interviews and observations and also narratives from my fieldnotes which were better represented by a more descriptive way of writing. Given the nature of the research, being able to understand the data from multiple angles and from more than one way of knowing seemed a better fit than relying on traditional triangulation.

Conclusions

In this chapter, I have outlined how I undertook the research, the research design and the reasons for some of my methodological choices. I have explained how a decolonising approach underpinned all aspects of the research and how I chose CPAR due to its compatibilities with the decolonising methodology and the participatory nature of the research design. I aimed for critical reflection rather than objectivity.

The study is small, with four families taking part, and I am very aware that this research only represents a small number of views and experiences. However, given the short time the participants had been in the country, our limited shared language and the fact that the participants did not share a language, the small group size meant I was able to provide a high level of much needed support. The small group size also helped us to quickly build good relationships and to carry out the research in a respectful and responsive way which allowed for individual views to be represented in depth. In the following chapter, I discuss the work with the Red Cross branches in Wales and Germany; I then discuss the findings from this fieldwork, how they relate to the Scottish context and how they shaped the teaching study in Glasgow.

4 Wales and Germany

Introduction

This chapter provides an overview of language learning for refugees in Wales and Germany following the discussion in the previous chapter which outlined the reasons for including these countries in the initial planning stages of the CPAR spiral. Here I consider language learning for refugees in Wales first before moving on to Germany, then drawing the findings together and illustrating how they shaped the study in Scotland.

Wales

Wales holds a unique status as the only officially bilingual country in the UK, meaning that refugees arriving in Wales have unique opportunities to learn the two official languages of the host community. As translanguaging originated in Wales, I was interested to find out if the approach of combining both English and Welsh was used in ESOL classes and whether this approach also extended to the inclusion of migrants' home languages.

Wales has four dispersal centres for asylum seekers: Newport, Cardiff, Swansea and Wrexham. Most refugees have not chosen to live in Wales specifically but have been placed there by the Home Office through the dispersal scheme with the majority being settled in Cardiff and Swansea. The overall landscape of refugees in Wales has also been shaped by the arrival of Syrian refugees through the VPRS which has resulted in refugees being resettled all over Wales, including rural areas for the first time. This is significant due to the elements of regionality which impact the 'micro' language ecology as some areas of Wales are predominately Welsh speaking and others are predominantly English speaking. The resettlement of Syrians throughout Scotland through the VPRS has had a similar impact there with small numbers of Syrians being settled in more rural areas across Scotland while Glasgow remains the only dispersal centre. Newport and Glasgow have similarities in this regard as they are both major dispersal centres within devolved UK countries.

The key lines of inquiry for Wales were:

- How are reunited refugee families currently supported with their language learning in Wales?

- Is translanguaging present within the learning of Welsh/English for refugees?
- How is the language ecology represented in teaching and learning?

During this stage of the research, I visited the BRC offices in Newport and observed one ESOL class, one AVAIL (Amplifying the Voices of Asylum seekers and refugees for Integration and Life skills) session and met with staff. I also interviewed five sector specialists to gain a better understanding of the wider context of language learning for refugees in Wales.

The following discussion is based on the interview data, my observations and key documents which are relevant to the lines of inquiry.

Nation of Sanctuary: Refugee and Asylum Seeker Plan

The Welsh Government has openly opposed the dehumanising policies of the UK hostile environment and much work has been done at local level to support refugee integration in Wales. In 2019, the Welsh Government declared that Wales would become the world's first 'Nation of Sanctuary'; a plan which was endorsed by the United Nations.

The Welsh approach to refugee integration laid out in the Nation of Sanctuary Plan has similarities with Scotland's New Scots approach. Both recognise the importance of a holistic, person-centred approach which begins from day one of arrival. In her foreword to the Nation of Sanctuary Plan, Rossella Pagliuchi-Lor, UNHCR Representative to the UK, praises the Welsh approach as 'humane' and 'pragmatic' (Welsh Government, 2019b: 4). The foreword also notes how welcoming refugees brings positive benefits for both refugees and communities and how this is a 'win-win'.

The Welsh Nation of Sanctuary Plan openly refers to the constraints of UK immigration policies and the detrimental impact they have had on refugees and asylum seekers. In the Plan, the Welsh Government states its commitment to 'continue to monitor and seek to mitigate the worst effects of UK Government welfare reforms' (Welsh Government, 2019b: 13) and to identify barriers and find solutions. The Plan also recognises the responsibility and opportunities that Wales has to support refugee integration in its role as a devolved UK nation. It outlines the breadth of work which the Welsh Government is undertaking to reduce inequalities, increase access to opportunities and improve relations between communities.

The Welsh Nation of Sanctuary Plan gives an informed and detailed overview of work across a broad range of services (including housing, employability, finances, employability, health, education, rights, community cohesion) and identifies organisations carrying out work in each of these priority areas. Each of the actions in the Plan aligns to the themes and priorities of Prosperity for All: The National Strategy for Wales and the goals of the Well-being of Future Generations (Wales) Act 2015, specifically, 'a more equal Wales', 'a Wales of cohesive communities' and 'a globally responsible Wales' (Welsh Government, 2019b: 5). The actions are also closely linked to Wales' Strategic Equality Plan 2016-20 (Welsh Government, 2019b).

Like New Scots, the strength of the Welsh Plan lies in the fact that it has been developed in consultation with refugees and key partner organisations (including 120 refugees and asylum seekers, the Equality, Local Government and Communities Committee, Welsh Government officials, the Wales Strategic Migration Partnership, Welsh Local Government Association, the Welsh Refugee Coalition and other stakeholders). The approach is holistic and recognises how work in one area also strengthens outcomes in another, e.g. supporting refugee volunteering schemes would contribute to Welsh society, while also supporting language learning, mental health and employability. The actions in the Plan aim to be mutually reinforcing (Welsh Government, 2019b).

In keeping with New Scots, the Welsh Plan also recognises the negative associations of the terms 'refugee' and 'asylum seeker' and the dehumanising impact of referring to people by their immigration status. Instead, the Plan encourages the use of 'people seeking sanctuary' as an umbrella term for refugees or asylum seekers from any background and recognises that these members of our communities are 'people first and foremost' (Welsh Government, 2019b). The Welsh Plan also acknowledges that people seeking sanctuary come from a wide variety of backgrounds and as such they have diverse needs. A one size fits all approach does not work.

The Plan also acknowledges the skills which people seeking sanctuary bring to Wales, that cultural exchange and learning is a two-way process, and that 'people from different backgrounds have much to share and learn from each other' (Welsh Government, 2019b). It also acknowledges the skills and knowledge of people seeking sanctuary as they are 'experts by experience'.

The Plan highlights the importance of ESOL learning and states the commitment of the Welsh Government to promoting essential skills for refugees and asylum seekers to improve employability prospects, social cohesion and school attainment levels for children (Essential Skills, English for Speakers of Other Languages and Digital Literacy remain the key priorities for adult learning provision in Wales). The Welsh Government commits to promoting ESOL in line with the 2018 Welsh ESOL Strategy and to continue with the development of ESOL Hubs across all four dispersal areas (Cardiff, Swansea, Newport and Wrexham) to improve collaboration between ESOL providers, support appropriate placement, and aid ESOL progression.

Language learning for refugees in Wales

The Welsh Government supports free ESOL classes for refugees, migrants and asylum seekers. Wales has its own ESOL Strategy which lays out the strategic objectives for ESOL delivery and coordination in Wales. The refreshed 2019 Strategy makes the language ecology of Wales clear and specifies what this means for language learning within the bilingual context:

> Being a bilingual society provides a richness that can make learning English all the more interesting, and our funded providers are encouraged to integrate the Welsh language into their ESOL classes where possible. Recognising and understanding that there are two languages in use in Wales is very important. (Welsh Government, 2019a: 13)

The Strategy encourages ESOL providers to integrate some Welsh into their ESOL classes to support learners to recognise and understand that there are two languages in use in Wales and that any official letters they receive will be written in both English and Welsh. The sector specialists I interviewed highlighted that this is particularly challenging for those unfamiliar with the Roman script and that Welsh place names and signs present additional challenges for learners. The ESOL Strategy explains how resettling Syrian refugees across Wales into predominantly Welsh speaking communities requires language provision which supports them to integrate. To this end, local authorities are permitted to use their Home Office ESOL funding to support settled people to learn Welsh, as well as English (Welsh Government, 2019a).

One of the main barriers to migrants learning Welsh is the fact that Welsh classes are not free in the way that ESOL classes are. The only evidence of financial support for learning Welsh comes from my conversation with Erica Williams, the ESOL Coordinator for the Wales Strategic Migration Partnership, who tells me about how well the VPRS is funded compared to other schemes:

> There's always a line in the guidance that they do recognise that Welsh might be an advantage but the ESOL funding is purely for English because they consider that to be essential for integration into the UK and to some extent that is true because you would be stuck if you didn't speak any English however […] an email did come round saying that the Home Office had considered the situation in Wales and if your Syrian refugees expressed a wish to learn Welsh and you were happy that they had a functional level of English then you could use the funding to pay for Welsh lessons.

Discussions with the sector specialists indicated that payment for classes is a complex issue. ESOL learners who wish to learn Welsh are encouraged to do so through Welsh for Adults provision which is funded by the Welsh Government. The National Centre for Learning Welsh has responsibility for the fees policy for Welsh for Adults and they are currently considering their policy on fees for refugees and asylum seekers (Scaife, 2018).

The issue is further complicated by the fact that Welsh classes are not a direct equivalent to ESOL classes. ESOL classes are designed to provide additional support for learners in terms of settling into life in the UK and the development of more general skills such as employability, whereas current Welsh provision is restricted solely to the development of language skills.

ESOL teachers' attitudes towards learning Welsh were also highlighted as having a significant impact on learners' opinions on learning Welsh. As ESOL tutors may be the only person from the host community that learners have contact with, their views on the Welsh language may influence whether their learners see learning Welsh as an essential part of their lives in Wales. Ruth Gwilym Rasool, the BRC Refugee Support Operations Manager, told me: 'What I found is that when people are going to ESOL classes that is pretty much their only contact with people from the host community, is their ESOL teacher so a lot of perception and knowledge about the country depends on that teacher'.

There are also important policy considerations for language learning for refugees in Wales. Although Wales has an ESOL Strategy, there is no equivalent 'WSOL' (Welsh for Speakers of Other Languages) policy. Dr Gwennan Higham, a lecturer at Swansea University, tells me it is positive that policies such as the Welsh Language Measure (Cymru Cynulliad Cenedlaethol, 2011) are in place: 'the latest strategy, the aim is to reach a million Welsh speakers by 2050 and there is, for the first time, slightly more reference to migrants and the fact that they should be included in the picture.' As Welsh lessons are delivered through the medium of English, this presents an additional barrier for migrants who have lower levels of English.

Visit to BRC Newport

Women's ESOL Class

On the first day of my visit to the BRC in Newport I attended a women's ESOL class. Seven learners attended on the day I visited although this number is usually higher. The class has an informal feel and is very welcoming. Theresa Mgadzdah Jones, the Refugee and Migration Support Coordinator, who organises the classes, comes along for the first part of the class to take the register and support the women with any issues that have arisen since they last met. There is the familiar sense of the ESOL class being a key point of contact for refugee women to come for support with a wide range of issues including housing, school, financial matters, childcare etc. There is a sense of community within this supportive environment and Theresa tells me that this is something she is working to foster among the women by encouraging them to meet for a coffee or take their children to the park together on the days when they don't have a class.

There is an excellent crèche facility downstairs in the same building with enough places for all of the children of the women in the class. The atmosphere is warm and welcoming with tea, coffee, water and biscuits provided and the women appear to feel very comfortable with the setting and with the staff. The classroom is a large room with one central table where everyone sits facing each other. I am made to feel very welcome and the learners are keen to know who I am, where I'm from and why I don't sound very Scottish! We start the class with an informal chat about why I am visiting, where they are from and how they feel about living in Newport. It's a really windy day and, as most learners walk to the class, some people haven't made it today due to the bad weather.

Most of the women in the group are in their twenties and thirties and we discuss how their children are learning Welsh (it's compulsory up to Year 9, GCSE level in Wales) but they themselves are not. I ask if they feel they need or want to learn Welsh and I'm surprised that only one person says they feel strongly that they do. Theresa feels this is due to the fact that Newport isn't such a strong Welsh speaking area and it is possible to live there without using Welsh at all. There is a discussion about how children come home from school singing songs in Welsh and that the mothers would like to be able to understand these. Theresa greets the class in Welsh saying *'Prynhawn da'* to the group (good afternoon) but this is the only Welsh that is used in the class today.

The classes cover general topics that are typical of most ESOL classes. Theresa and I discuss the importance of content reflecting real life scenarios such as speaking to someone from the council, parents' evening, speaking to the doctor and other everyday situations. It is also clear that the classes go beyond simply helping learners to improve their English. Theresa stresses the importance of encouraging the women to forge relationships with each other, of providing a 'safe environment' and practising English in social situations.

The AVAIL project: Collaborative, peer-led learning

The AVAIL project is a European transnational project 'for coordinating the development of refugee led participatory integration projects between refugees, asylum seekers and host societies by utilising and developing best practice in co-production approaches' (British Red Cross, 2020: 1). The project is funded by the European Commission and contributes to the smooth integration of refugees and asylum seekers through piloting, learning from, and embedding proven and new models of work that are based on participatory, peer and community approaches.

On my second morning at the BRC in Newport, I attend an AVAIL session to gain an understanding of the collaborative, peer-led approach which underpins the project. The room is divided into tables, one per language, each group supported by an interpreter. The sessions are for asylum seekers most of whom are newly arrived. Today's topic is 'NASS Support' and a representative from the Welsh Refugee Council gives an introductory overview of what this is and how it can be accessed (referring to it as 'house + money'). There is a lot of discussion about how to survive on the £37.75 per week that asylum seekers receive, how to use the 'Aspen' card and how this differs from a standard bank card, how to use cash machines and what to do about housing issues. There is an activity on which organisation to go to for help and a group activity with scenarios for groups to discuss how to approach common issues including problems with housing and letters from the Home Office.

Barriers to learning ESOL

In Wales, the key barriers for refugees to learn English are lack of childcare and long waiting lists to access ESOL provision. The crèche at the BRC Newport offices is essential and Theresa has worked hard to establish this through combining various pots of funding (although working in this way is difficult to ensure long term continuity and development of the service).

Theresa feels strongly that there is a clear desire for people to learn the local language:

> despite what the media says that people are not keen to learn the language when they come here, and they want to stay in their own communities I have found the absolute opposite. People want to learn, accessing the classes is so difficult and I've got a waiting list with over 70 women and I can't cope. My provision is not enough. I could run numerous classes and crèches. Thankfully we've got AVAIL and they can support those women for a few weeks

Erica also talks about the barriers of childcare and transport:

> They do stop women going and I've also heard of families where one week the husband would go and another week the wife would go but they would never be able to attend all the classes because one of them had to be home with the children or to meet the children from school.

Erica tells me about the importance of having informal opportunities to practise English such as volunteer support groups, conversation groups, drop ins and coffee mornings and how such opportunities could be made more multilingual:

> you've mentioned as well using their own languages in the class and I think I agree with you on this but it's not a universally accepted idea in

> the ESOL community. I think the feeling that if you do that, they won't be using English, but I just think it would help if you just had somebody who explained a few things now and again in class. I think they would learn quicker and feel a lot more comfortable

All interviewees recognised the issue of lengthy waiting lists and the goal most learners have to study at college for which there are insufficient places in Wales as there are in Scotland, due to insufficient funding. Erica explained that the issue of waiting lists is being addressed at a local level through the 'Regional ESOL Assessment Central Hub' (REACH) in Cardiff although there are some initial teething problems with people being entered on the list more than once. This system is similar to the Glasgow ESOL Access Register and the issues that have arisen while establishing a shared, central system to manage ESOL waiting lists in Glasgow.

There are also additional challenges for reunited families. Theresa tells me how women who come and join their partner can be at particular risk of isolation:

> I think when the first person arrives, gets refugee status and brings their family over, that first person gets a lot of support then sometimes when their family arrives, the individual who is here already might be very familiar with the services that are happening and say "I want this and this and this for my wife" however, on the other hand they could also just arrive and fade into the background and don't really get to do very much. Say if your husband is already here and he's working he's got a life set up for himself. You will come as a woman with the children, the children are going to school and you'll probably just stay at home. I think that is a huge challenge.

Ruth highlights the benefits of tailored provision which includes an 'informal approach to begin with', the very different needs that learners have and how initial support needs to build 'confidence to come into the classroom'. Ruth explains that an informal class with opportunities to progress into more structured accredited classes works well and that different groups have different needs:

> I think what we've found with the Syrian resettlement is those people who might not have been through any education and they were put in the same classes with those who had so there was that unease and not wanting to go to classes, or not being used to it and levels of concentration and different learning styles for different people I suppose.

English *or* Welsh? English *and* Welsh or English *then* Welsh?

I had hoped to find examples of how translanguaging is used to integrate Welsh into ESOL classes but in contrast I found that, with the exception of a few simple greetings in Welsh, most ESOL classes are taught monolingually. Translanguaging has not made the transition into the ESOL classroom in Wales as a recognised pedagogy and I could not find evidence of translanguaging being used to incorporate learners' own languages within the learning of English or Welsh either. Instead, languages appeared to be kept separate with English being the priority.

Theresa feels that the learners in BRC provision should have the option to learn Welsh:

> I'd always been told these people are here they need to learn English because we speak English, that's the main priority. My argument has also been "but we are in Wales and we speak Welsh and there are two official languages in this country and we should make sure that our client group, if they want to, they should have access to both". My experience is there have always been people who have been interested in Welsh, but they have never had the opportunity [...] When you're travelling around Wales, you see the signs are bilingual [...] it would be lovely for the women to be able to walk around and say "well ok 'bread' that's *'bara'* I know what that means, the word for 'Cardiff' now I know what that means" instead of thinking "just English", ignore the other one that's underneath.

The Welsh Language Commissioner Policy Officer explains that the system for learning Welsh is completely separate from ESOL. Those who want to learn Welsh are directed to Welsh for Adults provision for which they have to pay. However, this provision is not an equivalent to ESOL in terms of preparation for living in Wales, course content, how the courses are structured, and their aims. There are significant differences between them not just because ESOL is free, and the Welsh classes are not.

The Welsh Language Commissioner Policy Officer also explains the relationship between policy and practice telling me that, 'the previous 2014 ESOL policy contained a section that suggested that the Welsh language may be a source of additional difficulty for learners'. This did not present the Welsh language in a very positive light. The Policy Officer explains how the current, newly published policy removed that section and how this was a welcome change.

> So, on the one hand you have this issue of what happens at the ESOL side, how these individuals who undertake ESOL provision are informed about the Welsh language, how they are encouraged to learn it and how the Welsh language is portrayed. The second big difficulty is that once the individual is directed towards Welsh for Adults' provision it is not an equivalent provision as I explained. ESOL is not just for learning English, it contains a lot of other elements, skills for life, preparation to live in the community and support for job seeking.

Despite the focus on English only in ESOL classes, translanguaging is a known and understood strategy used in schools to operate between Welsh and English. All interviewees felt there could be benefits to bringing such multilingual learning into the ESOL classroom. This is reflected in my interview with Theresa:

> I haven't seen it used. I guess the reason I think it will work is because we've got Welsh schools where children are learning a bit of English and Welsh and we've got English schools where Welsh has got to be delivered and in that way I can't see why if we're running an English class why we can't have some Welsh thrown in within that class. With our Adult Learning Wales classes for example I've gone in and given the women some core phrases which our tutor has used and if I walked in to an Adult Learning Wales class the ladies won't say "good morning Theresa" they'll say *"bore da"*, they'll say *"prynhawn da"* and I think that speaks for itself. It shows that given the opportunity the ladies will learn and if they speak more than one language already learning another language is not going to be that difficult, is it?

Gwennan also tells me that ESOL classrooms in Wales are predominately 'English only' spaces:

> From top-down the focus is on English only from my interviews with government officials and ESOL teachers. Not surprisingly with Welsh teachers they said it was very important for equality and for jobs for migrants to learn Welsh [...] One of them said we're tied in with the Home Office and you can debate whether they should be learning English or Welsh and that's what I found interesting they were always saying English *or* Welsh, not looking at it as one repertoire like all the research today about multilingualism.

Gwennan also gives a clearer picture of migrants' own attitudes towards learning Welsh:

> What stood out in my research was actually what the migrants thought themselves and I spent a lot of time teaching Welsh to them and observing what they did afterwards and they very much were clearly challenging that monolingual ideology saying that "yes, Welsh *and* English". That categorisation wasn't there and lots of them referred to their own backgrounds, the fact that they in many cases they had other languages

Translanguaging?

In terms of translanguaging, it seems as if this has yet to transfer into the ESOL classroom. Gwennan tells me:

> Translanguaging is something that people certainly do as a practice all the time especially between Welsh and English but I think there's a lot of room to further the term and it's taking on a new form across the world and I don't think that's been developed so much in Wales

Gwennan tells me how translanguaging is understood to refer more to bilingualism in Wales rather than to multilingualism: 'I'm not actually aware of any examples with other languages involved. In my observation, Scotland is moving towards multilingualism more in terms of policy whereas Wales is focussing more on bilingualism and I think in the long run that's neglected a lot of different aspects with migrants with their own languages'.

In my interview with Erica, we discuss multilingual learning within the context of how ESOL is currently taught in Wales:

> What you've described is new to me. I know about language support in the classroom to help move things along to make sure that everybody has understood but obviously a multilingual approach involves everybody, it's more inclusive, and to me a monolingual approach ... there might not be many in the ESOL community in Wales who agree with me on this, but it just feels so confusing and I know from having taught French in school or having learnt languages myself it is so good to have somebody tell you what that means and then you practise and you use it but there's never this moment where you're really struggling to understand what's going on and then I think you can't form those words in your head because they don't mean anything to you.

Gwennan feels a more coordinated approach is the way forward: 'my vision would be to incorporate it into ESOL, into mainstream provision rather than doing something on the side and communicating from the beginning that you're in a bilingual country and we have some Welsh language provision.'

During our interview, Gwennan tells me about her former work as a Welsh language tutor and the resistance that she encountered when suggesting that migrants could learn Welsh: 'a few people actually laughed at the idea'. For several years she taught Welsh taster classes on St David's Day and this was a highlight of her role with 100–200 learners taking part over the course of a few years. The response from learners to the taster sessions was positive; however, there were tensions with the teachers who felt it was fine to teach Welsh on St David's Day but that the learning should not go beyond that or become a regular part of the ESOL classes.

Gwennan tells me that the reasons given for the negativity from ESOL tutors towards learning Welsh included ideas such as 'they have enough problems with English' or that there didn't seem to be a need to learn Welsh or the idea that learners would not be able to cope with learning another language. Some attitudes perhaps stemmed from the fact that the tutors themselves did not speak Welsh with one tutor saying, 'I live my life through English and I'm fine, so surely migrants don't need it either'.

We also discussed the idea that language learning is presented as a linear process, which requires mastering one language before the next. There is an assumption that learning another language before the first is fully 'acquired' would negatively impact the next (in this case, Welsh) rather than strengthen the linguistic repertoire and increase connections between new language and what is already known. The assumption that English should be learnt before any Welsh can be introduced reinforces the prioritising of English in contrast to an ecological approach which values other languages as an intrinsic part of the ecology in which they exist.

Theresa, Ruth and Gwennan also feel that Welsh could be introduced within the current ESOL system where the relevant structures and support systems are already in place. Gwennan tells me: 'I was just asking about introducing the Welsh language within the ESOL context, but it didn't seem to be something that people could understand very easily, it was either one or the other'.

The benefits of learning Welsh were clear to all interviewees. Learning Welsh would enable more people seeking sanctuary to take part in their local communities and to gain a better understanding of Welsh history and Welsh heritage, particularly where Welsh is a large part of the local language ecology. Ruth tells me:

> It's about integration into communities [...] I would say in places in the north, maybe Carmarthenshire and those areas you need to learn the language to be part of something [...] I guess it's a sense of a community [...] There is a drive for more Welsh language speakers, particularly children, and I would think traditionally Welsh speaking communities are now seeing the worth of sending their children to Welsh schools. There's a drive to have a million speakers and all of that going on and they're quite keen for refugees and asylum seekers not to be excluded from that. Because you know, it's about their children's future when they've had their lives torn apart, they care very much about their children's futures.

Erica further highlights the language differences of each local ecology and tells me how learning Welsh is essential in certain part of Wales and that not speaking Welsh would significantly limit employment prospects: 'You're not going to get a job in the public sector in Gwynedd or Anglesey or Conwy possibly Ceredigion and parts of Carmarthenshire unless you speak Welsh. There's a whole sector of employment that will be closed off to you if you're not a Welsh speaker. It *is* important'.

Ways forward for language learning in Wales

Gwennan feels that a more coordinated approach is the key:

> I find it really hard that people are working in their own boxes and I would like to see better cooperation [...] I would like to see possibilities for migrants in ESOL classes to be able to do Welsh in ESOL classes and it wouldn't be these very categorised ideas there would be more room for translanguaging and the Welsh language.

Overcoming current barriers is also key to improving language learning opportunities, Gwennan tells me:

> One of the barriers is attitudes and different ideologies which I thought had been overcome many years ago and perhaps I was naive when I was living in London that people still feel very strongly against the Welsh language for whatever reason. That was what was quite nice about migrants, they don't carry this linguistic baggage that many people in Wales do or the large proportion of the Welsh population who come from England. I know many of them do learn Welsh and have respect for it, but some just see Wales as an extension of England and there are some problems that occur with that.

The Welsh Language Commissioner Policy Officer tells me how important it is not to focus solely on English as the language of integration; 'there's an automatic equation being made between learning the language of the country and integration. We certainly believe that the Welsh language is absolutely essential to it'. The Policy Officer notes how the ESOL policy highlights that English skills are essential for community cohesion which may imply that that learning Welsh is not, which does not seem fair or correct, 'I think that the updated policy, published recently, acknowledges that the Welsh language is also important in this respect. However, as I explained, there is currently no separate policy for ensuring that the Welsh language supports such integration to the same extent'.

Implications for this research

I had hoped to find examples of translanguaging in practice in Wales, but this was not the case. I found evidence of the need for a tailored approach and recognition of the benefits of informal provision, particularly at the initial stages of arrival and language learning. All interviewees were positive about multilingual approaches; however, further questions are raised about why the translanguaging pedagogy used in schools doesn't transfer into the ESOL classroom. The interviews underpin the prioritising of English, the commonly held belief of languages needing to be kept separate, the gap between policy and practice in Wales, and the need for better coordination and cooperation between services.

The initial conversations in Wales contributed to the emerging foundation of the fieldwork in Scotland by raising the question of contextualisation and agency of place alongside the need to 'bring the outside in' (Roberts & Baynham, 2006), to make language learning representative of the local language ecology. I felt this acutely as I sat in the ESOL class at the BRC looking outside at the street in Newport where all the signs are in Welsh, yet the focus remains on only English with Welsh often ignored in the classroom.

These findings emphasised that there is little recognition of the idea of linguistic repertoire or of the benefits of multilingual learning in practice in ESOL classrooms in Wales, although all sector specialists agreed this could be beneficial. The conversations also showed a lack of understanding and practice of how to implement translanguaging pedagogy or incorporate learners' home languages within the context of teaching English/Welsh to refugees.

The interview data and my observations from the ESOL class clearly emphasised the need for language learning to be relevant and connected to the local context, e.g. through content which reflects real world situations and by introducing phrases and place names in Welsh, although this appears to currently be quite limited. The need for an informal, gentle start to language learning was also emphasised.

The impact of the physical ecology and environment was also shown as an accepted factor which affects attendance and learning, as it was understood that people would not attend their ESOL class because of the heavy rain. These factors are known and understood but could be brought more directly into pedagogy as part of an ecological approach which draws on Haugen's (1972) ideas on the interrelationship between language and the physical environment. I explore this in detail within the fieldwork in Scotland in Chapter 7.

Collaborative peer-led learning is already happening within the BRC through the AVAIL sessions. Although this approach does not currently extend to language learning for BRC clients, the transferability of such approaches was clear to me and emphasised the appropriacy of the CPAR approach which I intended to implement for the fieldwork in Scotland. In the second half of this chapter, I consider the findings from the fieldwork in Germany and how they further shaped the teaching study in Scotland.

Germany

Germany has 16 federal states which are governed by the central government in Berlin. This structure is similar to both Scotland and Wales's devolved status in the UK as the central government holds responsibility for immigration law and the support services are organised at local level. In Germany, the model for language learning for refugees is based on a 600-hour 'integration course', organised at national level by BAMF, the Bundesamt für Migration und Flüchtlinge (Federal Office for Migration and Refugees), and delivered by a range of organisations within each federal state. As refugees have been dispersed all over Germany, these courses are widely available and, in contrast to the lengthy waiting lists present in Scotland and Wales, they are quick to access for those who are eligible. I explore the integration course below as it forms the structure for how most language learning needs of refugees are currently met. In the following section, I provide some context for refugee integration and

Germany's response to the increased numbers of refugees it has received since 2015.

Germany's 2015/2016 Response

Since the peak of the 'reception crisis' (Phipps, 2019a) Germany has accommodated 1.2 million refugees, more than any other country in Europe (Der Spiegel, 2017). In Germany, refugees are resettled in areas where there is plenty of housing but low employment. 2016 saw asylum applications reach the highest levels in Germany's history with more than 800,000 applications received that year. More than 1.4 million people have applied for asylum in Germany since 2014, which represents more than 43% of total applications to EU countries (Financial Times, 2017). For comparison, this is four times the number of Italy, six times that of France and nearly 12 times that of the UK (Financial Times, 2017). According to the Organisation for Economic Co-operation and Development (OECD), refugees are expected to remain in Germany long term and Germany acknowledges that their integration is a 'long-term project which is expected to take decades rather than years' (Der Spiegel, 2017).

The lines of inquiry for Germany were:

- What can Scotland learn from Germany's model of language learning support?
- How does the support for language learning for refugees within the GRC compare with the work of the BRC in Scotland?
- Is a multilingual approach present within language learning support for refugees?

The following discussion is based on my interviews with five sector specialists, key documents which are relevant to the lines of inquiry, and my visit to the German Red Cross language school in Frankfurt.

Changing attitudes

The sector specialists told me how German goodwill for supporting refugees has changed since the initial response to the reception crisis. Between 2015 and 2016, 15,000 community projects were launched across Germany to support newly arrived refugees including volunteer-led language learning programs, mentoring and social events, which increased opportunities for informal, flexible support to learn German in addition to the government funded integration courses. These learning opportunities mirror the informal start to language learning which was highlighted as important in the interviews with the sector specialists in Wales.

Staff at the GRC in Birkenfeld explain how initially there was a strong sense of empathy and willing to support refugees:

> The work that volunteers did was very different to what volunteers do now. In 2015 it was more like meeting the basic needs of the people who arrived in Germany like giving them food, shelter and clothes and keeping them warm [...] You didn't really need to interact with them. Now we need volunteers to help the people who want to stay in Germany to integrate, to help them learn more German and to know how to behave in certain situations to deal with bureaucracy. It's a completely different kind of help and I think on one hand it's more challenging for people and on the other hand I've got volunteers who feel they always have to justify themselves for helping the refugees because there has been a lot of bad press lately.

Dorothee Hermanni, an Integration Project Officer in Berlin, also confirms that this initial support has waned over the past few years. She tells me:

> This great enthusiasm of Germans who said, "we want to help the refugees" is no longer so much true, many people unfortunately are more in the right-wing side when it comes to talking about refugees.

Dorothee also talks about how a more collaborative approach could signal a way forward and how this would encourage people not to see people as refugees but as ordinary people. This might also encourage people to see the skills which refugees bring to Germany. Dorothee tells me:

> Improvements would be that refugees are not perceived as refugees but that they are seen as ordinary people with potential as we all are. I think there is still a lot of work to be done, many people still haven't had any contact with "the migrants", "the refugees" and there is more need for more initiatives to do something to show they are no longer refugees, they are just people from another country. I think this is still new for many people. I think Berlin is an exception, many cool initiatives are located here but in the rest of Germany in the smaller cities I'm not sure how liberal and interested they are.

There are additional challenges for refugees arriving through family reunion as current German law restricts the total number of people permitted to come to Germany in this way to just 1000 people per month. This makes it very difficult for refugees to bring their family members to Germany; typically the process and bureaucracy can take a year to navigate.

Approximately one third of GRC branches provide support for refugees who are searching for their family members but there are no specific support services for reunited families once they have arrived in Germany. As is also the case in both Scotland and Wales, reunited families access language learning provision in the same way as other migrants.

Language Learning for Refugees in Germany

The integration course

The BAMF-organised 'integration course' consists of a language course and an 'orientation course' of a combined 700 hours of contact time. The courses are aimed at learners who 'do not speak German well enough to make yourself understood in everyday life' (Das Bundesamt für Migration und Flüchtlinge, 2018). A fast-track version of the course consists of 430 lesson units.

The content of the language course is standardised by BAMF at national level and covers important aspects of everyday life including work, basic and further training, raising children, shopping/trade/consumption, leisure time and social interaction, health, media and housing (Das Bundesamt für Migration und Flüchtlinge, 2018). It also includes learning to write letters and emails in German, complete forms, make telephone calls and apply for jobs, and is assessed by the 'German language test for immigrants' (DTZ). Full-time and part-time courses are available, with most learners attending full-time and part-time courses available only in 'exceptional cases, for example if you are employed' (Das Bundesamt für Migration und Flüchtlinge, 2018).

BAMF acknowledges people learn best with others who have similar interests and needs (Das Bundesamt für Migration und Flüchtlinge, 2018). Tailored integration courses are available including literacy courses, women's integration courses, parents' integration courses and youth integration courses which help prepare young people for apprenticeships or higher education. The sector specialists agreed there are plenty of opportunities for learners to access these courses due to the better model of funding organised at federal level.

The orientation course

The 'orientation course' forms the last module of the integration course. It consists of 60 lesson hours (30 hours for the fast-track version) and is assessed by the 'Life in Germany' test. The course covers the German legal system, history and culture, rights and obligations in Germany, community life, and German values, such as freedom of religion, tolerance and gender equality.

Learners who pass both tests receive the 'Integration Course Certificate' (Zertifikat Integrationskurs) which certifies that learners have gained an 'adequate knowledge of German and important basic knowledge about German society' (Das Bundesamt für Migration und Flüchtlinge, 2018). The certificate entitles learners to apply for German citizenship after seven years of regular residence in Germany (normally, the requirement is eight years) and is also a benefit when seeking employment. In the following section, I consider how the work of the

German Red Cross Language School in Frankfurt complements this provision.

Visit to German Red Cross Language School, Frankfurt am Main

To set up the fieldwork in Germany, I initially contacted the GRC headquarters in Berlin as it coordinates the work of the 19 GRC federal branches. I also spoke to staff at the GRC branch in Birkenfeld before staff in Berlin advised me to contact the branch in Frankfurt am Main (see Figure 4.1) as it has the most well-established language learning support for refugees through the dedicated language school based at its branch in Galluswarte, in the west of the city. This is not typical of GRC branches and is the only one of its kind in Germany.

I interviewed Natalie Tiranno, the manager of the language school, in preparation for the visit to the school in March. Natalie explained that the classes they offer are not the integration course but rather Deutsch für den Beruf (German for work).

On the day of the visit, I attended three classes, all at B1 and B2 level. There was a strong grammar and accuracy focus in all of the classes with the goal of preparing learners for the 'B1 plus' test. The groups are mixed in terms of participants with asylum seekers, refugees and PhD students all taking part together, an issue Natalie tells me is challenging due to learners' different academic backgrounds and previous experience.

The classes take place entirely in German. There is a great atmosphere which feels so familiar to me, partly as it feels much like ESOL classes in Scotland and also because it reminds me of the 'Deutsch als Fremdsprache' classes I attended as an Erasmus student here in Frankfurt over 20 years ago. The classes are warm with a friendly, supportive environment and I am made to feel very welcome by the learners and the teachers too who are all interested to hear about Scotland and my research.

Figure 4.1 The German Red Cross, Frankfurt am Main

The facilities at the school are excellent with several large, bright, airy classrooms set around a central reception area. Natalie's office is to one side of this area and I notice a steady stream of learners knocking on her door to ask for support with a range of topics, much like the additional support provided alongside ESOL highlighted in my interviews in Wales and also fundamental to ESOL in Scotland. The classes and the facilities are about much more than language. This is a community, a support network, a place to go to ask your questions, a lifeline, and a chance towards other opportunities.

Inside the classrooms, the tables are arranged in rows, all facing the front with the exception of the B2 class which is arranged in a U-shape. I notice this as ESOL classes in Scotland are typically set up to encourage interaction and conversation between learners. In each class there is plenty of laughter and chatting between the teacher and learners and between the learners themselves.

During the first class, the teacher tells the learners in German, 'we're a multilingual group; tell your classmates in your languages if they don't get it …'. Although this may not be an official strategy, there is acknowledgement of learners' own languages, their place in the session and the support that learners can give each other in their own languages. Similarly, in the B2 class there is confusion between the meaning of *'authentisch'* and 'authentic' in English. An Australian learner asks the teacher who turns to me and asks me in German if 'authentic' can be used in English to describe restaurants to answer her query. I explain in German that it can. This referring back to the learner's first language quickly answers the question. The session content is grammar/accuracy focused with activities based around choosing the correct verb, article, preposition etc. which supports learners with German's complex grammar rules.

Natalie explains that the language school provides classes for over 100 people each day with between 8–9 classes and how this capacity has increased from 4–5 classes due to demand. The language school is based in Galluswarte, a part of Frankfurt where many 'Gastarbeiter',[1] Turkish guest workers, were traditionally housed. There is now a large refugee housing unit for 400 people in Galluswarte and the GRC language school is located in this area due to its proximity to this accommodation.

Natalie explains that the classes are not exclusively for refugees and that anyone who receives unemployment benefits can attend; 'they're all mixed and this makes it difficult because we have people who have a PhD and they are sitting next to a person who has come from Afghanistan who may not be literate and has just learnt to read and write'.

The classes start at B1 level and focus on language needed for work and to prepare for the B1 'Deutsch für Zuwandere' test. The class content focuses on achieving this goal, with accuracy a priority and few opportunities to practise German in a less structured way.

The need for a flexible, tailored approach

Within the interviews, there were some criticisms of the rigidity of the integration courses both in terms of the structure and the content. Dorothee tells me:

> If you want to offer these language classes there are strict rules ... sometimes this is too strictly organised. There could be much more freedom because they do not look at what the people need, they just say "ok in this period of time you have to do this".

The fixed number of hours for the integration course and the expectation that learners will pass an assessment at the end of a specified number of hours does not account for the different pace at which people learn. It also does not account for the different starting points which people have due to their backgrounds and previous access to education. This rigidity illustrates the expectation of the correlation between input and output rather than understanding language learning as a non-linear process. As the content of the integration course is fixed and driven by the need to pass an assessment, it gives little scope for teachers to develop a curriculum based on learner needs.

Unsurprisingly, all interviewees noted that language learning was essential to integration. Staff at the GRC in Birkenfeld told me: 'if you can't speak the language, you won't have any chance to become a functioning member of society'. Natalie was more specific about the level needed:

> You need B1 level to get integrated in the working process. If you're under B1 level you can't work at all. I also think it's very important because you have to speak to everyone not just Germans [...] Germany didn't think about integrating people like the Gastarbeiter. They didn't worry about integrating them because they thought they would just go and now you see what this was. It's really sad because I think integration doesn't mean assimilation it means both sides learn from each other in the same way.

Natalie's observations from working closely with newly arrived refugees and asylum seekers clearly shows that integration should be mutual and a two-way process with adaptation from both sides. Natalie also highlighted the opportunities for socialising and finding common ground which the language classes bring as a vital part of improving understanding between learners:

> In the beginning people don't speak to each other and after a certain time they get along and they become friends, and this helps with racism and sexism and a lot of things and it's very nice. It helps with integration. They are all in the same situation. They realise "you have a kid like me and you like to cook too."

BAMF can also force learners to attend the integration course by threatening to cut their unemployment benefits if they do not attend regularly. Language schools are required to report back to BAMF on attendance which puts course providers in a difficult position. If they do not comply with the rules, they risk losing their funding to deliver courses.

There is a clear need for a tailored approach which is partially addressed by the creation of the specific integration courses detailed above. The participants told me that in Germany the majority of language classes are monolingual including those delivered by the GRC. Natalie tells me the reasons for this:

> In our classes it's only German because they have a higher level when they start. I worked with unaccompanied minors before and the lingua franca after a while was Urdu. Other learners would tell them in Urdu and I knew a bit of Arabic and there were two children, one from Myanmar and one from Ghana and nobody spoke any Hausa and this was bad because on the one hand you're helping people and on the other hand you're excluding others so I started using paper and drawing things so then everybody could understand. In our classes for example B2 level, they speak only German and of course there are two or three people who speak the same language and they help each other, but *we* don't do it.

These conversations also reflected the belief that the teacher must know the learners' languages well to be able to incorporate them into his/her teaching. This idea echoes definitions of code-switching explored in Chapter 2 where the learners' language is used to scaffold learning, e.g. by explaining grammar points rather than translanguaging to co-construct meaning. This question was immediately present in many of my interviews in Wales and also in informal conversation with colleagues in Scotland throughout the project. Natalie continues:

> I speak six languages, but I don't know Tigrinya or Farsi or Urdu so how can I? It doesn't work. I mean in our levels I don't see this is necessary and I think they have to be able to work in the target language, in German, if they don't, they are in the wrong level. This other thing we are discussing with the translanguaging is how far can you go? [...] and you can't have only teachers who speak Arabic, Tigrinya but of course it should help but it could also make them a little bit lazy. If I speak only German from the beginning, they learn quicker because they have to understand. They concentrate better. We use only the target language in foreign language classes so you can't always have the target language word and the Italian word right away you see the table and say "table" in Italian. I don't know if it's more difficult to use other languages. Sometimes using just one you really learn quicker.

There seemed to be an acceptance that learners above beginner level would benefit more from monolingual classes, delivered solely in German.

I explained further about the affective functions of incorporating learners' own languages as I hoped to do in my fieldwork in Scotland:

Sarah: I think for people who are new to the country it's also about recognising learners' own languages and how this can help with confidence and make people feel their own skills are valued.

Natalie: Yes, there you are right. You can say: "how do you say 'hello' in your language?" I know only one word of Tamil and I told a woman in one class and she said, "wow, you know my language!" I think when you talk about intercultural situations […] it's more or less like this but learning or teaching grammar things they have to know. I think it doesn't really help.

In Chapters 6, 7, 8 and 9, I return to how teachers can incorporate learners' own languages if they do not know them well and the impact this has on the balance of power in the classroom. My conversations in Germany showed a general lack of knowledge of the principles of translanguaging and how it can be used if the teachers do not know the learners' languages well.

An ecological approach?

The sector specialists also felt that there was a need to create more opportunities for people to practise German outside of class. Staff at the headquarters in Berlin told me that the integration courses could be improved as they take place in the morning from 9am–1pm and after class people go home to their families and don't have time or a place to interact with German people. Staff reported that often the only opportunity learners have to practise is grocery shopping and that they don't have other opportunities to practise their German language skills. The government could provide more opportunities for learners to practise the things they learn in the integration course.

The focus on grammar and accuracy could also be seen as unhelpful when it comes to practising German in real-life situations which form a more ecological perspective on language learning. Staff at the GRC in Birkenfeld told me that they felt the classes were too focused on theory and that this could have a negative impact:

When the refugees come to me, they all say, "the grammar is so hard, I don't know the articles" and I tell them that it's not important because people will understand you anyway and not to worry about having the grammar right because if you focus on that you will always end up scared to speak actual German and I think they're not really taught that. They're taught they have to have the correct grammar and exactly the right word.

> They don't know how to explain things in another way, they're very strict, I think. I would prefer it if they were taught different ways to communicate with people if they don't have the correct vocabulary, just to take the fear from them and to have something where people can practise with actual German volunteers.

Increasing opportunities for people to practise their language in informal, authentic settings could improve this. The staff at the GRC branch in Birkenfeld also told me about the flexible, volunteer-led support in the more rural areas in Germany:

> Now I have about 15 volunteers, because over time with the negative press people don't want to work in integration things in their free time anymore but still, I work with refugees and the volunteers. We've got a meeting point for women, which is once a week, we've got a language class on a voluntary basis, which is once a week, we've got a writing tutoring and some kind of partnerships for mentoring where citizens of the parish look after refugees and help them with everyday life – how to fill in forms, how to go to parents evening, stuff like that.

Accuracy as a goal

The rigidity of the content of the integration courses is also called into question in terms of the appropriacy of some of the topics and how these needed to be quickly adapted as part of a more sensitive, trauma-informed approach necessary to support refugees. It is vital that teachers know and understand that people in their classes may be recovering from trauma and loss while simultaneously building their new lives in Germany. It is also vital that teachers understand the impact such experiences can have on learning and know how to tailor materials and activities accordingly. Natalie tells me:

> We also have to differentiate between refugees and the normal integration class, now they understood since two years ago. When I was teaching young unaccompanied minors, I had a group and it was difficult to teach them as they were all traumatised. I couldn't use the book to talk to them about family because their whole family was dead. So, I had to invent new things to work with and they understood this and now the new books for refugees have different topics.

Natalie explains how these courses now have the same grammar content but with more appropriate and sensitively thought-through topics. There is also some evidence of these courses allowing scope to go outside the classroom and practise in real world situations:

> Normally, they ask the teacher to go outside for an excursion to let them experience not only the classroom but real life. So, what we did was go outside in the street and they had to ask people what time it was or how

to get somewhere or their homework was going to the supermarket and asking for something or to write down how much butter costs and they started to understand why this is important to teach them. It's for you, it's for your life and you have to get it.

Integration from 'day one' and the need to recognise existing skills

The need for integration from day one which forms such an essential part of the Scottish and Welsh approaches to refugee integration, is also highlighted through the conversations with the sector specialists in Germany. Dorothee describes the need for integration and support from 'a very early stage':

> Language learning is a key factor for integration, but it does not work well if you separate them and you say wait until B2 until they are 'allowed' to be part of something 'official' like a job. I would say the sooner they have the feeling they are welcome, and they are an equal part of a group the better. I also try to motivate people – go to a sport group, go to a cultural group and be part of something then the language of course will be much more successful.

Dorothee highlights the strain that people feel when their lives are put on hold and how people often want to get started with work or vocational training at a much earlier stage than is often possible. She notes how this can be a particular issue that needs to be addressed:

> they really have problems; and "now I'm 25 and I have to wait 6 months to repeat something and then I have to learn something for 3 years". It's very stressful for them and I would also advise that politicians really look at what the person has as professional experience. What does this person bring? Does he really need to start at zero level? This is also not good [...] There is movement in this, and people are discussing this. This is linked to the rigid thinking of local authorities especially in the field of school administration; they are super rigid and super inflexible and it's really a fight between people who work in the school and see the potential and say, "hey they can do things quicker, they are able to do it" and the authorities who say, "no we don't want to lower our standards."

Both New Scots and the Welsh Nation of Sanctuary Plan highlight how important it is to recognise the great many skills and experience which refugees bring to their host communities. Language can be a significant barrier which prevents people from being able to use their existing skills. Although the German system provides far quicker access to language classes, the interviews with the sector specialists evidenced similar barriers in Germany in terms of language, employment and training which prevent and delay refugees being able to progress with their lives. In turn, these factors can contribute to frustration and can impact mental health and wellbeing.

Intergenerational learning

Although interviewees were positive about the idea of intergenerational learning, it was hard to find evidence of provision where family members could learn together. In Birkenfeld, there was some evidence of family members learning together in an informal setting:

> There is one family with the grandma, the mother and the daughter and you can see they are all coming to the meeting place together. The grandma can't speak any German – if you say something to her even in very simple words she doesn't understand, she needs someone to translate for her. The mother is intermediate level of German and the daughter, because she's had a couple of years in a German school, her German is very near native and they're helping each other but I think the grandma is not very willing to learn the language because she doesn't go out that often. She's Syrian and she's got a Syrian community in her neighbourhood so she can still communicate with other people, but it's restricted to Arabic speaking people. For the mum and the daughter, they are really keen and willing to practise and it's nice of them to take the grandma along as well so she can at least hear a bit of German when she is with us.

The staff member told me she felt that this support system of working with family members worked well for this particular group:

> in this group it really works, they support each other, or they ask questions. Sometimes the granddaughter translates for the grandma, sometimes the mum helps. So, I think learning together for those three people works.

Aside from this one example, the sector specialists were not aware of any other opportunities for families to learn German together.

Implications for this research

The fieldwork in Germany provided an interesting comparison with both the physical ecologies of Wales and Scotland, and highlighted some of the strengths and weaknesses of the German integration courses, people's perception of these and the specific work of the German Red Cross Language School in Frankfurt am Main.

At structural level, Scotland can learn from the reliable and sustained model of funding which enables faster access to language classes provided by the BAMF, although the interviews clearly highlight frustrations regarding the rigidity of course content and the need for more specialised courses. There are also frustrations regarding the focus on accuracy, which takes a long time to achieve given the complexity of German grammar, and the need for refugees to be able to quickly communicate and feel part of society from an early stage without feeling that they need to speak perfect German. This focus appears to hinder learners' willingness to 'language' in their communities due to the fear of using incorrect grammar.

Conclusions: Shaping the Fieldwork in Scotland

The findings in Wales highlighted the dominance of English within the bilingual context, the position of English within linguistic hierarchies and how firmly embedded the idea of language separation is within ESOL contexts. In contrast, the findings in Germany emphasised the benefits of being able to quickly access extensive (600 hours) language classes within the existing German model of integration courses, some of which allow capacity for taking the learning outside the classroom to work on everyday communication through real-world tasks.

In both contexts, there was a lack of knowledge of the epistemological difference between translanguaging and code-switching when discussing multilingual approaches. There is a belief that it is only possible to teach multilingually if the teacher knows all of the learners' languages. Uncovering this belief highlighted the need to explore the fieldwork in Scotland from a position of 'linguistic incompetence' by committing to an openness to other languages and working from the translanguaging stance which I explore in full in Chapter 8. The pilot study was shaped by the themes outlined in this chapter combined with discussions with BRC staff in Glasgow, visits to BRC ESOL classes in Glasgow, and the foundation provided by the policies and academic literature explored in Chapters 1 and 2. In the following chapter, I return to Scotland to explore the pilot study as an introduction to the fieldwork in Glasgow.

Note

(1) 'Gastarbeiter' are migrant workers. The term refers particularly to those moved to West Germany between 1955 and 1973 as part of a formal guest worker programme.

Part 2

Beginning to Co-Construct a Multilingual, Ecological Praxis for Refugee Families in Scotland

5 Learning a Language is Hard Work

ቋንቋ ምምሃር ከቢድ ዕዮ እዩ
ஒரு மொழியை கற்றுக்கொள்வது கடின உழைப்பு
یادگیری زبان کار سختی است

Introduction

This middle section of the book explores how the participants and I took our first steps towards co-constructing a multilingual, ecological praxis for our research and teaching context. Freire (1970) used the term 'praxis' to describe the unity between theory and practice which are often seen as completely separate entities. Developing the teaching study in praxis describes the process of taking action in practice while operating within a theoretical framework of thought. Freire (1996) describes this as 'informed action'.

This section details the shift into the practical application of recommendations for multilingual, ecological approaches from the policy and literature review chapters, which we combined with the collaborative, reflexive nature of CPAR outlined in Chapter 3 to develop the teaching study as 'informed action' (Freire, 1996). Co-constructing our multilingual, ecological praxis in this way meant combining theory, practice and critical reflection on practice as equally essential elements of the project.

In this fifth chapter, I introduce the pilot study within the wider context of the fieldwork in Glasgow. Here I discuss the four learning sessions which formed the pilot and explain how this initial stage fed into the CPAR spiral by exploring how the participants and I began to establish our relationships and evaluate our ways of working before moving into the main study.

I chose to write the pilot study as a separate chapter because this initial stage is fundamental to understanding the participants' starting point for the research, and to understanding the significance of their commitment to the project. The chapter gives an insight into the challenges the participants faced and illustrates why this ecological and multilingual approach fitted this context so appropriately.

98 Part 2: Beginning to Co-Construct a Multilingual, Ecological Praxis

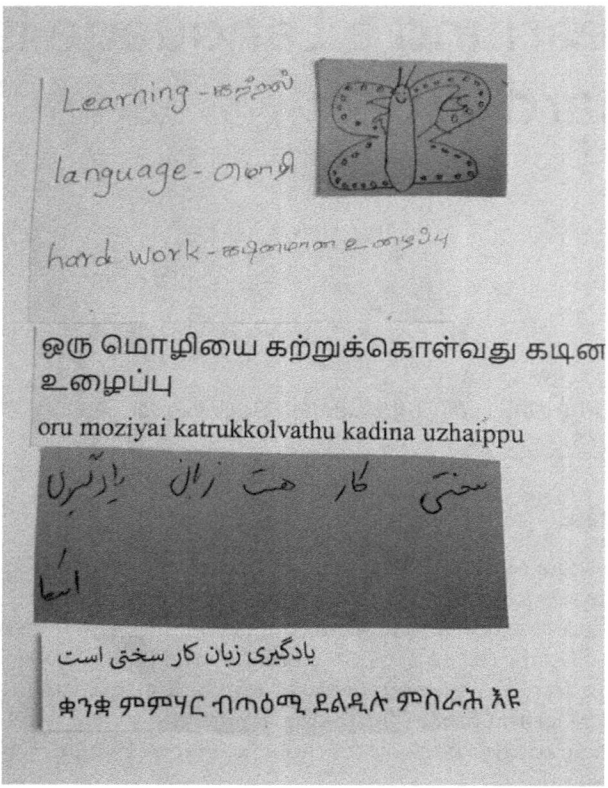

Figure 5.1 Reflections on the pilot study

Understanding the pilot study and its significance within the project is also essential to understanding the research process and how the key themes evolved from starting at 'day one'. The end point for the research, when the participants told me they felt 'empowered' to learn, would not make sense without understanding the starting point. I hope that by giving an honest account of the challenges the participants and I faced, others might learn from these experiences and be able to apply some of this knowledge to their own contexts, and in turn improve support for refugee women and children in the initial weeks after arriving through family reunion.

By discussing each of the first four sessions in depth, I intend to give a sense of how our relationships developed step by step to create our 'account' of ourselves and our positions within the research. I begin with an overview of each of the learning sessions before discussing the key themes which emerged and showing how they informed the main study.

Getting to 'Day One'

The BRC had several new clients who arrived through family reunion in the weeks before the pilot. The BRC staff told me they were keen to offer their new clients activities to attend in their first few weeks to help them settle in and we discussed the importance of being able to access support quickly during these vital first few weeks. We agreed that the learning sessions would work best for mothers with children of primary school age as this age group would be able to actively engage in the activities. We also agreed that women with children of primary school age were more at risk of isolation than women with children of pre-school age who can attend local community ESOL classes with crèche facilities, albeit, as discussed in Chapter 1, this provision is also limited.

The BRC staff and I agreed to invite people with elementary level English if possible as we felt they get the most out of the study. We agreed not to be too restrictive about this as we wanted to form a group with similar needs who could work well together. As participants had only just arrived, I knew they would not have had an English language assessment in Glasgow so it would be difficult to know their level of English or educational background prior to meeting them. I wanted to avoid a very mixed level group as this would make it more difficult to accommodate everyone's needs within the limited timeframe, particularly given the additional intergenerational aspect of the work. I also did not want to turn away anyone who wanted to participate, and I asked the BRC to keep me updated on the response so I could adapt plans as necessary.

I had initially hoped to deliver the sessions at the BRC offices in the centre of Glasgow as this was a familiar place for participants and I wanted to make the sessions as accessible as possible. This would have removed the need for an additional journey and additional travel costs for participants. However, due to the demand for meeting space at the BRC offices it was not possible for us to use a room there. Instead, we decided to hold the sessions at the School of Education at the University. This is only about a mile from the BRC offices; however, it is a bit too far to walk, particularly with young children, so this would mean an additional bus journey for participants. It also meant that participants needed to enter a large, unfamiliar building with several different wings and locate the room for each session. The BRC offered the support of travel tokens to cover the bus fare for the participants and also provided interpreters for the second hour of the first session so I could explain the aims of the research and have a full discussion with each participant to allow them to decide whether they wanted to take part.

I was keen for the sessions to feel as welcoming and informal as possible. Staff at the University suggested the children's literature library might work well as an informal space for the sessions (see Figure 5.2). Although the space is quite small and narrow, it is brightly lit and

Figure 5.2 All set – the children's literature library on our first day

colourful with low tables, children's books and comfortable chairs and feels less formal than a classroom, which I thought would work well for activities with younger children. It also had the additional benefit of being the only space in the School of Education available at the same time each week. I was concerned changing rooms each week would cause confusion and stress for the participants and impact their attendance as a result. I decided to hold the information session in the children's literature library and to discuss room options with the participants once I knew the size and the makeup of the group.

I had very little information about the participants before the pilot project. I liaised with the BRC staff about days and times, and they contacted potential participants using their telephone interpreting service to invite people to the sessions based on the criteria we had agreed. Two days before the first meeting, the BRC were able to pass a few key details on to me (names, ages of children, languages) of the people who might come. This helped me to plan the first session and confirm that the pilot could go ahead as enough people had shown an interest.

Day one

From the list of participants the BRC provided, I knew the families included Arabic, Tamil, Tigrinya and Farsi speakers. I knew the ages of their children and that they had all very recently arrived in Glasgow. I did not know how much English they knew or how much education they had been able to access prior to coming to Scotland. For our first meeting, I planned to introduce the research and break the ice through a few introductory activities to illustrate the nature of the sessions in the hope of fostering the participants' 'investment' (Norton, 2013), as outlined in Chapter 2. I wanted to find out what the participants wanted and needed from the sessions so that I could make the sessions as meaningful and collaborative as possible and to give them a shared sense of ownership of the project right from the beginning. This approach meant I could not plan the sessions before we all met, before I knew what they wanted to learn, their level of English, which languages they spoke, the ages of their children and their interests. I did not know what the language ecology of our group would be and how we would work together until our first meeting.

There were many unknowable factors at this stage, which also meant I could not be sure of exactly what my own role would be. I drew on Butler's (2005) 'account of oneself' knowing that this account can only ever be given in relation to others. My account of myself, who I would be within this research, and how the participants and I would relate to each other could not be known until we were together in the room as I did not know what they would need from me and how best we could work together.

I also did not know the size of the group or the ratio of adults to children. I had agreed with the BRC that the sessions could accommodate up to eight families. Would it feel like an adult focused group? Or a children's group? Or more equally balanced? I was committed to working with whichever families wanted to attend. This openness was necessary, it meant I entered the first session with many unknown factors but planning the sessions in advance would have created an artificialness rather than fostering the organic and participatory nature of the project which is central to CPAR. Having a predetermined plan would also have undermined the decolonising methodology described in Chapter 3 and the principles of translanguaging outlined in Chapter 2. To share power and collaborate meant leaving the process of deciding the content to those who knew what they needed best: the participants.

During the planning stages, I had many initial ideas about activities I felt could work well with a multilingual, intergenerational group, partly informed by my visits to the elementary/pre-intermediate level BRC ESOL groups the previous summer. These initial ideas included using picture books, origami craft activities or using disposable cameras to create photo stories of places in Glasgow to connect with an ecological approach – activities which I felt would have worked well with the participants I met at the BRC ESOL classes. It took time to liaise with the BRC and set up the pilot sessions, and confirmation of the go-ahead came just two days before the first session. Within the first 30 seconds of meeting the participants, I knew that none of the ideas I had had would be suitable. My fieldnotes below detail our first meeting:

Session 1

Monday 4 February, 3pm
It's a cold, wet afternoon as I trudge down Sauchiehall Street towards the Red Cross office on Cambridge Street in the city centre. Backpack on my back, full of activities and ideas for our first session. It's the kind of Glaswegian winter day that doesn't really get light at all. There is a constant drizzle and dampness in the air. I'm eager to meet the participants and see who will turn up today from the list of clients the BRC have given me.

I have already been to the University to set up the room for our meeting today. I have arranged the tables and chairs, put out snacks, cups and juice to welcome the participants when they arrive. Paper and pens, a portable whiteboard, an inflatable globe, a ball. A plastic tub of activities I can draw on depending on what I think might work best – paper, coloured pencils, stickers, sticky notes, marker pens and a box of flashcards.

I ring the bell and go up to the third floor to the BRC offices. I sit in the kitchen chatting with the staff member who has contacted the participants about the session, and she updates me on who has arrived and who has called to say they can't come. Then I collect the bus tokens that the BRC have offered to provide to cover the travel expenses for the participants. The BRC staff give me an updated list of six confirmed families, their names, the children's ages and their languages.

I enter the waiting room. It's very busy. I have been here several times before and it is always busy with people needing support of the BRC staff. 10 people look up at me. I smile and say slowly: 'Hello, I'm Sarah. Are you here for the English classes?'

10 blank faces watch me. No-one responds. I try my limited Arabic: 'Marhaba. Ana esmy Sarah'. I'm grateful that my name always seems easy in intercultural situations as 'Sarah' is also used in Arabic. One person looks up. One Arabic speaker perhaps? I look back to the list of names to check who is in my group as I think some people are waiting for other support services. We manage to identify three families from the list through my best attempts at pronouncing their names. There is confusion between the spelling of names on my sheet and how the participants pronounce their names. Some of the names are very similar to others. It isn't clear who is the mother in one of the family groups, both of the women look so close in age and it isn't initially clear who is with whom. Two of the husbands have accompanied their wives and children and one of the husbands tells me he will bring his son to the University later to meet us. I give him a map with the building and room number along with my phone number so he can find us.

It is awkward and clumsy. One of the participants sits alone in the corner of the room, not making eye contact. She stares blankly out of the window at the cold, grey afternoon. She lifts her eyes briefly to mine as I check her name and gives me a single nod in acknowledgement but does not smile. I hope she doesn't feel that she has to come if she doesn't want to. I cannot ask her more than 'are you ok?' She doesn't know me, and we don't have enough shared language to be able to communicate if something is wrong. I smile gently at her in an effort to provide reassurance and hope she will feel more comfortable as the afternoon goes on. The interpreters will meet us in an hour and I hope to find out more if she can bear with me until then.

I show the map to the University which the BRC have provided and give everyone their own copy. My name and phone number are on the sheet. I explain we are going to the University together and ask if that's ok. No-one responds but everyone follows me to the door and down the steps back out into the cold, grey afternoon.

This is where our story begins. In this waiting room, on this street, walking to the bus stop, pulling our coats up around our shoulders and faces, trying to shelter from the cold, Glaswegian rain. There is confusion and uncertainty but there is also risk and trust. They are trusting me by making eye contact and following me to the bus stop not really knowing who I am or what will come next.

Our walk is quiet with an air of anticipation and shyness. I chat and smile a lot, nodding encouragement and making as much eye contact as I can, not knowing how much they can understand. I need Tamil, Tigrinya and Arabic. The other Arabic speakers on the list have not turned up and I quickly realise no-one shares a language outside their family group.

I tell them the number of the bus and use my fingers to show 'four', 'Arbaa?' I attempt to say the number in Arabic. I feel lacking that I cannot do the same in Tigrinya and Tamil so check on my phone for the equivalent word for 'four'. It seems appreciated.

The bus comes.

(Fieldnotes 4th February 2019)

I knew instantly from this first meeting that the participants would need high levels of support. We would start at the very beginning as even basic greetings and saying their names in English were new. As we travelled to the University, I began to mentally adjust the activities for the session now I knew the number of participants, how new they were to Scotland and the languages they spoke.

The first few minutes in the BRC waiting room told me several things that would shape the project:

- No-one shared a language outside the family group. This would have implications for the relationships participants built with each other. It would also mean they could not support each other with translanguaging outside their family groups as I had hoped. I would need to find another way to facilitate multilingual learning.
- They were all at the absolute beginning of learning English. We would need to start at the beginning and take our time.
- All participants had been in Glasgow less than two weeks, this gave us common ground as a starting point.
- I needed to be able to support them in Tigrinya, Tamil and Arabic, particularly with the language needed to explain the activities. It was Monday and I would need to know some of this before our next session on Thursday.

I noticed how nervous and uncomfortable the women and children looked, particularly Semira who sat in the corner of the room alone, not making eye contact with anyone. When I smiled at her and checked her name, she nodded but looked away, and I wondered if she really wanted to come to the sessions at all. None of the group knew more than a few words of English and as they did not share a language outside their family group this would limit their interaction with each other. They could not support each other with peer translation. This was difficult as I wanted everyone to feel comfortable and supported from the beginning, and I hoped that the project would enable them to connect and make friends. It was important as the project was also the first contact the participants had had with any service in Scotland.

By focusing on the practicalities of getting from the BRC office in central Glasgow to the University I was able to introduce the participants to bus numbers, the location of the bus stops and how to use the travel tokens provided by the BRC. This introductory session situated the learning firmly within the context of Glasgow and within the context of integration from 'day one'. The session required a lot of knowledge that was new to the participants; the location of the bus stop, which bus to take, what kind of ticket to ask for, where to get off. None of the participants had any of the English or local knowledge to be able to do this. The burden of needing to ask for a ticket was eased by the travel tokens which could simply be put into a slot at the front of the bus and also meant participants did not need to explain the ages of the children to work out which tickets were needed.

We arrived at the School of Education, and I stopped to draw everyone's attention to the multilingual 'welcome' sign (see Figure 5.3) at the

Figure 5.3 Multilingual 'welcome' sign, School of Education entrance

entrance to identify all the languages we knew between us and we took time to try to pronounce each other's. I wanted to give everyone a sense of the University being a place where all languages were welcome as a starting point for our project. I also wanted to establish who could read in their own language before we reached the classroom. Participants were all able to point to their own language and tell the group how to say 'welcome' in their language. I pointed again to 'welcome' in English at the end of this activity, some of the participants repeated the word in English and we entered the main building together.

I led everyone up to the children's literature library. Everyone seemed relieved to have arrived; I offered snacks and drinks and suggested a five-minute break to settle in. By this time, it was 4.15pm, almost half of our session was over.

We tried a few introductory activities by standing in a circle and throwing an inflatable globe to each other to practise simple greetings in English and in Tamil, Tigrinya and Arabic and then asked each other, 'what's your name? where are you from?' The globe proved a useful tool for participants to show each other their country and then throw it on to the next person to ask, 'which language do you speak?' Everyone started to relax and smile, it was a good icebreaker and worked well to include the different aged participants. These activities also allowed me to get a sense of how much English the participants knew. Even these basics were new to the adults.

The BRC had arranged for interpreters to come along for the last hour of the session to support me with explaining the research aims and to gain informed consent. The BRC staff explained that interpreters are usually necessary and that they are used to having this support for their clients at first meetings, in contrast to the way that ESOL practitioners are used to working solely in English.

The interpreters arrived after these introductory activities, and I then explained the research aims and consent. I emphasised there was no obligation to decide in this first session if they wanted to be part of the project and explained they could think about it and let me know another day. I was relieved and delighted that everyone was enthusiastic, and they all agreed they wanted to take part. The interpreters supported this process by relaying the participants' questions to me, each working one to one with an interpreter. There was a shared sense of needing support as they were all so new to Scotland and all facing similar challenges. I emphasised the importance of their role in the research and that we would be trying out a different way of learning together and we would work collaboratively to do this. My fieldnotes below give a glimpse into this process:

> At 4.45pm Rushani's husband arrives with their son. I appreciate the effort he has made to bring his wife and daughter to the BRC at 3.30pm then to collect his son and bring him to University too. I know this has taken most of his afternoon. He shakes my hand warmly and I shake his hand firmly back and thank him. With the children, the interpreter and Rushani's husband and son there are now 13 of us crowded into the small room. There is a warm sense of coming together with the children eating all the snacks while I work with the parents and interpreters. The parents break off from our conversations now and again to tell the children off for eating too much.
>
> There is a sense of embarking on something important at this first session. We discuss what times are best to meet and how difficult they're finding it to get around. I find out that they all like Glasgow. I feel a shared sense of relief as they all agree how hard the last few weeks have been for them and I notice the adults shyly begin to make eye contact with each other. They can tell the interpreter, in this room, with the comfort of their children here, in their own languages, that this is not easy. The interpreters are listening carefully and so am I. We nod in understanding as it emerges how recently they have all arrived. I watch them count on their fingers. Less than two weeks. Last Thursday. 10 days. I explain we will work together in these sessions and ask, 'what can we do together to help you?' 'The bus', they tell me, 'getting to know Glasgow, buying food.'
>
> We laugh about the weather as the rain hammers down hard on the window and the wind whistles through the gaps between the glass and the wooden window frames. It is 4pm and now completely dark outside. As we throw the globe around, they ask where I'm from, I tell them I'm from England, that I found it difficult when I came here too. It will get easier. The interpreters translate my words an they all look at me with some recognition and nod.

(Fieldnotes, 4th February, 2019)

Deciding the Content of the Learning Sessions

At this first session, we discussed how the project could best meet the participants' needs. When I asked, 'What would you like to cover?', the room erupted into vibrant conversation, each participant speaking to their interpreter with everyone talking at once, giving their opinion on what they needed and all wanting to tell me at the same time. As everyone had arrived in Glasgow so recently, there was a sense of relief that they were struggling with similar issues and it was easy to agree the content of the learning sessions because of this common ground.

The participants chose to focus on getting the bus, buying tickets, food, everyday communication, greetings, numbers. This was a lively part of the session with a lot of nodding, laughing, and smiling and chatter in all of the languages present. At the end of the session, we put one of these requests into direct action by leaving the room together and going outside to wait at the bus stop together in the dark. I showed them the bus timetable, checked the bus number, gave out the travel tokens and waited in the cold with them. I took a photo of the bus number and timetable to use in our next session. When the bus came, I got on the bus with them, I reminded them where to put the token, I thanked them for coming, and I stepped off the bus and waved them goodbye.

There is solidarity in the immediate action of stepping outside the classroom and being physically present at the bus stop to show them how to use the bus rather than explaining it at a distance in a classroom. In doing this, I could see first-hand what the issues were and this allowed me to better support them. They could also see that I was 'in' this project alongside them. I was willing to step outside, stand next to them in the freezing February evening and wait for as long as it took for the bus to come. This action underlined that our project was not just about learning language in a classroom and that I was not a distant teacher figure standing at the front of the class at a whiteboard with a pen. It also meant that the issue of the bus became less daunting as it was something we had already begun to work together to overcome from day one.

In this first session we agreed some practicalities. Which days were best? Where did they live? How could they get here? What time worked best? How could we fit our meetings around school? Should we use a different room? What was the best way to keep in touch? I also checked phone numbers and we agreed to contact each other by text message when necessary. I agreed that I would text them ahead of each session to keep in touch and to remind them of our meeting; in return, I asked them to let me know if they were unable to make it. This initiated a relationship of mutual respect and collaboration which is key to the co-learning relationship, which García and Li (2014b) describe. I discuss how we embedded this foundation of mutual respect in the main study in full in Chapter 7.

I came out of the first session with my head swimming with ideas for the next few sessions. We would meet again on Thursday, in three days' time. I was very aware of the stage we were starting at and how much support they would need to get to the sessions. Would they come next time? We agreed via the interpreters that they would find their own way to our next class. I felt a significant sense of responsibility for their wellbeing and that these sessions should be an enjoyable, positive experience to build confidence in their own skills.

Participant Profiles

Three women and their children took part in the pilot study:

Semira

Semira is from Eritrea and speaks Tigrinya. She has a 10-year-old daughter. They were separated from Semira's husband for five years before reuniting in Glasgow two weeks before the pilot. Semira attended Primary School in Eritrea for three years then had to stop due to the war.

Rushani

Rushani is a Tamil speaker from Sri Lanka. Her daughter and son, aged 17 and 10, also attend the sessions. Rushani finished secondary school in Sri Lanka and learnt English as a foreign language for a few years at school. Their family was separated for several years and reunited in Glasgow a month before the pilot. Lakmini is Rushani's 17-year-old daughter.

Kamila

Kamila is from Sudan. She arrived in Glasgow two weeks before the pilot. She speaks Arabic and attends learning sessions with her two sons, aged 10 and 12. They were separated from her husband for several years before reuniting in Glasgow.

Session 2: *'Ciao Ciao'*

We agreed at the first session that the children's literature library was not a suitable room for our learning sessions (it turned out to be quite cold at that time of day, dimly lit as the daylight faded, and the narrowness made it difficult for us to move around and work actively together). The children in the group were also older than I expected (aged 10–17) so my idea of using the low tables for activities for younger children was not necessary. We decided that I would find a better alternative for our next meeting and agreed to meet at the children's literature library so I could accompany them to the new room.

Staff at the School of Education managed to find a science lab that was available each week at the same time. The room was large and bright with a good view of Kelvingrove Park. It had the additional benefit of a sink, which was useful for us to wash fruit (the preferred snack along with biscuits) and to fill the kettle which I brought to each session. The new room also had the advantage of a computer and a smart screen which proved to be a useful resource for using online dictionaries to show images and words in Tamil, Tigrinya and Arabic, and helped us understand each other.

On the day of the second session, I received several phone calls from the BRC staff telling me some of the participants had called to say that were worried about travelling to the University by themselves and had asked for someone to accompany them. I offered to meet participants at the BRC offices again but knew this could cause more confusion as some participants would come straight to the University and I would not be there to meet them. An hour before the session was due to start, the BRC called to let me know they had found a volunteer to accompany some of the learners while I met the others at the University.

We had agreed that the sessions would run from 4pm to 6pm. At 4.30pm, Kamila and Rushani arrived with the BRC volunteer but without their children. We moved to the teaching room, and I boiled the kettle to make tea and coffee, which was welcome as it was another cold day. Semira arrived 20 minutes later; I had left a note on the library door with my name and phone number and the new room number in an effort to help her if she turned up late. I was not sure how else I could point her in the right direction if I was not physically there to show her.

Fortunately, a member of staff helped Semira to find us in the new room when she arrived. Semira had not brought her daughter so I knew from the start of the session that the intergenerational activities I had planned would not be suitable! We now had a much bigger room for a much smaller group of only adults. I quickly adapted all the activities to suit the participants who were present. The three participants who attended all speak different languages so were not able to support each other with translanguaging.

The first stage of this learning process was navigating the journey to the sessions and we celebrated this success. After everyone had arrived, we focused on giving personal information: the basics of saying your name, where you are from, which languages you speak, addresses and numbers (to help with the use of the bus), tying everything back into the participants' own languages. Having only adults gave us scope to focus on their specific needs for this session.

I gave everyone a choice of how they wanted to travel to the second session rather than assume they needed my help as I wanted to strike the right balance between giving support and ensuring people feel welcomed but also not creating dependency. At the end of the session, I gave out the travel tokens and went to the bus stop with the participants. As we had worked on numbers in class and rehearsed the number of the bus we were waiting for, I was pleased that they could all tell me which number bus they needed to take back into town. Rather than waiting with them for the bus, I checked the time, checked they were happy to wait together and left them to wait without me. This was a small step to build their confidence in their own abilities from the start. I went back inside the building and watched through the window, where they could not see me, but I had peace of mind as I saw them get on the right bus together.

This session was hard work. I had prepared flashcards in advance with some key phrases in their languages to help us along. When I showed them to Semira, Rushani and Kamila their faces lit up, and I told them the equivalent phrase in English. The absence of the children and the interpreters made the session seem so much quieter. Without them, our group was stripped back to show just how very little shared verbal language we had and how hard it was to navigate with the few words we shared. We needed to constantly go back and forth between Tamil, Arabic, Tigrinya and English. In addition to finding a foundation for how to communicate, we were also trying to figure out how to work multilingually from this starting point and how to translanguage with these dynamics. I felt uncertain in this session. I hadn't done this before. By the end of the session, I had used every Arabic word I knew but that still left me lacking in Tigrinya and Tamil. As we concluded our work, I wondered whether they had enjoyed it. My fieldnotes below pick up at the point of ending the second session.

As we finish the session, I open the door for Semira, Rushani and Kamila. I smile and thank them for coming, trying to remember the word for 'goodbye' in Tamil, Arabic and Tigrinya. Semira is last to leave. I offer her the grapes and biscuits that are left, and she picks them up and thanks me. As she reaches the door, I put my hand up to gesture 'bye', she reaches out, presses her palm to mine, shakes her head and looks directly into my eyes, (I notice for the first time that we are the same height and close up she might be closer to my age and slightly older than I first thought). She pauses and corrects me with a smile and tells me in Tigrinya: 'ciao ciao'. *I hold her eye contact, smile straight back and respond with her palm still pressed against mine,* 'ciao ciao' *I tell her. We will do this in Tigrinya from now on.*

(Fieldnotes, Session 2)

Semira's actions reassured me that she understood the two-way approach I was trying to foster and her action of initiating interaction with me in Tigrinya showed me she invested in these practices by reciprocating the same way. I was grateful as I felt Semira was encouraging me that working between our languages was worth the effort.

Session 3: Another Dynamic

Four participants attended today: Rushani and her two children and Semira, which created a different dynamic again. As the children had returned, we started with a multilingual board race to review vocabulary from last time for giving personal information: name, surname/last name, postcode, telephone number, address. Being active in this way worked well and everyone seemed engaged. They seemed to enjoy the competitive element, particularly with Rushani racing against her own children. We worked slowly and reviewed all the key vocabulary in Tamil and Tigrinya as we went along.

For the next part of the session, we focused on free time activities with the aim of establishing what the participants might be interested in visiting in Glasgow while covering vocabulary for activities such as cooking, relaxing at home, visiting museums, playing sport, going to the park (we moved over to the window at this point to see Kelvingrove Park), again giving the names for all of these activities in both Tamil and Tigrinya alongside English. We then personalised the activity by working in pairs, asking 'what do you like doing?' Most of this language was new so we worked at a slow pace, moving back and forth between English and their languages and giving plenty of time for repetition, consolidation and making notes.

Rushani's children managed this more quickly and easily than the adults, so they worked together while Rushani and Semira worked together at the same pace, then we swapped pairs once everyone had practised. I noticed that when we worked as a whole group, Rushani seemed less confident, and I could see her copying her son's work. She seemed less confident in this session than she had in the previous one when her children were not there. I wondered if this was because she was aware they already knew some of the vocabulary that was new to her, and I questioned whether she found her children's support helpful or whether it held her back from working out the answers herself. The classroom dynamic in this session was interesting as three learners shared a language and Semira was the only Tigrinya speaker, which significantly limited communication between the group as a whole. I tried to mitigate this by splitting into pairs and working with Semira one to one using Tigrinya and English.

After introducing some of the language to talk about activities, I linked this to places in Glasgow using images of Kelvingrove, George Square, Kelvin Hall, the Hunterian, the People's Palace. Rushani's children seemed very interested and excited about this and we talked about places we could go as a group. No-one recognised any of the places I showed them, which made me wonder how much they had actually been out in Glasgow. I tried to link this into the map to show how close we were to some of the places they were interested in. We agreed to go to the Hunterian Museum in one of the sessions with the aim of connecting our learning to the University, the local area and the outside world in keeping with the ecological approach.

This session made me work hard to engage the different age groups and to make sure that Semira felt involved and comfortable with the three other participants who were from the same family. It was also important to make sure that the parents were not left behind as many of the English words were new to them and it took time to practise. Working multilingually helped the three Tamil speakers to support each other. Semira and I worked together, using an online dictionary to check that we had the right word, and this worked reasonably well. The games and being active were well-received, and I decided to include activities that get people up and moving around in subsequent sessions.

Session 4: ዐፍጥ ረ፭ቱ (I Like Sweetcorn)

I arrived at the room at 3.20pm and started to set up, eager to see who would turn up today. This always took a little bit of time as I needed to move the tables, set up snacks/drinks and materials, and make sure the room was warm.

I planned to start the session with an interesting expression on the screen in Tamil or Tigrinya to get everyone's attention as soon as they came in. This served to increase the visibility of other languages, following the principles of translanguaging in Chapter 2, and also aimed to support the development of a stronger multilingual identity (García-Mateus & Palmer, 2017).

At 3.30pm Semira arrives, she slowly opens the door and looks into the room to find me arranging tables and chairs. She smiles widely and greets me confidently in Tigrinya: 'Selam Sarah!' I look up to greet her in the same way 'Selam Semira!' Semira continues to coach me in Tigrinya as we set up the room together, boil the kettle, put out snacks, learning the words for each item in each other's language as we go along. Her increased confidence is significant to me as I know she has had the fewest opportunities to attend formal education and she has the least English in the group. I notice the contrast between how confident she is today and how she appeared at our first meeting when she sat quietly in the corner of the BRC waiting room not making eye contact.

(Fieldnotes, Session 4)

At 3.58pm my phone rang with Rushani's husband telling me his family were going to be an hour late due to an appointment. Initially I was concerned that Semira would be uncomfortable working one to one for the first hour. I explained this to her, and she said this was ok and we got started with reviewing vocabulary from our last session.

We started by reviewing giving your name, country and language and asking each other these questions. We took time to translate each of the words into Tigrinya at Semira's own pace, making notes as we went along.

As it was just the two of us, we were able to slow the pace to map everything between just English and Tigrinya and this allowed us to get to know each other better. I was pleased to see how comfortable Semira appeared to be with me.

Semira had told me at the previous session that she enjoyed cooking, so I had planned activities based on food. I explained this to Semira and showed her the food flashcards I had prepared. Her face lit up. This was a topic of genuine interest for her and we spent time going through each item and giving both the English and Tigrinya word. It was a simple activity but felt like a genuine multilingual exchange. We sorted the cards into piles of 'I like' and 'I don't like'. Facial expressions were important to this process and Semira seemed to enjoy miming eating corn (her favourite food), which made me laugh. I began to make sense of some of the characters in Tigrinya and the corresponding sounds within the food items we were working on. At one point, Semira reached over and wrote my name in Tigrinya on my notepad.

Part way through the session, Semira removed her headscarf, and I noticed how relaxed she seemed, laughing as we mimed and drew different images to communicate. It was important to take plenty of time to learn and practise all the new words and working in Tigrinya created a more level playing field as I relied on Semira to tell me how to pronounce each word in her language.

Working only with Semira gave me time to focus on how translanguaging can work with just one learner and one other language at a time. I saw these interactions as going far beyond code-switching as they underpinned the capacity of translanguaging for transformation. Our ways of communicating drew on the broader epistemological base of translanguaging, the openness towards other languages, and the fluidity of moving back and forth between languages as part of a linguistic repertoire which enabled us to use all our linguistic resources.

Rushani and Lakmini arrived and Semira put her headscarf back on. We continued working on the same topic together as a group, making a note of vocabulary in all the languages present, sorting pictures into piles of 'I like' and 'I don't like'. Semira was able to tell Rushani and Lakmini some of these new English words when they arrived, and I was glad to see this confidence in her. When Semira left, she said goodbye to me in Tigrinya again and she looked so much happier, relaxed and more confident than she had done on the first day in the BRC waiting room.

Learning from the Pilot

This section draws together the key themes which emerged from the pilot and identifies the learning that we carried into the main study that followed. Key themes began to emerge as early as the first session; these crystallised through the process of working closely together and analysing my own observations, fieldnotes and the data generated from the group interview at the end of the pilot, which I draw into the discussion and analysis in the discussion chapters in Part 3.

Relationships

The relationships within the project were grounded from the foundation that participants were all roughly at the same stage of learning English (beginners, all able to read and write, and knew the Roman alphabet). This created symmetry with my own role as I was also a complete beginner of Tigrinya and Tamil; I knew some basic Arabic, but this only helped me communicate with Kamila.

In addition, the participants all shared a real newness to Glasgow; having been here between two weeks and one month, they were facing similar challenges in terms of finding their way around the city. This shared common ground helped to build a sense of community, teamwork and meant they could understand each other's situation and help each other.

The small number of participants, the nature of our work and the fact that no-one shared a language outside the family group meant that I worked closely with each of the participants to establish our ways of learning together from day one. Semira, Kamila and Rushani had my personal phone number from our first meeting and our mutual reliance on each other for communicating necessitated a good working relationship.

Through my own lack of knowledge of their languages, my linguistic incompetence, the balance of power shifted away from me and away from English. This changed the ownership of our sessions and enabled Semira, Rushani and Kamila to take the lead in their own languages. This became a powerful tool to the extent that Semira held my hand at the end of the second session to correct me from saying goodbye to her in English, telling me in Tigrinya '*ciao ciao*'. I could see the intentionality and determination in her facial expression as she did this. My responding in Tigrinya was important as it created the openness for her to arrive early and greet me in Tigrinya in subsequent sessions, knowing she could trust me to respond in the same way. Swain and Lapkin (2000) found the use of learners' home languages enhanced interpersonal interaction and I already had a strong sense of this at this early stage.

The characteristics of a co-learning relationship (Brantmeier, cited in García & Li, 2014b: 113) were embedded in the study:

- All knowledge is valued.
- Reciprocal value of knowledge sharers.
- Care for each other as people and co-learners.
- Trust.
- Learning from one another.

Our learning environment was based on:

- Shared power among co-learners.
- Social and individualised learning.
- Collective and individual meaning-making and identity exploration.
- Community of practice with situated learning.
- Real world engagement and action.

These concepts define the co-learning relationship which formally shaped our work. The reality of our co-learning relationship was a far more up close and personal account, based on lack, humility and human interaction in a space with little shared verbal language.

The pilot showed the 'messiness' of our genuine human interaction and the need for gentle, accommodating support which allowed for lateness, misunderstandings and confusion. It was not about being able to understand every word, but more about learning that the detail of what is being said, the exact words, the grammar, the not-quite-right pronunciation don't matter so much. It is the languaging that matters, the trust and working together within an environment in which you feel comfortable to take the risk of trying out something new. For the participants, this meant trying to work in English for the first time. For me, it meant working in Tigrinya, Arabic and Tamil for the first time.

It was clear that the ecological approach, the languaging in the outside world rather than in the bubble of the classroom, would be central to our work. In our context, the New Scots theme of 'integration from day one' needed 'support from day one' which was accessible, appropriate, sensitive and ethical.

It is important to acknowledge that a certain level of confidence and determination was needed to attend the sessions and also to recognise that Kamila did not return after the second session. When I spoke to her husband, we agreed that a volunteer from the BRC would accompany her for the second session but that she would come by herself for the third session. I think coming by herself seemed too difficult for her. Perhaps too much, too soon. I texted her to encourage her to come but had no response.

It was clear how much emotional labour was required from me to facilitate these initial sessions. This took the form of phone calls, sometimes via the BRC telephone interpreter system, text messages, liaising with BRC staff to provide support, and checking that everyone was ok. This support and communication was vital at this stage and it was essential that it was carried into the main study. All three of the participants' husbands called or texted me at some point during the pilot to check the arrangements we had made. I reflect on the significance of their support and encouragement of the project in Chapter 7.

The significance of Norton's 'investment' (2013), discussed in Chapter 2, also began to emerge as a key theme within the pilot. The nature of the learning environment we created together was essential for learners to want to learn and to feel 'invested' in the process. The decolonising approach also contributed to this theme. By working multilingually, we created a more balanced relationship which further contributed to their investment in the research.

By the third session, the participants seemed comfortable with the way we were working together. This was shown by Semira's body language: removing her headscarf, appearing relaxed, laughing, sitting close to me, and the contrast with the first time we met in the BRC waiting room when she sat alone in the corner making very little eye contact and looking uncomfortable.

Semira's investment in the project was clear to me when she started to initiate interaction with me in Tigrinya, by touching my hand at the end of the second session and telling me *'ciao ciao'* in Tigrinya. This became our way of saying goodbye at the end of all subsequent meetings, and I would never revert back to English. I had the sense that she was trying to remind me of the words she had taught me in Tigrinya, and I was careful to always respond in Tigrinya rather than English. Our sessions prioritised what she *could* do rather than what she could not, and I felt that reaching this level of comfort had happened more quickly than it might have done had we worked solely in English. Working in Tigrinya enabled her and I to quickly connect in a meaningful way as co-learners and co-teachers on a more equal footing.

Intergenerational relationships

The families appeared to enjoy spending time together in the sessions. In the interviews, Rushani told me that she found it helpful that her daughter could help her in class when she didn't understand something. I also observed that some mothers lacked confidence with written activities, waiting to see what their children had written, then copying their work. Children also translated for their mothers in class, which the participants explained happens in their daily lives, and I questioned the impact of this on the mothers' confidence and whether this reaffirms this dynamic.

The participants were all also genuine reunited families, and I felt that I was reaching the intended group of people through the partnership with the BRC. All participants had experienced the trauma of family separation and were now adjusting to living together after significant periods of time apart. Different participants attended on different days which altered the dynamics each time. These fluctuations allowed me to try new things but made preparation challenging as I needed to adapt activities for whoever turned up each time. The small group size allowed me to personalise activities and give plenty of individual attention, which was important at this stage.

Place

The New Scots theme of 'integration from day one' (Scottish Government, 2018) came to life in the pilot study. As the participants were so new to Glasgow, our work became a genuine exploration of this theme in very practical terms, not two months or six months after arrival but within their very first few days. Their newness and the fragility of their situation contributed to the shape of the study as a whole and brought the concept of liminality to the fore (which I discuss in full in Chapter 7).

The participants needed orientation-style activities such as using the bus, getting to know the local area and buying food. The ecological approach prioritised taking the learning outside and made this meaningful within the physical context of Glasgow. Levine (2020: 84–85) notes: 'context is everything. A curriculum based on action research, whether with youths or older adults, is always and necessarily context contingent, meaning that the first step in planning is to identify the aspects of local context that lend themselves to a curricular project based on authentic situations'. For us, this meant more than drawing on the context for our classroom-based learning. It meant actually being together in the place and learning in it together. As I write up this research, I do not remember all the vocabulary or grammar points we covered together, but I do remember standing at the bus stop with Semira, Rushani, Kamila and their children. I remember how the cold wind and rain felt on my face as I peered along the road in the dark to see lights of the bus coming around the corner and Semira telling me the word in Tigrinya for bus is '*awtobus* ኣውቶቡስ'.

This is situated learning within a specific physical ecology, and it is this connectedness to the place and the people which makes it meaningful. This is what integration from day one is. It is support from day one – a showing, an accompanying. Woitsch (2012: 237) explains how in the intercultural field 'language learners walk, and we as teachers offer a certain kind of company'. I found this accompaniment central to both our relationship and to our work connecting our learning to the physical context. I explore this fully in Chapters 6 and 7.

Our learning was not based on a flashcard in a classroom with a picture of a bus. Instead, it was grounded in the need to remember the language for using the bus because it's freezing this evening and your ability to get home to your family depends upon it. Language learning from day one is not an ideal or something which is nice to have, it is essential. To survive. To be able to buy food. To be able to get out in the city. To live and to thrive. These first days are vital because they set the tone for all that follows.

The pilot took place at a key stage of 'integration': the point of becoming acclimatised to a new country, a new city, a new climate. The impact these external factors had on the learning was visible from our very own 'day one', and I began to consider the meaning and significance of 'place'. Was this term different to 'context'? Contextualised learning is key in ESOL, but our experience felt like something more viscerally connected to the physicality of the new surroundings. The cold, the weather, the shape of a city and learning to get around. The wind, the rain, the bus, the interconnectedness of these dimensions as an ecology in its own right. I began to consider definitions of 'place' within refugee integration, human geography (Kale *et al.*, 2019) and language geography (Shuttleworth, 2018). Chapter 7 explores what I began to term as the 'ecology of place'.

Language

In terms of pedagogy, the pilot allowed us to trial translanguaging strategies and to see what worked best for us in praxis as 'informed action' in the manner which Freire (1996) describes. We started from the point of increasing visibility of other languages, e.g. mapping single lexical items across languages to build confidence and starting each session with a word or phrase in their languages. This initial work highlighted the importance of the wider pedagogical interactions such as the additional time I spent with Semira setting up the sessions. It could be argued that this was not part of the project and yet, in some ways, this time we spent together had more significance and importance than the actual content of our 'official' time together. The fact she turned up so early spoke more than a thousand words in any language. She was voting with her feet and with her physical presence.

Linguistic identity began to emerge as a key theme, especially at the start. We were entering a liminal space, a process of adaptation and change. When you don't have English, your linguistic identity, repertoire and identity are Tigrinya. I began to visualise what this looked like; a repertoire consisting of languages other than English yet, through monolingual pedagogy, being limited to communicate in the only three words you know in English: 'hello', 'yes' and 'no'. The same level as my Tigrinya. I questioned the social justice and ethics of such an approach.

In terms of practical implications, a monolingual approach would not have got us very far. We needed as much common ground as possible, and I needed to meet the participants halfway. It felt exhausting to only use English. The pronunciation of a string of new English words looked strange and uncomfortable for them. When asked 'Where are you from?', I noticed their furrowed brows. When we tried in Tamil, it was my voice which sounded strange, my mouth which would not make the right shapes to fit the words. My brow was furrowed, not theirs. It gave them a break, a chance to take a breath, to lighten the mood and to build their confidence. Our pedagogical interactions were deliberately open and based on such human interaction, as Woitsch (2012: 236) notes, 'language pedagogy needs emotions, wonder, awe, and magic'. This was our own 'colourful mixture of discovery and learning' (Woitsch, 2012: 236). This balance of 'labouring and resting' (Polwart, 2019) with each of us picking up the others' language is two–way mutual integration itself, with effort on both sides.

This way of working showed linguistic hospitality and participant investment. I had to learn to facilitate translanguaging in languages I did not speak and I had to do this from 'day one' because, without this meeting halfway, there would have been far less communication between us. Their day one was also my 'day one' as I began to reconsider everything I had ever done in the classroom.

Norton's (2013) 'investment' was central to the project and linked to the place of their languages in our work. I knew the challenges the participants faced to come to class, particularly as we started the pilot at the beginning of February when it was already cold and dark at the time when participants needed to travel to the sessions. During the group interview at the end of the pilot, participants told me how useful it was to have their own language included and how this gave them power. They wanted and needed to use their languages as part of learning. This was both a practical and an ethical necessity. I draw on these findings in full in Chapter 9.

Conclusions

The orientation-style topics the participants requested highlights their specific needs at the point of arrival before being able to enter the 'system' of more formal language learning. At this stage, the participants urgently needed immediate support with the practical aspects of their daily lives: how to use the bus, finding their way around, local places, how to buy food and introduce themselves.

This chapter has highlighted the challenges which we faced as we began to co-construct our multilingual, ecological praxis and to shift into the practical application of the theory, policy and methodological recommendations identified in the first three chapters. Participants recognised this stage as 'hard work' when reflecting on this experience as we created the Spring School poem entitled 'Learning a Language is Hard Work' shown in Figure 5.1. It was 'hard work' to travel to the sessions, to begin to learn each other's languages and to find ways we could work together.

In the following three and a half discussion chapters, I analyse the main study and illustrate how the themes identified here developed over the course of our five months working together, and how I began to develop an 'ecologising' of language learning based on relationships, place and language/languaging. In the following half chapter, I discuss how we carried our learning from the pilot into the main study as part of the CPAR spiral.

5½ Uncovering Three Ecologies

Introduction

This half chapter sits in the liminal space between the pilot study where the participants and I met and the first of the three discussion chapters in which I present the findings from the main study. In this chapter, I discuss how we moved from the pilot into the main study, I give an overview of the learning sessions and discuss the development of the three 'ecologies' which emerged from the data, and I draw together the ideas laid out in the policy review, literature review and methodology chapters.

Moving into the Main Study

Due to the significant support participants needed and the effort they had made to take part in the pilot study, the participants and I decided to move directly from the initial pilot stage into the main study. This allowed us to build on the foundation we had established during the pilot without losing momentum. Developing a good working relationship and getting to know each other formed a significant part of the pilot. As the ways of translanguaging were also new to all of us, moving directly into the main study allowed us to continue to develop our praxis while the strategies we had started to develop were fresh in our minds.

The participants and I also agreed that I would ask the BRC if they had any more clients who would like to join the main study to enable translanguaging outside each family group and also to give a better chance of the project being able to continue if some participants dropped out. It would also allow the participants to make valuable social connections with others who had arrived through family reunion. Despite well founded reasons for trying to expand the group, this proved to be a difficult process, which I explore in Chapter 6. Three new families came along to an information session but only one of them joined the project for the main study, which meant our group consisted of a total of three families: three mothers and three daughters.

The participants: Yasmine

Yasmine is from Iran. She has been in Glasgow for five months and has a five-year-old daughter, Rana, who also attends the sessions. Yasmine finished high school in Iran and is also studying ESOL at college. She was separated from her husband for several years and reunited in Glasgow five months before we met.

Semira, Lakmini and Rushani continued from the pilot study into the main study. The addition of Yasmine altered the dynamics of the group as her daughter was five years old, significantly younger than the other children in the group. Kamila did not continue into the main study and this also shifted the linguistic ecology of our group as we no longer had an Arabic speaker. Instead, we included Farsi for Yasmine. This meant I could no longer make use of my limited Arabic, the only language within our ecology of which I had any prior knowledge. From the start of the main study, I needed to know some Farsi in addition to Tigrinya and Tamil.

Shaping the study into an iterative spiral of CPAR

At the end of the pilot study, we held a group interview to gather feedback and discuss the main study. This discussion enabled us to plan the next phase of the project as part of the iterative CPAR spiral, following the process of Plan – Act – Observe – Reflect – Re-plan – Act. I reflect on participant engagement and how effective this approach was in Chapter 9.

We initially agreed the main study would consist of seven two-hour sessions, starting in the middle of February and running until the end of April. In Session 8, I invited interpreters so I could check in more detail how the participants felt about the sessions, whether they were happy with how things were going and the topics we were working on. At this point, the participants asked if we could extend the project as they wanted more time to work together. We also agreed we would co-deliver a workshop as part of the upcoming UNESCO RILA Spring School in May. This checking in enabled us to shape the project together.

Extending the project made sense as it gave us more time to learn together. Learning a language is a slow, laborious process and, given the starting point for all of us, the time taken to establish getting to the sessions and consolidating the group, it did not make sense to stop when we all felt we were only just beginning. This also fitted well with my own beliefs and experiences as a language teacher as, at this level, so few hours might have felt superficial in terms of helping the participants settle into life in Glasgow. I was keen not to remove this support at this crucial stage.

We initially extended the project to 10 sessions. Then, after another request to carry on, we continued until the end of June, which we felt was a natural end as it coincided with the end of the school term. The participants' confidence in asking to extend the project twice illustrated their investment and commitment to our work, their enjoyment of the sessions and their role in shaping the project. At the end of the project, Yasmine was due to move to London to be closer to family but Lakmini, Rushani and Semira wanted to continue. It was a hard decision to finish the project at that point and again I felt some tension between my roles of researcher (working within the remit of my PhD fieldwork) and facilitator/teacher (knowing how long it takes to learn a language and wanting to give as much support as I could). We had 14 sessions in total for the main study, usually meeting once a week on Monday afternoons from 4–6pm in the School of Education. At the end of the project, I supported the participants with finding suitable local community ESOL classes so they could continue with their learning.

The learning sessions

Each learning session had a different objective and often also a different dynamic depending on who attended. Sometimes we worked in the classroom, in other sessions we took trips to the local places detailed in Chapter 3, making the most of our proximity to places of local interest in the West End of Glasgow. The adults were all present for almost all of the sessions. Yasmine always came with her daughter. Rushani and Lakmini were almost always there. Semira attended almost all of the sessions and her daughter also came to four of the sessions.

Despite some disruptions, I tried to establish routines so everyone knew what to expect and understood what I was asking them to do. I felt this was particularly important as I knew other factors in their lives were less predictable. The ecology of our relationship was formed through time spent together developing these ways of working. I tried to establish activities that could become familiar, for example by making other languages visible in the classroom as suggested in the CUNY-NYSIEB guide (Celic & Seltzer, 2011) by starting each session with a phrase on the screen in one of their languages. Whoever arrived first helped me to do this in Tamil, Tigrinya, or Farsi. This action built on the multilingual practices we had started to establish in the pilot and ensured that our language ecology was always visible and shown to be central to our work. This small action of starting each session in their languages also contributed to the decolonising methodology by decentring the position of English at every session.

The participants seemed to appreciate this familiarity. The repetition also served as a pedagogical tool as completing tasks became quicker and smoother with practice. I observed they became more confident working on activities that were similar to ones we had done before. We worked at a slow pace and built in repetition to build confidence and consolidate our learning, beginning each session with a review of what we had covered the previous time and opting to build the project around the few essential topics the participants had requested.

Choosing content

The participants chose to focus on the following 'everyday' topics for the main study:

- Using the bus.
- Time.
- Health, body and making appointments.
- Visits to local places.
- Money and paying for things.
- Food and shopping.

I developed materials and activities around these topics using a combination of realia, authentic materials such as bus timetables and maps, materials which participants brought to our sessions and materials I created specifically for the project. On one occasion, for the topic of 'health', I used some of the SQA National 2 materials to explore how I could adapt them for multilingual activities.

I revisited their list of chosen topics frequently to check that everyone was happy with what we were covering. Yasmine was less keen to let me know what she wanted to learn and told me: 'I'm happy for you to decide, I trust you and I think you know best what we need' (Interview 2). This may have been due to cultural differences or personality; it reminded me of my students in Japan and their reluctance to tell me anything that might be perceived as being critical of their teacher. I felt this showed Yasmine had a more formal view of our relationship, perhaps based on cultural norms where it would be the teacher's sole responsibility to direct the learning. I noted also that this dynamic did not seem to occur with Semira, Rushani or Lakmini. In Semira's case, this was perhaps because she had not had the chance to get used to more typical dynamics of education, rather than the collaborative approach we took, due to her education being so disrupted.

Three 'Ecologies'

Over the weeks and months working together, and later as I worked through the process of analysis, crystallisation and writing up, the subthemes which emerged pointed to three overarching themes which held wider significance within the study: (1) relationships, (2) place, and (3) language and 'languaging'. These broad themes were so fundamental to our work that I began to recognise each of these as an 'ecology' in its own right with an interconnected web of links between them.

The boundaries between each of these ecologies is porous. This porosity is appropriate and necessary as it connects the internal elements of the project (relationships, language) with the world outside (the place, the policy context). An ecological approach is grounded in this interconnected nature of contextual factors and their reciprocal influence on each other: 'pull one string, metaphorically speaking, and all the others will move in response' (Van Lier, 2010: 4).

These 'ecologies' form the structure of the three discussion chapters which follow in which I make a case for an 'ecologising' of language learning. This approach is holistic and views language learning not as a discrete entity but one which is bound within the physical context, the linguistic context (other languages known and how these interact in the mind) and the context of the relationships which shape it. I discuss the agency of each of these three dimensions within the process of language learning and consider how these three 'ecologies' intersected and were brought into contact in our work. The discussion explores what happens when we draw together the multilingual approach laid out in the translanguaging literature in Chapter 2, the decolonising methodology in Chapter 3, and the ecological approach in terms of the physical environment.

In Part 3, which follows, I begin a shift towards an ecologising of language learning by framing the presentation and discussion of the findings from the main study within the three ecologies of relationships, place and language/languaging. I begin by discussing the relationships within the project which formed the foundation of our work, and I explore the agency of these relationships as we built on the findings of the pilot study.

Part 3

Towards an 'Ecologising' of Language Learning

6 Ecology 1: Relationships

> If we are going to do this, if we are going to decolonise foreign language pedagogy, let's do it and let's do it as an attempt at a way of doing it. The only way to decolonise is to do it. It needs some forethought but ultimately it needs actions which are redolent with decolonising attempts ... It needs people who are able to embark on such a journey and return with tales to tell of what happens when decolonising is attempted in foreign language learning
> Phipps, 2019b: 5

Introduction

In response to the calls for 'decolonising' methodologies laid out in Chapter 3, the fieldwork in Scotland can be understood as a 'tale' of one such attempt to 'decolonise' foreign language pedagogy. As Phipps (2019b) suggests, forethought and planning is necessary and important, but ultimately the only way to decolonise foreign language pedagogy is simply to 'do it', to put the principles of 'decolonising' into action in practical terms and then share these experiences with others. As Freire (1982) notes, we should be 'learning to do it by doing it'.

This chapter illustrates how the participants took part 'on different terms' (Smith, 1999) due to our intentional decision to work collaboratively and multilingually by applying the principles of decolonising methodologies. As the fieldwork progressed, I began to understand this shared relationship as an 'ecology' in its own right, a blend of intercultural modes of communication situated within the physical and linguistic ecology of the project. This language learning in a broader sense explored different ways of 'knowing beyond – or *beside/s* words' (Thurlow, 2016: 503).

The ecology of our relationship contextualises our place from which to 'know' (Butler, 2005) each other by drawing on feminist care ethics (Gilligan, 1993; Noddings, 2012). Noddings (2012: 777) explains how establishing a 'climate of care' should not require extra effort 'on top' of other things, but instead it should provide a foundation which underpins all we do as teachers because 'when that climate is established and maintained, everything else goes better'.

It is important to start here because these intercultural relationships, the way we interacted with each other, serve as foundational concepts for the ecology of place and the ecology of language and languaging in the two chapters which follow. We embedded ethical intercultural relationships within our language learning through the wider pedagogical interactions within our work, particularly when verbal language was not the easiest way to communicate.

This chapter explores the relationships between the research participants and me, and between the participants themselves. It considers intergenerational relationships and support from family members outside the project. I refer to Brantmeier's (cited in García & Li, 2014b) co-learning relationship throughout this chapter, as it is relevant not only to the translanguaging pedagogy we favoured but also to the wider themes of intercultural research and decolonising methodology embedded in our work.

Stopping and Starting, Disrupting, and Establishing

Although the main study directly followed the pilot, we had an initial few weeks of disruption when we tried to increase the group size to accommodate new participants. Our relationship and the participants' investment in the project were tested during this period of transition. In my fieldnotes below, I describe the process of trying to expand the group for the main study and the impact this had on our fragile, developing relationship.

Session 5

Our session felt unsettled and frustrating today. The BRC staff member who tried to assist the new participants with getting to the session got lost, ending up halfway along Byres Road, a mile past the School of Education, and then had to catch another bus back to meet us. With all the confusion it took over an hour and a half for them to travel from the BRC office to the School of Education and I think the idea of needing to do this the following week seemed a near impossible task. Our session was in full swing when the new people arrived just 30 minutes before we were due to finish. This left half an hour to explain the research, answer questions, and facilitate a couple of activities so all the participants could get to know each other a bit and understand the project.

I tried to facilitate activities for Lakmini, Semira and Rushani, who had been working on language for using the bus and buying tickets, while also explaining the research to the new participants and trying to engage everyone. Semira, Rushani and Lakmini seemed uncomfortable with so many new people (four families; four mothers and seven children in total) suddenly coming into the room which now feels like 'our' space. Rushani, Lakmini and Semira seemed very shy to interact with the new people and trying to navigate this was difficult with so little time. The new participants asked questions with the support of the interpreters, agreed they would like to be part of the project and signed the consent forms. We finished the session and I gave the new participants the information they needed for next week.

(Fieldnotes, Session 5)

After the session, I texted everyone to check if they were coming the following week. Two people texted me back in Farsi, and I used online translation tools to translate our messages so I could also respond in Farsi. Rushani, Semira and Lakmini did not respond to my messages, and I worried they would not return.

These interactions reminded me of the fragility of our developing relationship. At the start of any course, I always feel there is a limited window of opportunity to engage everyone. In this case, I needed to quickly show that this project would be useful, enjoyable and a positive experience. I had carefully nurtured my relationship with Lakmini, Rushani and Semira during the pilot, and this session made me feel that that work/relationship was now at risk. I had the sense they might not welcome the change in dynamics that 11 additional people would bring. Would this still feel like their small, well supported group? Would they still feel the same sense of ownership and be able to shape the study with me? Would they feel confident to tell me if they did not? The new participants included two Farsi speakers, one Tigrinya speaker and one Tamil speaker – a perfect linguistic fit. The language ecology of the new group meant everyone would have someone to work with outside the family group, which would enable us to explore translanguaging more widely.

My observations and concerns proved to be well founded at the next session when only one of the new participants came and Lakmini, Rushani and Semira did not respond to my text messages. My heart sank.

Session 6

Only Yasmine came today. This is the first time that Semira, Rushani and Lakmini have not come and have not replied to my messages. It was the first time that Yasmine and I have worked together; we had already chosen the topic of 'health' and we tried a few activities to establish how much English Yasmine already knew. I kept an eye on the clock and wondered if Lakmini, Rushani and Semira would arrive late. I worry not only about the impact of the last session but also about their wellbeing.

It is an intense session with Yasmine and I working closely with her five-year-old daughter. I try to work in the same way that Lakmini, Rushani, Semira and I have established by checking back and forth between Farsi and English, but I can see this feels strange to Yasmine as she has studied ESOL at college here and isn't used to working across languages in this way. The others are not here to show how we usually work and bring life to the activities I have planned to support their chosen topics. It is hard to give a sense of how the sessions have been without anyone else for Yasmine and her daughter to interact with.

After class I text Rushani and Semira to see if they are ok but there is no response. I plan the next session but know that if they don't return I will need to speak to the BRC again to see if we can engage more participants, which would effectively mean starting again with a different group. I cannot go ahead with the project with only one participant.

It seems a long time to wait until the following Monday to see who will turn up.

(Fieldnotes, Session 6)

This was an uncertain time as I did not know if I was planning the next session for Rushani, Semira and Lakmini or just for Yasmine and her daughter. I sensed how fragile the participants' commitment to the project might be and was very aware of how easy it would be for them not to return. I did not know what other factors might influence their decision to come or not but I understood how much support they needed in these first few tentative weeks as New Scots. I knew they had enjoyed the pilot and thinking they might not return made me uncomfortable. These factors illustrated how precarious this period in their lives was and how important it was to feel comfortable with the group in terms of their relationship with me and with each other. In the following section, I explore trust and risk, and the balance between these themes and their investment in the project.

Building Trust, Taking Risks and 'Investment'

Session 7

4pm. I have set up the classroom and I wait to see who will arrive. I'm concerned that the fieldwork will all fall apart at this stage.

The progress of this project hangs on who walks through the door today. It is not just the progress of the study that worries me but knowing that Semira, Lakmini and Rushani and I had started to establish a way of working together that I could see was helping them. I want them to benefit from this project as much as they can. I feel a sense of having let them down, perhaps having misjudged the impact of increasing the group size. It is difficult to balance the components of the project; the role of the BRC, feeling I need to have a large enough group for the research to 'matter' and also the tension between my role of researcher and teacher where I want simply to be able to support the participants as best I can.

Unless they come today, they won't know that there is a strong chance that none of the new participants will come. In trying to expand the group I may have lost both groups. I am left with Yasmine who is unaware of these dynamics and seemed disappointed last week that she was the only participant. She asked last time, in Farsi through her phone – 'the others?'

I hear footsteps and chattering along the corridor. I have propped the door open so I do not miss anyone and am now sitting watching the doorway intently. The footsteps slow outside the room... Slowly Lakmini, followed by Rushani and then Semira appear in the doorway. I can't believe they're all back! I'm delighted to see them, to know they are ok and that they are going to give this another chance. They walk in, smiling and we greet each other warmly with 'Selam', 'Vanakkam' 'Hello'. There is no explanation about last week but we are pleased to see each other again. I'm relieved that we will have another chance to build this slightly larger group and to welcome Yasmine. It also means that Yasmine's daughter will have other people to interact with.

I ask if they're ok and they each tell me they are. Not knowing if they would return made planning this session difficult and as I greet them I mentally reconfigure the plan for today. I ask them to wait and I run back up two flights of stairs to the office to borrow our shared kettle and grab tea and coffee from my desk drawer. I run back down and show them the kettle – 'Coffee? Tea?' I ask. They smile in appreciation, make their hot drinks and we start a board race to review some of the words we have learnt for talking about health and the body. I know this is an activity they enjoy and I want to show Yasmine the type of activities we have found enjoyable together to help us with our ongoing review and vocabulary building. There is a great energy in the room, everyone takes part, laughing, smiling and competing with each other. It feels good that Yasmine can now see our work in action and be properly welcomed into the group. I hope that if the session goes well today they will all return next week and we will be able to consolidate the group.

We continue to work on health and body as a review, mapping single lexical items across languages. As this is the way we worked on food, the participants are now familiar with what I am asking them to do. It also demonstrates to Yasmine how we have developed ways of working to include all our languages.

The rest of the session goes very well and we finish up and say goodbye in all our languages. I close the door and start to tidy up. I can plan now. I decide not to invite anyone else to join our group – it isn't worth the risk and disruption.

(Fieldnotes, Session 7)

This experience showed me the fragility of the ecology of our relationship, its newness and the emotional labour, care and nurture needed at this stage. We would have a smaller group because of this, but I felt that if they engaged and came each week it would work well because I would be able to work closely with each of them. I accepted that we would not be able to translanguage outside the family group and, although I was concerned this would limit us, I viewed this as one of the key challenges of the relationship between theory and practice. Although they had not verbally told me they preferred the small group, they had made it clear this was their preference. I had to listen to them and to ensure the project was based on what was best for each of them. The project responded to real life as part of an ecological approach, and I did not want to risk losing Rushani, Lakmini and Semira. We had started this project together, and I felt responsible for them. Listening and understanding their needs went far beyond verbal language in our situation.

This session was a turning point for the project as it consolidated the makeup of the group. Our new language ecology would include Farsi. The ecology of our relationship would include Yasmine and her daughter. Lakmini, Rushani and Semira still formed the majority of the group, it did not feel like such a drastic change to include one additional family. I appreciated their risk in returning and giving the project, and me, another chance.

The fact that they returned despite what may have been an uncomfortable, unsettling experience illustrated their commitment and 'investment' (Norton, 2013) in the project. They returned because the benefits outweighed the difficulties of coming to the sessions. Semira told me at the end of the pilot: 'Yes, because it's a good experience for us and we're hoping to learn more that's why we have to do that. I come because this is helping me'.

The time and care taken to build this relationship was essential. Noddings (2012) describes this foundation as 'relations of care' and explains how these elements need to be established for everything else to go well. Caring for each other, not only as co-learners but also as *people* is also part of a co-learning relationship (García & Li, 2014b). This caring and development of trust was also key to establishing our own unique community of practice. Given the circumstances through which the women had arrived in Scotland, this foundation was even more essential to enable them to take part in the project and to feel comfortable coming each week.

This human interaction and care for wellbeing, which is grounded in the feminist ethics of care, is a fundamental part of intercultural research and permeates throughout the different elements of this research. It is present within the social justice aims of translanguaging, the decolonising methodology, the collaborative CPAR approach and the gendered nature of language learning. Compassion is also key to a human ecological approach, as Levine (2020) notes.

Over the weeks, which became months working together, we became increasingly comfortable and familiar with each other. This development of trust in the project and in each other was shown at the end of Session 9 when Semira seemed deep in thought, then told me: 'next time, my daughter come'. This was unsolicited. Semira had attended the sessions alone up until that point. I do not know the reasons for her decision. Was it because she saw how Rushani and Lakmini enjoyed the sessions together? Or did she need the support in Tigrinya? Or was it more about trust?

Brantmeier (cited in García & Li, 2014b) also notes that trust is an essential part of a co-learning relationship, and I understood this as key to the foundation of our shared work. Trust was shown again in Session 11 when Rushani, who always came with her daughter, attended alone for the first time as Lakmini was taking a college assessment. I was unsure whether Rushani would feel comfortable coming alone, particularly as she would need to take the much-talked-about two buses without her daughter's support. I know it was not easy for her to travel alone yet she overcame this to come to the session, illustrating her personal investment and trust in the project as the benefits outweighed the difficult journey for her.

Individual investment

The theme of investment in Chapters 2 and 5 carried very clearly into the main study. I knew some of the challenges the participants faced to come to class, I had seen them first-hand and stood in the cold, dark February evenings waiting for the bus with them as we all stamped our feet up and down, trying to keep the children out of the road. Their attendance and commitment to come to the sessions despite a challenging journey echoes the 'investment' that Norton (2013) describes and was evidenced further by their participation in the sessions, their enthusiasm and their patience with each other.

After the initial disruption with establishing the group, the attendance for the sessions was almost 100%. When someone was absent they always let me know in advance. This also showed the mutual consideration and respect we had for each other. In addition to coming to every session, no-one ever arrived more than a few minutes late. This meant that we could make the most of our time together, as we could go on short trips to local places after school but before closing time. I discuss our work outside the classroom in more detail in Chapter 7.

Semira's investment was clear to me throughout the project: by her attendance, arriving early and helping me to set up the room, in the way she participated in the interviews and in her careful teaching of me in Tigrinya. Working in Tigrinya enabled her and me to connect in a meaningful way that was not related to her English language level, which, as Simpson and Cooke (2017) note, promotes an improved sense of self-worth. My fieldnotes illustrate the significance of the time we spent together outside of the learning sessions:

Session 8

Semira arrived at 3.20pm today and helped me to set up again. She seems to enjoy this time and we have established simple routines for doing this together. I try to remember the words in Tigrinya for the items as we set up: ብስኮቲ *bshkoti,* ወይኒ *, weyni,* ሻሂ *shahi,* ቡን *bun,* ዋንጫ *wanča – biscuits, grapes, tea, coffee, cup. These are our own shared rituals. She is the only one who comes this early, knowing I will be here. On this* *occasion she opens the door and finds me eating an oatcake, a late lunch on what has been a busy day. She laughs at having caught me. I show her what I am eating, tell her the name, explain that it's Scottish and offer her one. She wrinkles her nose, shakes her head, declines, and laughs while looking at my oatcake. I don't know how to say it in Tigrinya and she doesn't know how to say it in English but we both understand that the dry, beige oatcake looks unappetizing to her.*

There is a quiet, calm sense of companionship in this work of setting up together. She chooses to be here, to come 40 minutes early before the others arrive. We meet here in the classroom with a quiet, companionable understanding of things we cannot explain to each other verbally, in this space between our languages. Leaving her home this early means that she does not bring her daughter as there is not time to collect her from school. This time together is as important and necessary as the time within the learning sessions. It is not just what happens within the class time of 4–6pm which makes this project, it is the building of our relationships, the establishing of this context in which to learn, to share, to redefine these parameters of relationships of learning and of being (together).

Rushani and Lakmini arrive at 3.50pm followed by Yasmine and her daughter who arrive a few minutes later and run in apologising. The dynamic shifts again as it is no longer Semira and I alone within our language ecology of Tigrinya and English. I have a sense that this project means something more to Semira than to the others. I am aware that she has the least formal education. Her expectations seem different and there is a different sense of balance between her and I. I never feel that she sees me as a formal teacher. As she sees me fumbling with the cables for the screen, I press the wrong button so rather than display the Tigrinya expression that I want to show, the screen retracts back into its tube near the ceiling – 'No!' I exclaim and repeatedly press the button to try stop it but it's too late. We look at each other and laugh. I am clumsy and human in this interaction and she seems to enjoy this part of our sessions, the bits that only she sees while we are setting up.

(Fieldnotes, Session 8)

By consistently arriving early, Semira showed me how much she invested in our work. As (Block, 2007: 75) notes, language classes form an important part of the process of 'reconstruction and repositioning' within the liminal phase of refugee arrival. It was also significant that Semira consistently initiated conversation with me in Tigrinya and this was key as each of these interactions can be understood as an 'act of identity' (Pavlenko & Blackledge, 2004). Here, Semira was reminding me that she was not just a learner of English, she was a fluent Tigrinya speaker, she was my Tigrinya teacher and my equal. By initiating these multilingual interactions, Semira also began to develop a stronger multilingual identity (García-Mateus & Palmer, 2017) by using her full linguistic repertoire to develop her English.

The sense of how much this project meant to Semira was shown further when the interpreters came for the interviews later in the same session. I noted Semira's body language. At first, Rushani, Semira and Yasmine gave short, polite answers, simply answering the questions but not giving much detail. My fieldnotes below explore Semira's response to the interviews:

I notice Semira listening intently as I reiterate the purpose of the research and I watch her sit up straighter when I tell her how important her role is and how much her opinions matter. The interpreter carefully explains this to Semira. I wait and listen to her very carefully give long, considered responses about what these sessions mean to her. Semira and I look directly into each other's eyes with the interpreter acting as our mouthpieces. It is a source of ongoing frustration that we cannot speak to each other in such detail without the interpreters but this seems the next best thing.

Seeing the way Semira responds shows me how seriously she is taking this project and I think she sees this symmetry in the way I nod and smile while keeping eye contact as the interpreter translates her words. I am confident of her investment and I have a deep respect and appreciation for the way she carefully considers her responses and speaks at length. The speaking at length is what we are missing – our conversations with each other are usually limited to short, measured chunks which can be translated, understood to make meaning. We 'language' through snippets of Tigrinya, English, and body language but the depth and the detail are what is lacking and I feel this acutely. The interaction with the interpreter, while it is necessary and it is my door to understanding how she feels about the project, is also hard to watch as I cannot ask Semira myself. How easy it is for the interpreter to ask Semira in detail in Tigrinya while I struggle to remember the word she has told me at least five times for 'chicken'. My linguistic incompetence is a tool, a feature of our translanguaging during our learning sessions, but it is something else during the interviews. I am lacking in their languages. I cannot meet her further along the English – Tigrinya continuum as I would like and if I could I think we both know we would have a lot more to say to each other.

Semira tells the interpreter that she did not finish primary school in Eritrea because of the war. I gently tell her how well she is doing in our sessions. I listen carefully in return, speaking slowly and checking her words for the interpreter to repeat back to her so she knows I have understood what she is telling me. By slowing down my pace of English I hope that Semira can catch some of what I say, this feels more respectful than speaking as if this form of English, the one that the interpreter and I use, is a secret language, one which is inaccessible, impenetrable to Semira, Rushani, Lakmini and Yasmine.

(Fieldnotes, Session 8)

In addition to this interaction underlining Semira's investment and commitment to our work, it also showed the mutual respect we had for each other and for our respective roles within the research. This mutual respect was key to both the decolonising approach and to the co-learning relationship that García and Li (2014b) describe. We were mutually reliant on each other to make this project work, and I could see that Semira's confidence grew as a direct result of emphasising the leading role she played in the group and in the project as a whole. As the only Tigrinya speaker, Semira's interpreter worked one to one with her to directly relay her individual views to me. I observed that she took great pride in understanding that her views were much valued and sought after. Her opinions, ideas and experiences were important enough for a third person to listen to, translate and relay back to me. They were important enough to be written down, discussed, recorded and returned to her for checking. Semira had had few opportunities to attend school due to the war in Eritrea, and I felt how deeply she invested in our work and in finally having her chance to learn.

The fact that these conversations could take place in Tigrinya was also significant. As I noted in Chapter 2, settling into the host community is dependent upon the development of a dually compatible identity which connects between the self and the new context as part of ecology. This also requires having a voice and having both the right to speak and the right to be heard (Van Lier, 2004b: 82). Tigrinya was fundamental to Semira's identity. It was her strongest language and she could not use it to her full advantage in class with me, due to my lack of knowledge. This barrier was removed during the interviews. Semira could finally speak in full, considered responses to the interpreter who was also from a refugee background. She could give detailed opinions to the interpreter, knowing she would understand. I was now at a disadvantage, and I had to wait for Semira to finish and for the interpreter to translate before I could be part of the conversation.

These interactions were key to the principles of decolonising and researching multilingually. In addition to Semira wanting to tell me more, I felt she was also showing me who she was in her own language – an articulate person with plenty more to say than I could understand. I understood her participation in the interviews as an 'act of identity' in the way that Pavlenko and Blackledge (2004) describe. The identity she enacted by using Tigrinya at length was more powerful than the subordinate student identity which Norton (2013) warns can be created by using only English and, as Canagarajah (2011b) notes, can be considered developmental and deficient. Semira wanted her voice to be heard in Tigrinya and rightly so. By valuing the position of Tigrinya and English in the interviews, I hoped to support the participants to develop their multilingual identities and their voices which, as Van Lier (2004b) notes, is part of ecological practice. In response, by listening carefully, I hoped to also increase the audibility which I discuss in Chapter 8.

I note similar investment from Yasmine during the final interview, as she gives extended answers, considering each response and speaking in depth for the interpreter to translate. The interpreters comment on how great the project is; I have a sense of inviting them into something which has become quite special to each of us within the private ecology of our relationship and, from the interpreters' comments, it feels this is visible to them too.

Finding Common Ground

Throughout the project, I found participants were keen to know more about me and there was a sense of trying to find what our 'common ground' was. In these conversations, I reflected on Butler's (2005) 'account of oneself'. In Chapter 3, I discussed my account of myself in terms of my language biography and my teaching experience; however, I found that the 'account' of myself that the participants were most interested in was as of me as a woman, a mother, a person who is also not from Glasgow. In the sessions, they were keen to know if I had children. Boys or girls? How old were they? A photo? How long had I been here? Our place in our families as women and as mothers gave us a position from which to understand each other. As the project explores the gendered nature of language learning, I found my position in the research was also shaped by my experiences as a woman and a mother also with children of primary school age. These were markers of the common ground between us because they are factors which transcend the boundaries of language and culture. These commonalities formed part of the foundation of how we understood each other and the way that we checked in with each other when we met, by asking how each other's families were.

My own position in the research was fundamentally shaped by participating as learner (García & Li, 2014b) from a position of linguistic incompetence. I was multiply disadvantaged as I tried to get to grips with all three of the participants' languages. This finding sits firmly at the intersection of the two ecologies of relationships and language, and was central to the project as it brought symmetry to our roles. I discuss this in full in Chapter 9.

Emotional Labour and Ethics of Care

The emotional labour required from me to facilitate the sessions continued throughout the project. This took the form of phone calls, sometimes via the BRC telephone interpreter system, text messages, liaising with BRC staff to provide support, and generally checking in with everyone. I texted participants before each session to remind them of the time we planned to meet and to confirm they were coming, and in return they let me know if they could not come or if they were going to be late. This worked well for almost all of the sessions with the exception of the disruption when trying to enlarge the group. This two-way process, balance and reciprocity was embedded in how we worked together.

This emotional labour also took the form of quietly noticing how people responded in the sessions, and this stepping back became a vital part of how we worked together. Paying attention and receptive listening are a fundamental part of feminist care ethics (Gilligan, 1993; Noddings, 2012), which are based on the premise that humans are inherently relational and responsive beings. They emphasise the connectedness and interdependence between people, and are grounded on the idea of voice and the need to be listened to carefully. As Noddings (2012) notes, from the perspective of care theory, such receptive listening is more than an intellectual tool, it is the basic attitude that characterises relations of care and trust. The 'receptive listening' which Noddings describes here goes hand in hand with the audibility I return to in Chapter 8. I found that stepping back to observe and notice created space for Semira, Rushani, Lakmini and Yasmine to fill the space themselves. This was an essential part of creating a balanced, collaborative and decolonising relationship as a foundation for our work. By not taking the lead, I emphasised the equality in our relationship and the fact that the participants were equally responsible for our work. As Phipps (2019b: 89) notes, this sharing of power is essential, without it 'there can be no decolonising'.

Emotional labour also meant creating a welcoming physical space (explored in full in Chapter 7). It was cold and dark at the time the participants travelled to the University, so I made sure hot drinks and snacks were available when they arrived and that the room was warm and comfortable. We took a break halfway through each session to keep energy levels up, which was particularly important for the children and helped establish a good routine for learning.

As the ecology of our relationship developed, we also accommodated the precarity and disruptions in each other's lives with a sense of mutual understanding of these challenges. We met at a time of profound change in the participants' lives, and the process of becoming more settled in our ways of learning together mirrored a wider sense of becoming more settled in their lives outside the project as New Scots within the physical ecology of Glasgow. I return to this theme in the following chapter as it connects with the ecology of place.

We developed a sense of caring for each other and each other's children (perhaps as we would our own, as we had established our position from which to 'know' each other as mothers of primary school aged children), a warmth, a sense of fun and friendship and of mutual support. This emotional labour provided a sense of stability. I made sure I was always consistent; I would always do as I said, they knew they could count on this and in return I asked the same from them. This worked. We were honest with each other and discussed alternatives when we needed to change plans.

As the project developed, the participants became more comfortable interacting with each other directly, and I tried to encourage this as much as possible. I could see how difficult this was with so little shared language, so we showed our commitment and care for each other in other small ways. Semira, Lakmini and Rushani were always kind and encouraging in their interactions with Yasmine's five-year-old daughter. They were always patient and, where shared language was lacking, they showed mutual encouragement and understanding with body language, smiles and eye contact.

Participants also became more comfortable with how they interacted and viewed me. Lakmini was 17 at the start of the project, and for the first few weeks whenever she wanted to ask me something she was very shy and would call me 'teacher'. Each time, I responded by smiling and gently reminding her to call me 'Sarah'. She gradually got used to this, a few times starting to call me 'teach ...', then laughing and changing to 'Sarah'. This became less and less formal and in Session 9, as I was engrossed in helping Yasmine, Lakmini called me by knocking loudly on the table three times in rapid succession to get my attention and shouting, 'hey Sarah!' By this stage she was confident enough that I was no longer a formal 'teacher' figure and that it was also OK to shout loudly to me. She also felt confident to take my phone from me when we visited the Hunterian (Chapter 7) to show me a better way to take a selfie. This gradual reduction in formality also happened between the participants, as shown in my fieldnotes from Session 9:

Semira arrived a few minutes after everyone else today and looked for somewhere to sit. There were plenty of empty chairs but Yasmine noticed Semira's hesitation, rather than interject I waited to let Yasmine act as host to emphasise that I am not in charge here in our shared space. Yasmine removed her handbag from the chair next to her and shouted 'hey!' followed by 'sit' to Semira. Semira looked surprised but took the seat next to Yasmine with a smile. Once both women were sitting they looked at each other and nodded, perhaps unsure of which language to use or how to greet each other. Our efforts to talk to each other are clumsy, but this is overridden by the desire to communicate, make ourselves understood, and help each other.

(Fieldnotes, Session 9)

This is 'languaging', 'a mode of exploration and embodiment, to allow a flow of action, impressions, natural conversation, showing and relationship' (Phipps, 2013a: 22) which I discussed in Chapter 3. Verbal language was lacking but by using all resources, including gesture, we could communicate what was needed in the moment. Here Semira and Yasmine combined language and gesture to co-construct meaning as a creative improvisation specific to their context (Canagarajah, 2011b) and needs in the moment. Their need to use all resources and their success in communicating brings us back to Becker's (1991: 34) statement that 'there is no such thing as Language, only continual languaging, an activity of human beings in the world'. In this case, our care and mutual consideration for each other was the priority, we would language as necessary to convey this to each other.

Our care for each other and for the children in the group was shown further on our visit to Kelvingrove Museum. I discuss this trip in full in Chapter 7 but refer to my fieldnotes from our walk back through Kelvingrove Park here, to illustrate our ways of caring for each other:

Session 11
  The museum is starting to close and we are asked to leave. We head downstairs and back out the other side of Kelvingrove Museum, facing Kelvin Hall.
  We begin walking along Kelvin Way then step back into the park, walking slowly together. It is quiet and companionable. Rana runs off ahead to the playpark. Yasmine calls her daughter gently back and we walk on but she runs off again, this time much faster in the other direction. Suddenly Semira yells – 'Ey... RAAAAANNNNNAAAAA NOOOOOO!' so loudly that we all turn around to look at her in surprise. I have never heard Semira's voice so loud. Yasmine and Semira only have the barest of direct communication in our sessions yet our bond and sense of community and togetherness is clear. There is a strong sense of caring for each other and a shared responsibility for the children in the group which extends to telling each other's children off and keeping them safe. Rana looks startled, she looks at Semira with surprise and quickly returns to walk alongside the rest of us in shock at being told off by someone other than her mother. Yasmine looks at Semira and smiles, in acknowledgement that this act is ok with her. Semira strides on through the park. She has succeeded. In Scotland, we are not so free telling each other's children off. Rana stays with us until we reach the park gate at the other side. We smile and laugh at each other, understanding that Rana would not come back to us when her mother called her but she recognised this as a more serious issue when Semira called her back.

(Fieldnotes, Session 11)

Feminist ethics of care highlight the importance of close personal relationships for women, and it was clear that these close, comfortable relationships were important to all of us. The fact that we were working as an all-female group had a specific impact on this research. The example here shows how Semira felt our collective responsibility for Yasmine's daughter. We were not only women in this research, but also mothers working with our children present. Feminist care ethics suggest that women learn to think about ethics in terms of care, responsibility and interdependence in relationships, in contrast to men who depend on ethics of justice (Gilligan, 1993). Women's capacity for care is seen as a strength and it was clear that these caring relationships had an important role to play in our work.

Creating a 'climate for caring' was fundamental to the foundation of the research and our intercultural relationships. As Noddings (2012) notes, this time spent building a relation of care and trust is not wasted. Noddings (2012) explains that caring cannot be reduced to empathy; dialogue is fundamental in building relations of care and trust, and we must ensure we listen carefully to strive for empathic accuracy. My understanding of empathetic accuracy also included listening using all my senses, it included observation as there was not much verbal language to tune in to. Instead, I listened by observing, stepping back, checking in, comparing all the 'data' available to me, reflecting on what we were learning and making adjustments as we went along as part of the CPAR spiral.

Yuval-Davis (2011) notes how feminist ethics of care transcend cultures and instead are based on interpersonal relationships. Our respect and care were mutual, which Yuval-Davis (2011) argues is essential, rather than one person in a more dominant position caring for someone needy. This mutuality permeates throughout the project; it was reflected in our co-learning relationship, the balance of power in our work, and also connects to the liminality and 'communitas' (Turner, 1969) I explore in the following chapter. The following section illustrates how we embedded these principles in our pedagogy.

Embedding Mutual Consideration and Wellbeing as Pedagogy

We embedded this mutual consideration in our work both inside and outside the classroom, as the examples in this chapter illustrate, but I was conscious that we lacked verbal language to express feelings and emotions. In Session 7, I introduced an exercise on greetings to enable us to describe feelings and tell each other how we felt. My fieldnotes below detail our work to bring this to life:

We practise adjectives for describing how we feel to answer, 'how are you?' I show images of faces. We review: 'good, fine, happy, bored, angry, sad' and we write the words for each of these in their languages too. These nuanced adjectives for emotions are harder to be precise and to pin down.

If someone doesn't 'get' the word and doesn't know the word in their language, I use the computer to check, which usually brings recognition. We have become used to this way of checking and they are good at letting me know when they don't understand. I can't tell whether what I am showing them on the screen is correct, so I watch their faces for their reaction – whether there is recognition, confusion, or blankness.

(Fieldnotes, Session 7)

In the next session, I was keen for them to be able to tell me how they were feeling, partly to extend our ways of greeting each other but also so that we could express our emotions to each other. To do this, we worked on single lexical items again across all languages, creating a multilingual map of facial expressions. After working through the language for this, I ask Lakmini, 'how are you?' She smiles and slowly puts together, 'I'm happy ... in your class'. I appreciate that she has extended this beyond the simple 'I'm happy/I'm fine' to give more meaningful detail that she is happy because of the class, and I feel it confirms that she is becoming more comfortable in the group. I answer her by smiling back and telling her, 'I'm happy you're here'. This work begins to initiate a foundation of being more able to express emotions and we practise this activity at the start of all subsequent sessions.

The Place of Ritual and Familiarity

We began each session with the same ritual of boiling the kettle and making coffee. We know each other's drink of preference – coffee for Semira, water for Yasmine, tea for Lakmini, Rushani and me. Not too many biscuits for Yasmine's daughter. Grapes are popular with everyone. There is a sense of community in the act of preparing and sharing this food and drink.

After break we review body parts as a bingo game, I'm impressed by what they remember. They shout out – 'leg, arm' etc. 'Mouth' causes confusion and sometimes sounds more like 'mouse' so I use the screen to show a picture of a 'mouse' and contrast this with 'mouth'. Everyone laughs and we check the words again in their own languages to reinforce understanding. There is a lot of laughing in this session. I think it helps that we are all women as we go over body parts. They point freely to each other's bodies and to mine.

As we are finishing up, I notice Semira wants to tell me something. She tells me in English: 'next time – my daughter' and points to our group. 'You're going to bring your daughter next time?' I search my brain for the word for daughter in Tigrinya that she has told me. Wlad? She looks at me blankly. I try again, slowly and raise my intonation at the end to show I am asking her if I have the word right. Wlad? ወላድ ? Semira nods, confirming 'mmm', smiling that I have remembered the word. I ask her daughter's name and we agree – next time. I am looking forward to this. Semira tells the others too: 'Next time, my daughter'. Everyone smiles and nods 'yes' with great enthusiasm.

(Fieldnotes, Session 9)

It has taken nine sessions for us to reach the point where Semira feels comfortable enough to bring her daughter. I recognise the length of time it has taken for us to build this relationship, this trust and familiarity, and for Semira to know us all well enough to feel she can introduce her daughter. This trust is particularly important for intergenerational work within the context of working with refugee families as this extends to trusting another person/a group of people with your child. Bringing your child to a group activity with people you do not know well is an even more significant decision during these early weeks settling into a new country when family members are also adjusting to living together again.

Intergenerational Relationships

In this section, I explore the family relationships which impacted our work. I begin by considering the relationships within the learning sessions before discussing the support outside of the project.

Introducing Semira's daughter: Another shift in dynamics

At this point of the discussion, the ecology of our relationship intersects with intergenerational relationships and their impact on each individual family and on the group as a whole. My fieldnotes from Session 10 reflect the impact of Semira's daughter joining us:

It's starting to get lighter outside at the time our classes start. Semira brings her daughter for the first time and I feel her sense of pride as Awet introduces herself confidently in fluent English. Everyone welcomes her to the group. Awet looks like a smaller version of Semira and this starts a discussion on whose children look like their mothers. We talk about their daughters who are now all in the room and decide which features are similar – Eyes? Hair? Mouth? When it's my turn I show them a photo of my eldest son. They are surprised and laugh at how blond his hair is and we check how to say this in all our languages. No, he doesn't look like me at all. I show my youngest son – oh, yes! (he looks just like me) – dark eyes, dark hair – same.

We now have a 5-year-old, a 10-year-old a 17-year-old and 3 women in our all-female group. Everyone is on time today and there is a sense of excitement in the room, a sense of being ready to start the session and welcome Semira's daughter.

We review our work from the previous week and practise answering 'how are you?' Awet shows how easy this is for her. She is incredibly confident and chatty for a 10-year-old. This is the first time Semira has someone to work with in Tigrinya. Awet is quicker and tells Semira the answers in Tigrinya, she is also quick to correct my Tigrinya! Semira looks proud of her daughter. It alters the dynamic between Semira and me as her daughter translates for her rather than us speaking directly to each other. I am careful not to initiate this. Semira and I have established our own way of communicating. They can now all translanguage in their family groups which makes it much more evenly balanced and easier for me to facilitate.

Rushani and Lakmini give me the homework they asked me to set them last time. It is beautifully presented and Rushani hands this to me with a sense of pride – a clear plastic wallet with careful handwriting that they tell me they have worked on together at home. I check it carefully and tell them how well they have done.

We do a board race which I've found works well with all age groups. People shout out and correct each other. Some of the children playfully complain when their mothers get the wrong answers. We line up in teams and I make a chalk mark on the floor for them to stand behind to race to the board. Semira is very fast; she tells me she likes running and it's good that this comes in useful as it balances the skills each of the participants use in the session. They run to erase the numbers I have written on the board then to write the new ones I call out. Everyone is engaged and it's good to get moving.

(Fieldnotes, Session 10)

Throughout the project, I tried to find ways that would engage all the different age groups. I found that activities which required physical movement worked well. The participants enjoyed games and particularly those with a competitive element. I also found that these activities worked well given the participants' different stages of learning English, as it encouraged them to use their other skills such as the example above of Semira being a fast runner in the board race. In the following section, I discuss the specific needs of reunited families.

Intergenerational learning: Addressing specific needs of reunited families

During the project, there were many examples which illustrated the benefits of mothers and their children working together. Lakmini and Rushani attended every class apart from one together and it was clear that this brought them both comfort. Lakmini turned 18 during the project; a birthday which was marked in between our sessions by a beautiful celebration with family, cake and friends. She proudly shared photos of the celebration with us the following week.

Lakmini and Rushani were both at beginner level of English at the start of the project but, as we worked together, Lakmini began to gain more confidence, to pick up words in English more easily and more consistently than her mother. Lakmini supported Rushani, and they seemed to really enjoy working together. Rushani often checked with Lakmini when she did not understand, and Lakmini explained for Rushani in Tamil when something was not clear. At times, I observed Lakmini become frustrated with her mother when she took longer to grasp something. Lakmini would look to me and roll her eyes. I always smiled back and supported Rushani as I did not want to feed into this dynamic. I noticed a balance between support and dependency between the two of them.

The dynamic between Semira and her daughter was similar in terms of her daughter providing support, although Awet was 10 years old and therefore not able to work in quite the same way. Semira's daughter worked with her using Tigrinya, supporting her when she did not understand. Awet was also extremely confident, often jumping in and asking questions when I was explaining something and frequently answering when I had asked someone else a question. Her presence in the group altered the dynamic and made it more possible for Semira to take a back seat. I questioned this dynamic throughout the project as I wanted Semira to maximise the opportunity of our sessions, and I felt she was more focused on her own learning without her daughter present. In the interviews, she told me that she was 'happy either way' with her daughter present but also that she liked to learn alone. Semira decided when she wanted to bring Awet and when she preferred to come alone, and this struck a balance which seemed to work well for them both. She had support from her daughter in some of the sessions, and in others she could focus solely on her own learning.

The situation for Yasmine was different as her daughter was only five years old. This meant I had to adjust the activities so that her daughter had her own learning outcomes to work towards. This was difficult as she did not have other children of a similar age to work with, bringing a different dynamic in terms of intergenerational learning and the pedagogy we adopted; importantly, it also made it possible for Yasmine to attend the sessions. In the final interview, Yasmine told me that both her and Rana had enjoyed the sessions, and that if her daughter had not been allowed to come, she would not have been able to take part. It removed the need for additional childcare which is so well recognised and documented as a key barrier to learning for many refugee women (Chapters 1 and 4).

The intergenerational learning aspect worked very differently for each of the three families but there were positive benefits for each of them. Yasmine told me in the final interview: 'I'm very happy in this class and actually I enjoy being with people from different countries and different ages.'

Rushani told me: 'It's ok to have different age groups people but preference is for this age, teenagers. They can grasp quickly compared to younger age groups so they can pick up what you're teaching very easily'. Due to this, Rushani decided only to bring her daughter and not her and son to the sessions. She told me: 'Yes, so this age group is ok. This age group will be fine compared to kids.' Semira also felt it was good to have her daughter's support and told me: 'My daughter is picking it up very quickly and I can learn from her. It's really useful.'

Attending the same sessions had the added benefit that participants could work together and practise outside of class. Semira told me this was important for her and her daughter. It also gave the families somewhere neutral to go to take part in an activity to take their minds off any problems they might be having, with the aim of providing a distraction and a common purpose. They could also support each other's learning in between sessions, which supported translanguaging as they worked together in their own languages.

I asked participants if they would like tasks to complete at home and gave them these at the end of each session. Rushani and Lakmini seemed to take particular pride in this, and returned their work to me, beautifully written, carefully thought through and kept flat in a plastic folder. I checked their work carefully and took time to sit with each of them to go through their work together. The first time I did this, I sat with Rushani first; she moved her bag to make space for me, and carefully listened to what I said and showed her. I felt this emphasised the sense of investment and value she placed in the classes and in our interactions. After I gave back their work, I noticed Rushani and Lakmini check my written comments together as they had clearly worked on this together; there was a sense of a shared task and helping each other.

Semira also felt it helped her to have her daughter in the sessions and told me: 'Yes, it helps when we can work together in Tigrinya'. I asked her how she felt about having the children in the group and she told me: 'I think it's good. I'm happy to be here with my daughter. She can help me.'

Rushani had similar thoughts and told me: 'I feel it's good, it's very comfortable to have my daughter here with me. We can help each other if we don't understand. Sometimes if I don't understand, I can understand from my daughter'.

I asked Yasmine if she enjoyed the sessions and she told me: 'Yes, definitely and yes, my daughter enjoys it too. I couldn't have come if I didn't bring my daughter, I didn't need to worry about someone to look after her when I came here. If you didn't accept her in the class, I couldn't attend this class'.

Semira told me: 'Yes, we did both enjoy studying together when we study together here. Because you helped us with the language and we start from easy English because English is hard to learn. When we start from basic it's really good and when we go home, we practise together and we learn together and that's good'. Semira also told me: 'Yes, it really helped us to practise together and now my daughter can read and speak better than me but when I started, I didn't feel confident and I couldn't read and write in English but now I'm getting it, so it's been really good'. At the end of the project, one of the key findings which the participants agreed was: 'I enjoyed working in my own language with my children in the class'.

The importance of trust and family support

Trust was also an important element within the intergenerational dimension of this work. Not only did the participants put trust in me and in the project themselves, they also trusted me and our project enough to bring their children along. The hesitation in Semira bringing her daughter to the sessions shows that this was an important decision for her. She tried the sessions by herself first, then after having experienced them and getting to know me and the other participants, she told me in Session 9 that next time she would bring her daughter.

For these women, I had a strong sense of how supportive their husbands were and the significant impact this had on their ability to take part in the project. Rushani's husband accompanied his family to the first session and stayed for the remainder of our meeting so he was present while we worked with the interpreters to discuss the details of the research. All three of the participants' husbands called or texted me at some point during the project to check the arrangements we had made. This additional support was important as it enabled them to take part, and it was good to know the participants had this support at home. It showed me their husbands were encouraging of the project and of their participation. Lack of family support is recognised as a barrier to learning (Scottish Government *et al.*, 2017), and it was clear that this was one barrier that this particular group of women did not have to worry about. It also helped that the husbands knew me, knew who I was and had my phone number. This helped to build the trust that is so fundamental to a co-learning relationship (García & Li, 2014b).

I asked about the impact of being the joining family member in the final interview. Semira explained her husband had been in Glasgow four years longer than her. She told me: 'My husband is quite good at English and he's studying too. I don't speak English when I'm with him!' I asked about the impact of this imbalance for Yasmine and she told me: 'for places like the GP or shopping I can do it independently but for other stuff my husband does most of the communication.'

Yasmine felt this was a real source of anxiety and disappointment for her: 'it's been very difficult for me because I've been here for a year and I just try my best to improve my English and I also ask my husband to help me and I use google translate to help me improve my English as fast as possible'. Yasmine told me she felt 'very frustrated' that she needed her husband to communicate for her.

Semira told me how difficult this was for her too: 'yes, it's really difficult and you feel it and you ask yourself when will I be able to speak and really understand? It's a big pressure'.

Yasmine told me: 'I feel sad and it's bothering me because I really like to be independent and doing stuff for myself not asking someone to do a favour for me. I really love to improve my English'.

Semira and Yasmine's comments give insight into the frustration of being the arriving family member with less knowledge of English and the resulting impact this has on family dynamics. Arriving in this way often creates a dependency on the family member who has already been in Scotland for some time. As the refugee sponsor in most cases is the husband/partner, this creates further difficulties for women and results in language learning remaining a gendered experience. The participants' determination to come to the sessions and the effort they put into the project gave me the sense of how strong and independent they were, and how important they felt it was to improve their English to be able to gain more independence and, crucially, to be able to speak for themselves.

Conclusions

In this chapter, I have explored the relationships within the project as an ecology in their own right by presenting the findings that illustrate the agency of these relationships in our work. I have brought the fragility of these relationships within these tentative few weeks to the fore by showing the participants' hesitation to participate in a larger group, and illustrating how they overcame these concerns by investing in the project and taking the risk of returning to our class.

Close interpersonal relationships and feminist care ethics were important and relevant for us as a group of women; these concepts underpinned all of our work as we established our common ground as women and as mothers. Establishing these relationships necessitated a high level of emotional labour and nurture, and was often grounded in moments of 'unknowingness' as we relied on communicating with very little shared language.

We embedded mutual consideration and wellbeing in our project, and drew this into our classroom learning via language learning activities which explored emotions and talking about our own wellbeing at the start of each session. The findings clearly show how fundamental these relationships were and highlighted the comfort the participants took in learning with family members in their own languages. The additional trust needed to support the intergenerational element of our work was shown by the participants' decisions to bring their children to the sessions. The ongoing support from family members outside the project was also essential to the project and overcame the lack of family support which is a known barrier for many women.

The importance of good relationships and the ethics of care formed an essential foundation from which to explore the key themes in the following chapters. These were particularly important within the context of family reunion at the point of arrival. Without this trust, mutual consideration and care, the project would not have produced such rich findings, and the participants may not have been able to participate in the project at all. In the following chapter, I move from the ecology of these relationships into the physical ecology and the agency of place, before discussing the third ecology of language and 'languaging' in Chapter 8.

7 Ecology 2: Place

> An ecological approach is where what happens in the classroom
> responds to aspects of the context and the context is also created
> out of learning, teaching and language use
> Kramsch *et al.*, 2010: 8

Introduction

This chapter explores the physical ecology of the project by drawing on our work outside the classroom. Here I introduce each of the places in which the participants and I worked together, and I highlight their relevance and agency within the research. I present the themes which emerged and the literature which emerged alongside them by putting an ecological approach into practice, and I consider the interdisciplinary nature of the project by drawing on the fields of intercultural research, human geography and anthropology. The ecology of place is situated within the framework of the three ecologies of relationships, place and language, as I explore different understandings of 'environment', 'place' and 'context' within language learning. I then discuss why 'place' has particular agency within the context of New Scots adjusting to life in Scotland in these first tentative weeks.

Defining 'Place' within an Ecological Approach

As discussed in Chapter 2, the connection between language, 'environment' and 'context' is present throughout the literature on language ecology. Haugen (1972: 325) initially defined language ecology as 'the study of interactions between any given language and its environment'. Similarly, Van Lier (2006: 20) reminds us that with language 'it's context all the way down'. Kramsch and Vork Steffensen (2008) also emphasise that language should be studied in connection to its natural surroundings and the personal, situational, cultural and societal factors that collectively shape it. While carrying out the fieldwork, I began to consider how understandings of 'context' and 'environment' might differ, and how the project could remain true to Haugen's (1972: 325) definition of the 'social and natural environment' as an understanding of the physical place in which our language learning was situated.

In ESOL settings, where learners are living in the host community and need English to be able to communicate every day, contextualising language learning for learners' lives is seen as necessary and important. This is shown, for example, through the range of ESOL courses available including vocational classes for specific work and study contexts. The Scottish Qualifications Authority provides ESOL learning and assessment materials created specifically for learners in Scotland to support them with settling into their lives, e.g. by using Scottish place names and Scottish culture as a basis for learning. 'Context' tends to be used as a very general term within theory and research about language learning; it encompasses a variety of understandings and perspectives which include social, political, geographical, institutional and individual factors.

In this chapter, I explore an understanding of 'environment' as 'place', grounded in human geography as the physical context, the environment, in which the learning is situated. This physical understanding of 'place' allows for the weather, the walk, the park, the greenery, the scenery, the 'Dear Green Place' of Glasgow, and the connections that people make with place in a human and embodied way. This is in contrast to understanding 'context' as supporting people to access and manage the system of integration which necessitates navigating benefits, work or study options. The goals of 'work', 'study' or 'progression' are difficult to reach within these first tentative weeks when adjusting to a new physical environment comes first and includes a different climate and navigating the layout of a new city.

The two-way reciprocal relationship between language and environment offers an understanding of the agency that the physical ecology has on language learning and is particularly relevant within the context of New Scots. During the fieldwork, I found there was a necessary but often overlooked stage of settling in which may not be encompassed within current understandings of 'integration', and the findings point to the need for orientation-style activities based on and connected to 'place'.

Understanding 'place' as the physical environment includes embodiment and sensory experience. It allows for 'languaging' (Phipps & Gonzalez, 2004) within the physical environment, in this case Glasgow, a superdiverse and multilingual city, and allows us to recognise language learning as a dynamic process through which there is a reciprocal relationship between place and language. Phipps (2009: 661) notes how the concept of 'languaging', which I explore in full in Chapter 8, is different from learning in classroom contexts to 'the effort of being a person in that language in the social and material world of everyday interactions'.

The learning takes place 'out there' in 'the whole social world, not just in the classroom' (Phipps, 2008: 222). This understanding of the agency of place also has implications for how we understand 'integration' and what is needed to support the human aspect of settling in and making this new physical setting feel like 'home'. To return to the idea of this study as a tale of decolonising, which I began the previous chapter with, 'any decolonising foreign language learning endeavour worth its salt will need to remember the intimate connections between land, language and its need of the air for speech, anywhere to find articulation' (Phipps, 2019b: 8). Over the course of the project, I begun to consider these connections to the physical environment more deeply, and I turned to human geography to explore this theme.

Human Geography, New Scots and Making a New Home

> Language can be conceptualised as a space of belonging in itself, providing a sense of being 'at home', and lending articulation to all of the emotions that go alongside such a sensibility
> Shuttleworth, 2018: 21

In Chapter 1, I explored the policy context for 'integration' and the need for refugees to 'integrate' into the host society. The 'indicators of integration' (Ager & Strang, 2004), on which the New Scots Strategy (Scottish Government, 2018) is based, recognise the importance of cultural knowledge. This process of orientation and settling in also incorporates aspects of liminality, as refugees enter a space between the known and the not yet known, necessitating elements of identity reconstruction in linguistic and cultural terms. Understood in more human terms, integration is about more than getting to grips with structures and functioning within society, it includes adjusting to a new climate, a new landscape, a new physical environment, perhaps in the way that Haugen (1972) initially described.

In considering 'place', I draw on ideas from human geography and in particular the work of Kale *et al.* (2019) in New Zealand with their exploration of multisensory experiences through which former refugee and host society residents develop, maintain, negotiate and co-construct feelings of homeliness in Wellington, Aotearoa New Zealand. Understandings of 'home' have become increasingly significant within responses to the international humanitarian crisis (Kibreab, 2003). Kale *et al.* (2019) note how the need to belong and to feel at home in a known social and geographic space is fundamental to identity. For refugees, many of whom have experienced war, oppression and poverty, the need to feel at home is a 'primary yearning' (Kale *et al.*, 2019: 2).

The sense of liminality and identity reconstruction I touched on in Chapter 3 is also present in Shuttleworth's (2018: 79) work on language geographies of refugees in Glasgow: 'for refugees and asylum-seekers, there is often a question of affiliating with "here" or "there", with destination or origin places'. There is a duality within this understanding of home. Shuttleworth (2018) notes how, during the process of settling in to a new country, migrants can be stuck between the past and the present as they connect their previous home with the new home in their host country.

For refugees, feelings of attachment are developed through familiarity, knowledge and regular bodily interactions with place (Kale *et al.*, 2019). Ahmed (1999) also suggests the act of leaving a home creates a duality which includes the place of origin and also the current context. The process of finding others who have similar experiences of leaving home and 'becoming a stranger' leads to the creation of a new 'community of strangers', who share a common bond of adjusting to the host community (Ahmed, 1999). 'The forming of a new community provides a sense of fixity through the language of heritage – a sense of inheriting a collective past by sharing the lack of a home rather than sharing a home' (Ahmed, 1999: 336). Butler and Spivak (2007) note how people seeking asylum often live in parallel realities, being here and also being there, a process of 'belonging and not yet belonging' (Pöyhönen *et al.*, 2020: 59). This sense of belonging is understood as 'the multiple, constructed and contested relationships with people and places' (Pöyhönen *et al.*, 2020: 59).

This new home and new community are also experienced in linguistic terms. It is these connections to each other, to place and to language which are fundamental to an 'ecologising' of language learning as 'people seek out places and experiences where they feel as though they are connected to something beyond themselves' (Kale *et al.*, 2019: 2), where they feel safe, secure and valued.

As the participants and I worked together and as our relationships developed, we became a community in our own right, closely connected to the place in which our learning and relationship building took place. In linguistic terms, acknowledging this liminality, this embedded 'being here and also being there', meant connecting our learning to the participants' own languages and home countries by bringing these connections into the learning process as much as possible. We achieved this by talking about differences and similarities when working on food, weather, buses, tickets and different ways to travel. Working in this way brought the idea of place as an important part of identity into our learning alongside language. In the following section, I consider our key 'places' and how these were brought into our work in a meaningful way.

Combining Project and Place

As I explored in Chapter 5, holding the learning sessions at the University presented challenges due to the need to travel on the bus and find the building. Rushani, Semira, Lakmini and Yasmine's determination to overcome this barrier indicated their investment in the project. Often the weather was challenging. It was dark and cold with very heavy rain on several occasions. They often told me they felt cold even though I always made sure the room was well heated for their arrival. Trying to mitigate physical discomfort was an important part of supporting the participants to attend and was underpinned by the ethics of care outlined in Chapter 6.

Although the University was not as convenient as the city centre BRC office might have been, it brought us other opportunities due to its physical location. During the interviews, I sensed the participants' pride at taking part in a class at the University, and I felt this contributed to their investment in the sessions. Perhaps this also encouraged a sense of belonging to Glasgow as a place and connected us to the University as a place to come for future courses/activities. The proximity to other places of local interest was also important as we could leave the School of Education and be at the Hunterian, Kelvingrove Park or Kelvingrove Museum in 10 minutes on foot (even when walking at the pace of a 5-year-old).

In the pilot study, I described the situated context of the project, from initially meeting at the BRC offices in the centre of Glasgow, the journey to the bus stop, travelling on the bus to the University, trying out the children's literature library and settling on Room 347 as our preferred learning space. As I explored in Chapter 5, the BRC office where we met on the first day of the pilot, was a starting point for the journey to the University and for our project and, as such, it can be viewed as a liminal space between arriving in Scotland and embarking on the journey of the project together. With its initial support services, the BRC office is associated with those challenging first steps between the old and the new. As the project progressed, I considered whether meeting at the University helped with the sense of moving on from that initial stage. As we moved into the main project, the theme of the physical ecology and the agency of place remained central. The key places in the main study became:

- The participants' home countries, brought into the learning space through the medium of the participants' own languages. This allowed us to connect with the idea of 'home' as a physical place from which to know this new place.
- The BRC Office on Sauchiehall Street.
- The children's literature library in the School of Education.
- Room 347 in the School of Education, the home of our classroom-based learning.
- Kelvingrove Park.
- Kelvingrove Museum.
- The UNESCO RILA Spring School at Heart of Scotstoun Community Centre.
- The Hunterian Museum.
- The University and Cloisters.
- The bus stop on Eldon Street.

These places are set within the wider ecology of Glasgow, within the context of the participants' lives and their journey through family reunion to be reunited with family members in Glasgow. Although these are local places (see Figure 7.1), they are set within the national and global contexts, and they are linked and interdependent as part of an ecological

Ecology 2: Place 155

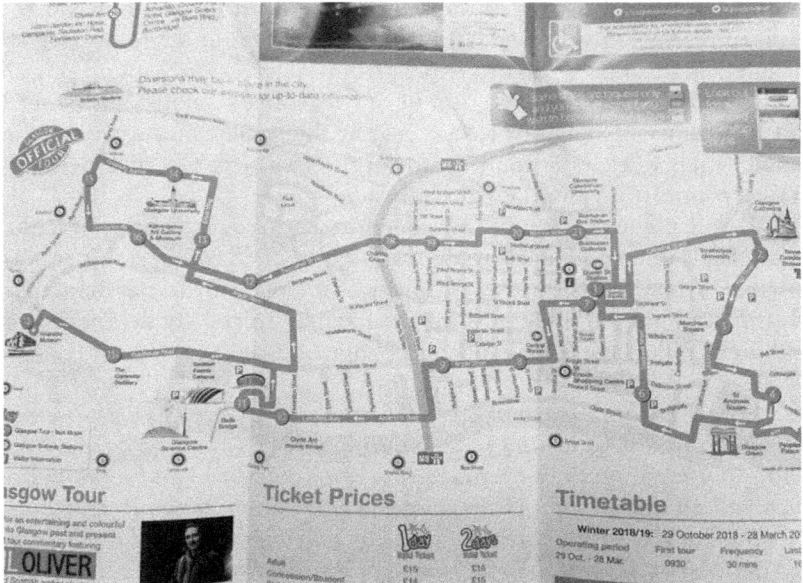

Figure 7.1 Photos and maps used to show local places of interest

understanding of 'place'. The connection between the global and the local is also fundamental to the CPAR approach outlined in Chapter 3.

Situating the learning within Glasgow in an obvious way was important, and this was supported by taking our learning out of the classroom as much as possible. This was fundamental in terms of language learning; it also introduced participants to local places to visit with their families to support the New Scots theme of 'integration from day one' (Scottish Government, 2018) and help them to contextualise their lives here. It made the learning specific to the physical ecology of Glasgow with its place names which are unique and difficult for non-Glaswegians to know how to pronounce and spell, e.g. Sauchiehall Street, Buccleuch Street, Buchanan Street. This also fitted well with the CPAR approach and the orientation style activities the participants requested.

We chose places to visit by looking at leaflets, maps and checking online together. To facilitate our learning outside the classroom, we sometimes needed to change the day we met as the museums were closed on Mondays. Their enthusiasm to do this echoes Norton's (2013) 'investment' and the mutual respect discussed in Chapter 5 as it required everyone to turn up on time. We also worked together to make arrangements which necessitated good communication. In the following section, I highlight the key themes which emerged and explore how these were woven throughout the fabric of the project.

Ritual, familiarity and place

In Chapter 6, I discussed the importance of ritual and familiarity in terms of the ecology of our relationship and how I found it important that the participants knew what to expect from each session. I found this also extended to the physical location of our learning sessions. The stability and continuity of being in Room 347, at the same time, with the same people, each week was important. On the two occasions we needed to change rooms this caused great confusion.

When I made the room bookings for the sessions it was difficult to secure the same room each week. On two occasions when this was not possible, I booked the closest room to 347, texted the participants in advance and arrived early to show them where to go. My fieldnotes from Session 11 reflect the impact of this change of place:

Our usual room was not available today due to the exam timetable. I booked the closest available room, three doors along the corridor, put a note on the door to our usual room with an arrow and left the door open so I could hear if anyone arrived late. I knew they might not read the note but the combination of this, the text messages and my listening and watching for their arrival, I hoped would mitigate any confusion.

After setting up the new room, I went back to Room 347 to find Rushani, Yasmine and Rana waiting for me. I explained the room change and took them to the new room. Semira had not arrived so I kept popping out into the corridor to check for her which felt disruptive to the session. The new room did not have a kettle or sink, so I used the staff kitchen to make drinks at break time but Rushani and Lakmini seemed disappointed that the learning environment was not the comfortable space they are used to, which has started to feel like home to us. I am not sure what happened to Semira today. I don't know if she arrived and left due to the room change and not being able to find us.

(Fieldnotes, Session 11)

The room change seemed disruptive and it took time for Rushani and Yasmine to adjust. The fact they had both gone into Room 347 and expected to have our session there, despite text messages and a note on the door further, underlines the high levels of support they needed at this stage. This was also the first and only session that Rushani attended without her daughter and, despite the confusion with the room, she did very well to attend this session, to travel alone and negotiate the room change and then participate in the session with only Yasmine, Rana and me. Their commitment to attend the sessions despite these challenges again underlined their investment in our work.

In Chapter 6, I also discussed the importance of the kettle and making hot drinks together at the start of each session. This ritual connected us to the feeling of Room 347 being our physical 'home' for the learning sessions, the importance of which Kale *et al.* (2019) recognise within human geography and refugee resettlement. The idea of feeling of 'at home' is also associated with embodied, sensory experiences, such as making coffee to enable a feeling of familiarity through 'sensory stimuli that provoke memories or positive associations' (Kale *et al.*, 2019: 7). By making tea and coffee together, we connected this ritual to which hot drink everyone drank in their home country and how these drinks were made. I learnt the importance of coffee and coffee making in Eritrea from Semira and tea in Sri Lanka from Rushani and Lakmini. These simple rituals incorporated all of our senses: touching, tasting, smelling, seeing and hearing which served as a 'link to familiarity and security of home(lands) and also provide comfort, building on a homely sense of community and belonging through recollection and remembrance' (Kale *et al.*, 2019: 3). The importance of such associations cannot be overlooked in making people feel at home as part of a more human understanding of integration way from 'day one'.

Shuttleworth (2018) notes the significance of these embodied experiences and how connecting such experiences to pre-migration lives becomes important as refugees and asylum-seekers settle into their new communities. Shuttleworth (2018) also notes that spaces in which such gatherings take place are a 'space of care', helping to overcome community boundaries and providing a space in which to share and learn about others (Conradson, 2003; Piacentini, 2008, cited in Shuttleworth, 2018). This 'space of care' provided a physical context within which to situate the ethics of care explored in Chapter 6.

In Chapter 3, I introduced the concept of liminality as a state of 'betwixt and between', a concept which is clear here as the participants adjusted to their new homes and made connections to the rituals of their former homes. Turner (1969: 80) extends the concept of liminality to include 'communitas', which sees society as 'unstructured or rudimentarily structured and relatively undifferentiated' as it 'emerges recognizably in the liminal period' while sharing a common experience through a rite of passage. The concept of 'communitas' connects to the balance of power and the mutuality within the ecology of our relationship (Chapter 6) and the mutuality of our languaging, which I discuss in Chapter 8. Turner (1969: 81) notes how 'each individual's life experience contains alternating exposure to structure and communitas, and to states and transitions'. This 'communitas' within a liminal phase where social structure is disrupted was present within the decolonising, collaborative approach we took as it disrupted the balance of power. This was clearly shown in Semira's observations that she and I were 'the same' and 'equal', which I discuss in Chapter 8.

Shuttleworth (2018) found understandings of home to be fluid and dynamic within the context of refugee integration and that, as a result, people find multiple sites of belonging, which may not necessarily be their 'homes' and may instead be other places where they are able to share aspects of their identities. Our work encouraged a sense of belonging to the physical ecology and to the ecology of our relationship within the unstructured, liminal communitas that Turner (1969) describes. All of these aspects were grounded in increasing familiarity and settling in. Van Lier (2004b) also recognises this process of adapting to a host community within an ecological approach and notes the impact this has on identity as people create new identities to reconnect their sense of self to the new environment, new culture and new language.

Session content as orientation

In the initial information session, interviews and ongoing dialogue the participants confirmed that they wanted to explore the local area and that practical, orientation-style topics were what they needed. In Interview 2, Semira told me she needed help with language for 'everyday life', and I was careful to make these experiences as authentic as possible rather than working solely within the 'ecological niche' (Kramsch *et al.*, 2010) of the classroom. There is safety and security in the haven of Room 347 with its coffee, warmth and biscuits and our comfortable small group, but this work also needed to be balanced with trying out 'languaging' within the places we selected to visit together. Rushani and Lakmini told me they needed 'basic information. You've taught us how to get the bus, how to go to the doctor, we are comfortable with these topics'.

At the end of each meeting, I asked the participants whether the session was useful for them. I recognise that this was a limited way of gaining meaningful feedback due to our limited shared language; however, it contributed to my overall impression of whether they were enjoying the sessions and reinforced the role of collaboration in deciding the content of the sessions while feeding into the CPAR spiral. During the group interview at the end of the pilot, I asked whether this approach was useful, and the participants confirmed these were topics they needed. Rushani told me: 'Yes, it's very practical.' The Tamil interpreter continued: 'they're going on the bus and they don't know how to buy a ticket or how to talk to the driver ... for example, I'm going to this place. I need a ticket to ... which type of ticket?' Cultural differences were also highlighted as a learning point as the participants told me that in Sri Lanka return tickets do not exist, and they are expected to buy a single ticket for each journey. This highlighted the importance of having someone to ask about such matters at this stage of settling into their new lives. These topics helped to develop closer connections to Glasgow and to their new lives.

Acclimatising to a Glaswegian climate as orientation to 'place'

Weather, and challenges with weather, formed a key theme in our work and presented genuine difficulties for the participants when travelling to and from our sessions. It was frequently cold, wet and dark when we met. Throughout the project we often talked about the weather by way of introduction at the start of our meetings. On several afternoons, we had extremely heavy rain and the participants arrived soaked and windswept. Arriving at our usual room and feeling comfortable enough to remove wet layers of coats and scarves to dry them on radiators in our all-female group showed the impact and discomfort caused by a climate that is very different to their home countries. We quickly covered a variety of language to describe the local weather: heavy rain, drizzle, dreich, windy, stormy, cold, brighter, lighter, warmer, sunny. The shift in the language needed as the weeks went on, and we moved from winter to spring to summer, mirrored the changes in weather outside. We experienced these changes as an 'embodied geography' (Kale *et al.*, 2019); as Gibson reminds us, 'one sees the environment not just with the eyes but with the eyes on the head on the shoulders of the body that gets about' (Gibson, 1979, quoted in Woitsch, 2011: 207). Such things can only be experienced as embodiment as they incorporate the use of all senses in *seeing* the darkness as we waited for the bus, *feeling* the cold wind on our faces and the rain against our skin, and the *smell* of the grass being cut as we walked across the park together. We *watched* the rain from the classroom as we *listened* to it hammering so loudly against the window one afternoon that we could not hear each other speak in any language. The significance of these embodied experiences of place and the impression made by them is mirrored in the first two lines of the Spring School poem (shown in full under 'The Spring School'):

'Scotland
Cold, dark and wet'

By the last weeks of the project, it was no longer dark when we finished our sessions. The passage of time from winter to summer, albeit a Glaswegian summer where coats are still necessary, also mirrored the easing of the participants' process of settling in, adjusting identities as a liminal process. By summer, they had become more familiar with their surroundings and the journey. It was warmer and lighter and being in Glasgow, in this new place, was also now easier as they had started to become more acclimatised to life here, to the place and the climate.

The idea that intercultural language learning is not detached from being and living in this world is a key premise of Woitsch's (2012) research, 'Walking through the Intercultural Field', and it connects with the question Tim Ingold raises in his book, *Being Alive: Essays on Movement, Knowledge and Description*:

> Why do we acknowledge only our textual sources but not the ground we walk, the ever-changing skies, mountains and rivers, rocks and trees, the houses we inhabit and the tools we use, not to mention the innumerable companions, both non-human animals and fellow humans, with which and with whom we share our lives? They are constantly inspiring us, challenging us, telling us things. (Ingold, 2011: xii)

Our experiences of learning ecologically acknowledge the significance of the physical aspects that Ingold describes, and I found these to be parallel to Haugen's (1972) description of the physical environment, particularly in terms of the interconnectedness between mind and nature which Ingold describes:

> Experience, therefore, cannot mediate between mind and nature, since these are not separated in the first place. It is rather intrinsic to the ongoing process of being alive to the world, of the person's total sensory involvement in an environment. (Ingold, 2011: 99)

Our total sensory participation in our environment was part of our embodied experience. It was part of 'languaging'. We were indeed 'alive to the world' ourselves, as an intrinsic part of the physical ecology.

Mobility and embodiment

We also connected to the outside world by travelling together. This process of not only *being* in the physical ecology but travelling together within in it mirrors Woitsch's (2012) study referred to above. Woitsch (2012: 187) refers to the appropriacy of 'ethnography on foot' as a method for intercultural work as it 'underlines those moments of intercultural learning which are centred in orientation', for example 'the first strolls in an unknown town; walking with maps in search of specific places; or moments of getting lost and suddenly remembering the way'. These mobile, intercultural experiences grounded in orientation and sensing were highly relevant to our work.

Our mobile research extended beyond Woitsch's (2012) 'ethnography on foot' to 'ethnography by bus' and, on one occasion, 'ethnography by taxi'. These experiences became an embodied way of learning, being, communicating and interacting with the physical ecology. These methods became our way of knowing each of the places and understanding their physical location and how to get from each of these places to the other. These shared experiences bonded us a group, for example on the walk back across the park from Kelvingrove Museum when Semira shouted at Yasmine's daughter as she ran off into the distance (Chapter 6).

Incorporating such methods gave us insight 'into the way people and place combine' (Moles, 2008: 31). Perhaps due to the lack of verbal language and the embodied clues needed for us to communicate in the place of verbal language, this was particularly evident in our work. We were all physically in the space in which we were working, both in the classroom and also on the bus, standing, walking, waiting, seeing, smiling, being physically present together.

In describing 'the intercultural body', Woitsch (2012) notes that the significance of the learner's relationship to her/his learning environment significantly exceeds Kramsch's (2009) understanding of it as external stimuli which brings us back to an understanding of physical place as an agentic factor within language learning. The 'physicality of the experience', which Kramsch (2009) highlights, corresponds with Woitsch's (2012) perspective on the 'intercultural body', and points to the significance of embodied experiences within language learning and the connections to place.

Layered simultaneity and connecting to place

Kelvingrove Museum, Session 11

Everyone arrived on time and seemed keen to go to Kelvingrove today. This was important as our time was limited between the children finishing school and the museum closing at 5pm.

We walk across the park together on this beautiful sunny afternoon, chatting as much as we can. We notice the blossom, how green the grass is, the trees, and the squirrels and give the word for these in each of our languages. I explain that it's a five-minute walk across the park and check that this is ok. I hold up my fingers to indicate 'five' and try to remember the word in Tigrinya, Farsi, and Tamil. For once it isn't raining and we all laugh about how often it rains on Monday afternoons. We turn along

Kelvin Way and along the road which takes us to the back of Kelvingrove, it has only taken us a few minutes. I open the door to the museum for them.

I stand back as we enter the beautiful main hall and watch Semira, Lakmini, Rushani, Yasmine and Rana look up and around smiling and taking in the new surroundings. I point out the organ on the first floor and pick up floor plans from the information desk to give to everyone.

The central hall is taken up by 'Dippy' the diplodocus who is currently on loan to Kelvingrove and we start our exploration here. One of the staff asks if we would like her to take a photo of us all together in front of Dippy and we all crowd in to do this.

We have prepared for our visit today by talking about what we might see inside Kelvingrove. I simplify the contents of the museum and indicate that upstairs are 'paintings' and downstairs are 'animals' for the purposes of choosing where to go next. I show the different items in each area of the museum using the floor plan and ask 'what would you like to see?' Rana wants to see the animals and Lakmini wants to see the paintings, so we agree to start on the ground floor and then go upstairs. We walk into the 'natural history' section on the ground floor and see 'Roger' the stuffed elephant. Yasmine uses her phone to ask me, typing in Farsi and then translating into English: 'is it real?' I check the word for 'stuffed' in Farsi and show her. It is hard to explain any of the exhibits in any of our languages so we spend most of the time looking and sharing the experience of being in this place together for the first time. I am careful to step back and see which exhibits they are interested in rather than lead. Our communication is limited but everyone appears to enjoy being here together and I hope that this will introduce them to Kelvingrove so they know how to get here, it's free to get in, when it is open and that it's good for families and adults too.

We head upstairs to the paintings and look down over the balcony to the room below with all the head sculptures suspended from the ceiling. 'Faces' Lakmini says, 'yes!' I say. We each choose which is our favourite and try to explain why we like it.

There is a sense of comfort and companionship despite our limited ways of communicating. This languaging, this trans-languaging in this place, outside the classroom. I notice a couple watching us as we work between Tamil, Tigrinya, Farsi, and English with me in the middle.

Everyone agrees that Kelvingrove is beautiful. Yasmine types in Farsi into her phone and tells me 'I will come back with my husband'. Good! I tell her, smiling and nodding. Semira and Rushani agree they will come back too.

The museum is starting to close and we are asked to leave. We head downstairs and back out the other side of Kelvingrove Museum onto Argyle Street, facing Kelvin Hall. I point to Kelvin Hall and explain it is for sport. We take a photo together in front of the museum and I send it *to Semira, Rushani and Yasmine on WhatsApp. They receive it straight away and seem pleased to have it. I hope they can use this to show their husbands, their friends and maybe come back together.*

We begin walking along Kelvin Way just as the bells of the University chapel start to ring out at 5pm. Semira grabs my arm in excitement and exclaims 'Sarah! Church!' and then she points to me. 'Yes – University church' I tell her, she tells me the word in Tigrinya 'ቤተ ክርስትያን beete krstyan'. *She is telling me she is Christian, I think. This is important to her, she wants me to know this part of her identity. It also connects her life, her religion to this place. It contextualises this place for her in a way that is personal and meaningful.*

(Fieldnotes, Session 11)

Semira telling me that there is a church is significant. Kale *et al.* (2019) recognise the need to create familiarity and to connect the previous known place with the new. At this stage, Semira's vocabulary in English was limited to just a handful of words for food and basic communication. It is significant that she knew the word for 'church' in English and that she wanted to tell me she knew this, noticing the sound of the church bells within the physical place. This interaction echoes the 'layered simultaneity' shown in the lithograph in Chapter 2 to illustrate 'layers of historicity and identity, as well as presentness in every utterance' (Van Lier, 2010: 3). Kramsch (2008) also recognises that meaning is 'multiscalar', 'reflexive' and 'historically contingent'.

Within an ecological approach, language is connected not only to the physical environment, it is 'the enactment, re-enactment, or even stylized enactment of past language practices, the replay of cultural memory, and the rehearsal of potential identities' (Kramsch, 2008: 400). Kramsch (2008: 392) notes that such encounters are not 'discrete, bounded events' but instead are 'open-ended and unfinalizable patterns in a web of past and future encounters'. Semira's utterance connects not only to the here and now but to the cultural memory to which Kramsch refers.

Semira's utterance contains several layers of meaning; it connects this place to her previous place and lets me know that she knows this word in English. She knows this is a church, she recognises the sound of the bells ringing within this new landscape and, importantly, she wants to share this with me. She looks at me, says, 'Sarah – church' and her meaning is ambiguous to me at first. At first, she is telling me that she has noticed the church, and she then repeats the words again with raised intonation, pointing to me. 'Sarah – church?' 'Yes' I say. Is she asking me if that *is* a church? Or is it more personal, is she asking if I *go* to church? If I am Christian too? If this place has significance for me too? It is important for her that I know that she knows what this sound is, and it seems she is seeking to find the common ground between us in terms of whether I also go to church, echoing the concepts of Butler's (2005) ways of 'knowing' each other explored in the previous chapter. Kale *et al.* (2019) found that multi-layered connections such as these enabled individuals to (re)construct their cultural identities in their new city, which enhanced feelings of homeliness and belonging. The physical gesture of grabbing my arm highlights our embodied way of being together in this space, the growing sense of trust and familiarity between us and the 'intercultural body' which Woitsch (2012) describes.

The layered simultaneity here also connects to Pennycook and Otsuji's (2014) idea of spatial repertoires, which Canagarajah (2017) expands to include 'spatiotemporal repertoires' (Levine, 2020). Levine (2020) notes how language is dependent upon both spatial and temporal context which includes the person, place, time and purpose of the interaction. Rather than being individual, biographical, or something that people possess, 'repertoires are better considered as an emergent property deriving from the interactions between people, artefacts, and space' (Pennycook, 2016, quoted in Levine, 2020: 41). I find this also to echo the literature on identity explored in Chapter 2 as it considers identity not only in terms of *who* we are to each other, but also who we are in this place, this context and at this particular moment.

Kale *et al.* (2019: 3) recognise that 'the aim of resettlement should not be to encourage former refugees to simply start over and create new attachments to a new place, but to enable them to mediate between past, present, and future experiences, needs, and desires so that they can maintain valued aspects of their identity, manage grief, and regain a sense of safety and stability'. The process of connecting old and new, known and not yet known runs throughout the project and is mirrored within the ecology of language in the next chapter as we connected known language with new language through our multilingual practices.

Bringing the outside in

Just as it was important to create a comfortable, well supported place in which to hold our learning sessions, it was also important to connect this classroom-based learning with the physical ecology in a meaningful way. This meant preparing for our classroom trips by supporting the participants with useful vocabulary, showing images of what to expect, and then reviewing and learning from these experiences once we returned inside. It was important to make the connections between the classroom-based learning and the physical ecology as direct as possible. The extract from my fieldnotes below illustrates how we connected our work inside the classroom with the physical ecology through our trip to Kelvingrove Museum.

Session 11

We start the session by chatting about our trip to Kelvingrove last week. I ask 'where did we go? What did we see?' Everyone is engaged with this activity and can tell me 'Kelvingrove Museum'. We go over to the window and look out across the park towards the museum to confirm the direction we took last week.

We stand at the whiteboard together with board pens and make a multilingual list of everything we can remember from the museum with the children drawing pictures when they don't have the word. This openness to recall the items in whatever mode suits each person best works well and we quickly have a long list on the board. When a word is unknown we check using the computer or phones to translate from Tigrinya, Farsi and Tamil:

- Museum
- Faces – big faces
- Elephant – stuffed – 'Roger'
- Animals
- Birds
- Dinosaur – Dippy
- Paintings – lots of paintings
- Shoe – big shoe
- Elvis
- Tiger
- Mummy
- Piano – organ
- Fossils
- Plane
- Big eggs

Through this activity, we piece together an account of our trip, a picture of Kelvingrove through their eyes. I am impressed by how much they have taken in and I feel this confirms the trip was worthwhile. 'What did you like?' I ask and we each make sentences and ask each other this simple question. Lakmini tells us she liked the paintings, Yasmine's daughter liked Dippy and the animals. Semira liked the paintings too.

(Fieldnotes, Session 11)

Preparing to take the inside back out again

Session 9

We discuss the upcoming University 'Refugee Integration through Language and the Arts' Spring School and use a previous activity on dates/times as a basis to check arrangements for meeting. I write the meeting place, date, day, and time on the board and take Rushani, Semira, Lakmini, Yasmine and her daughter downstairs to the entrance to show them exactly where to meet.

We move on to work on developing a poem for the Spring School based on the topics we have worked on for the past few weeks and the Spring

School themes of 'Labour and Resting' which we interpret into the labour of learning a language. I take their comments and the key themes from the interviews as a starting point and we weave together the lines to create a poem in all of our languages. We call it 'Learning a Language is Hard Work'.

(Fieldnotes, Session 9)

In addition to the multilingual poem, we also plan to hold a 'languages café' as part of the Spring School workshop (see Figures 7.2 and 7.3) with Semira, Rushani and Lakmini taking turns to teach a few key phrases in Tamil and Tigrinya. We prepare for this by taking turns being the 'teacher', coming to sit in the seat where I usually sit and teaching each other the phrases we have prepared together in Farsi, Tamil and Tigrinya:

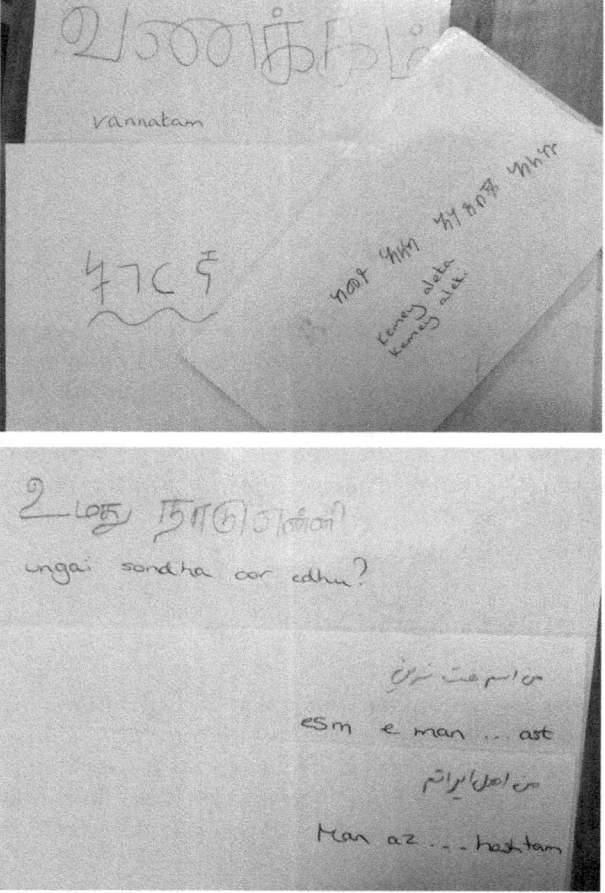

Figure 7.2 Prompt cards for the Spring School workshop

My name is …
What is your name?
I am from …
Where are you from?
I speak …
Which languages do you speak?

For my own benefit, I write down a transliteration so I can remember how to pronounce each of these phrases in Tamil, Tigrinya and Farsi (even though Yasmine won't be there we want her language to be represented). Together we create sheets with the names of their languages which I laminate for us to use as a warm-up activity at the workshop.

Awet has drawn a butterfly for us to add to the poem. I remind everyone of the meeting arrangements for the Spring School as this is the last time we will meet before the event. Rushani and Lakmini seem clear on this, but I can see that Semira is unsure. This is made more confusing as it's another bank holiday next Monday, and I explain we can't have a class then as the building will be closed again. They seem disappointed. I call Semira the next morning through the BRC interpreting service to check in with her, our conversation goes as follows:

'Selam *Semira! It's Sarah!* Kemey aleka? *How are you?*
Aaaaah Selam *Sarah! I'm fine.* Kemey aleka? *How are you? I hear Semira smile down the phone when she recognises my voice, she sounds pleased to hear from me.*
I ask the interpreter to explain we are going to the Spring School together on Thursday morning and that we will meet downstairs at the entrance to the School of Education at 9am. Everyone needs to be there on time. Is that ok?
I hear Semira smile again when she understands the details which were not clear before. Sometimes her daughter will answer the phone for her, but she knows my number now and answers my calls herself. I don't know if this is because she knows it is me or because I can bring an interpreter into the call if needed.
Semira thanks me for calling and tells me that she understood about the Spring School but wasn't sure of the time or where we should meet. She says she's looking forward to it and she's glad I called. I ask the interpreter to tell her that I'm glad she is going to come and that I'm really looking forward to going there together.

(Fieldnotes, Tuesday 22nd April, 2019)

This interaction underlines the mutual care and respect we had for each other, the ongoing emotional labour which underpinned our work, the need for a multilingual approach and the high levels of support needed to facilitate our learning. This was particularly true when we needed to change plans.

168 Part 3: Towards an 'Ecologising' of Language Learning

The Spring School

9am Thursday 2 May 2019

It is a beautiful sunny morning on what will become a warm bright day. I have arranged to meet Semira, Rushani and Lakmini at the School of Education at 9am so we can travel to the Spring School together. The event is in Scotstoun, in the west of the city, none of the participants have been there before.

Today is the first time we have arranged to meet in the morning and on a Thursday, which meant explaining a different day, time and meeting point and a trip to an organised event. I am hoping they will come today as I want them to be part of the workshop and take their part in sharing our project.

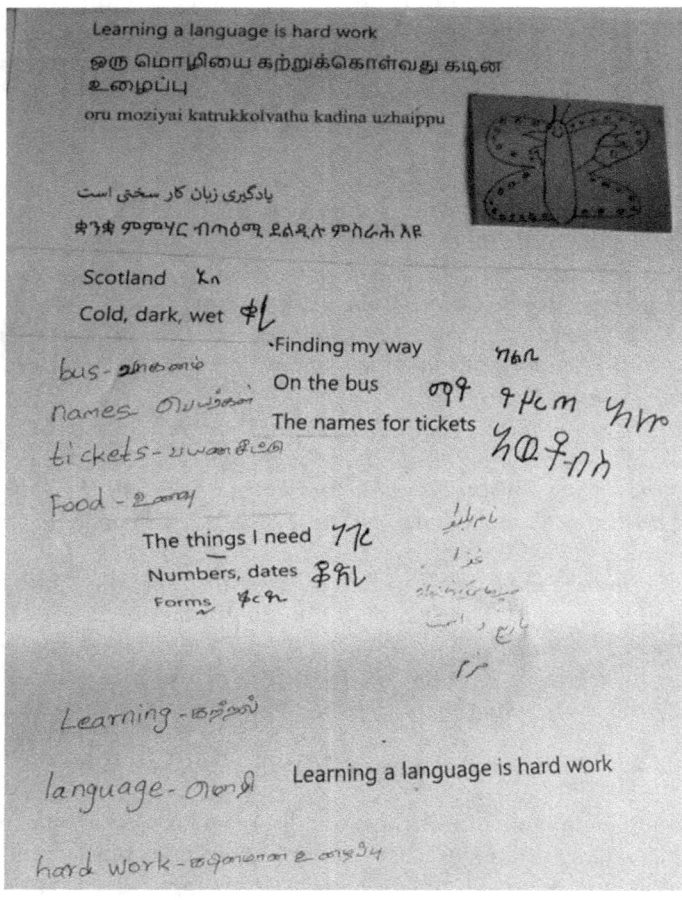

Figure 7.3 The Spring School poem

I go upstairs to the office and take the travel tokens from my desk drawer. I have booked a taxi for 9.15am. I carry the box of materials down the steps, out into the beautiful sunny morning and I wait at the entrance.

No one arrives.

At 9.10am the taxi arrives, and I explain to the driver that I am waiting for the others, he agrees to wait.

I wait ... I wonder if they will come. They usually let me know if there is a change of plan, but I also know they have many things going on in their lives. I start to mentally reconfigure the workshop in case they do not turn up. I hope they will come as I think it will be empowering for them, but I am also acutely aware it may seem daunting. I hope they feel they know me well enough to tell me if they don't want to come.

I call Lakmini, no answer. I call Semira, no answer.

9.30am. They are still not here, and the taxi driver is starting to get impatient. How much longer should I wait? I need to set things up at the other end and if I have to do this alone, I need to adjust the workshop activities to deliver the session alone. More than anything this is their work and I don't want them to miss the opportunity to share it with others. Doing the workshop without them would feel wrong.

9.35am. I manage to get through to Lakmini through the phone interpreting system. I ask if they are coming today and she tells me they are on their way.

9.40am. Rushani and Lakmini come around the corner, they smile when they see me and I ask if they're ok – they say 'yes, ok' and we hug each other. Semira comes around the other corner just a couple of minutes later. I'm so pleased to see them, relieved and glad they have come. I do not want to speak on their behalf. I will support and guide them but it feels important that we all stand up together and share our work in the same way that we have worked together – collaboratively.

Ok – I say, 'let's go'. Lakmini asks – 'bus?'. I tell them 'no – today – taxi' and point to the waiting black, shiny, seven-seater taxi. Rushani's eyes widen and she says 'wow!'. She smiles widely at us all and looks to her daughter, nudging her with her elbow. They both raise their eyebrows. I ask again if this is ok for them. I turn to catch Semira's reaction and notice she looks impressed. The door opens automatically and Rushani, Semira and Lakmini wait for me to get into the taxi first but I hold back and reach out my hand saying, 'after you'. They pause, then step into the taxi first and sit next to each other in the back seat, I perch on the seat opposite them, facing backwards and give the driver directions.

I wish I had taken a photo of Semira, Lakmini and Rushani sitting together in the taxi facing me with their huge smiles, looking excited and I consider this for a moment but I don't want to take the focus away from this simple pleasure of us setting out on this trip together, so I leave it. As we travel, we drive past the University and turn left along Kelvin Way. 'The park' Semira says, then we turn right along Argyle Street, past Kelvingrove. Rushani recognises this and points and says 'Kelvingrove Museum', we all nod. We are 45 minutes later than planned but it's a beautiful morning and we are now setting off with a purpose. Everyone seems excited.

We arrive at Heart of Scotstoun community centre and go inside to find the first session underway. We try to creep in and find seats together near the back. Lakmini, Rushani and Semira sit and I tell them I will come back, I need to go into the other room to set up for the workshop. Our session will start at 11am.

I set up in the other room, make sure my PowerPoint is working and move some tables around. When I have everything ready, I go back into the main hall to sit with Rushani, Lakmini and Semira.

The presentation finishes and it's time for a coffee break. We go out into the café and I make coffee for everyone which we take with us into the workshop room. I ask Lakmini, Rushani and Semira to stick the laminated cards with their own handwritten words for 'Tamil', 'Tigrinya', 'Farsi' and the other languages I have prepared, onto the walls. They smile when they recognise their own handwriting, but I am still aware that they cannot really know what the session will hold, and I'm concerned that it might be intimidating for them. There is another session running at the same time as ours so I'm not sure how many people will choose our workshop.

Semira, Rushani and Lakmini go to sit at one of the tables. I put chairs next to mine at the front and I ask them to sit with me – 'is here ok?' They look nervous when they realise they will be facing everyone. I nod encouragement and they laugh and say 'ok'.

The room quickly fills up and I watch Lakmini's, Rushani and Semira's faces, smiling reassurance although inside I'm also feeling nervous. I quickly count – 35 people. The chair for the session introduces us and I start my first slide – 'welcome' in Tamil, Tigrinya and Farsi – 'Khosh amadid, Verruga, Merhaba' I slowly say and I watch Lakmini, Rushani and Semira's faces. I see smiles and recognition as we connect our ways of working in our other place, our classroom, to this new place in the workshop. I'm nervous, for me and for them! I speak slowly to explain our project. I introduce myself and I turn hopefully to Lakmini, Semira and Rushani, gesturing that it is their turn, unsure of how this will go. I am silently willing them on but I know this act of asking them to introduce themselves to such a large group has the potential to either make them feel shy or to empower them. I know they can do this and I hope I have not misjudged how they might feel in this setting. I ask Lakmini first as she is the most confident ....

I need not have worried, there is a slight pause then Lakmini is on her feet, standing, tall and proud as she shouts out to the room, in a voice much *louder than my own introduction: 'I'M LAKMINI! I'M FROM SRI LANKA!' (I am stunned and proud, to see her jump up with so much confidence, her voice so loud). I ask Rushani next ... she follows her daughter's lead 'I'm RUSHANI, I am from Sri Lanka' (this is confidence I have not seen before in Rushani) and then Semira. Semira who is usually so softly spoken ... she hesitates and looks across at me, I nod to her, silently willing her on ... I see her fists clench in determination ... she stands up and shouts louder than anyone to the full room: 'I AM SEMIRA, I am from ERITREA!' Her volume rises as she shouts 'ERITREA' and I hear the pride in her voice. I am stunned and delighted by this confidence and momentarily my mind flashes back to the image of Semira sitting alone, looking scared and not making eye contact on the first day we met in the BRC waiting room. No-one else in the room knows the significance of what Semira has just done. We have come a long way. Her achievement is not lost on me.*

I clap for Semira, Rushani and Lakmini and everyone joins in to welcome them. I have a lump in my throat and tears in my eyes. I am taken aback, so proud of them and what achieving this will mean to them. They are here to be heard. To be seen. I thank them for coming and I tell them slowly that I am happy they are here. 'Yekenyeley' (thank you) I say in Tigrinya 'Nanri' in Tamil.

I blink back my tears, turn to the audience in front of me and just as they have done their part in introducing themselves, I pick up my role of presenting our project to the group. Lakmini, Semira and Rushani watch me and smile. We are a team.

(Fieldnotes, May 2nd, 2019)

Learning from the Spring School

The Spring School represented a snapshot of the project. It combined our collaborative, decolonising ways of working by putting their languages first within an authentic context situated within the physical ecology and the broader society. It brought all of these elements together. It was the only session when we connected directly with other people, other members of the University community and the local community beyond that.

Our workshop showed me how their confidence had grown and how they used the skills we had developed together to be able to participate in the session. It connected the ecology of our relationship and the ecology of place by demonstrating to others what we had been working on, allowing us to transpose our ways of working into a different setting, a different and unfamiliar place.

I felt moved that they had trusted me to come out of our comfort zone of the classroom, and its immediate surroundings, to come with me in a taxi to an event when they did not know what this would entail. All the elements of our co-learning relationship were present during our workshop: the mutual respect in working together, the sense of being valued and important that came with taking a taxi together, which was paid for by the University; and the collaborative approach of delivering the workshop together. Their participation emphasised the mutual trust in our relationship. They trusted me to come with me and take part. I trusted that they would turn up and do what we had agreed on together. This experience also addressed the balance of power in our work. I was vulnerable in this session, unsure if they would turn up, worried when they were so late and uncomfortable at the thought of having to carry out the workshop without them. I needed them just as much as they needed me.

This experience intersects with both of the other ecologies as it evidences the ecology of our relationship and the ecology of language within the physical location of the Spring School. Watching Lakmini, Semira and Rushani shout out their introductions also challenged my own perceptions of their levels of confidence in other physical settings. I came into the session concerned that they might not feel confident introducing themselves to a full room of people and acting as 'teacher' of their own languages, outside the niche of our classroom. I was wrong about this, and the experience highlighted how much of a barrier language is in terms of confidence and showing your natural character.

An ecological approach also allows for the learning to be localised; 'pedagogical decision making therefore entails studying situations "locally", in their own terms' (Tudor, 2003: 8). Tudor (2003) refers to this concept as 'local meaningfulness', allowing for the role of 'environment' to be much more than a passive backdrop for language learning. 'It replaces these views with a conception of the learning environment as a complex adaptive system, of the mind as the totality of relationships between a developing person and the surrounding world, and of learning as the result of meaningful activity in an accessible environment' (Duff & Van Lier, 1997: 783). As Moore *et al.* (2020) note, this concept is also present within translanguaging pedagogies as they respond to local realities and, as a result, look different within each specific context.

Learning has to be observed in authentic surroundings (and not with the limited view of 'inside' and 'outside' the classroom); there is a need for greater authenticity and fluidity in our understandings of this. The Spring School provided an authentic setting and one that I hoped might build the participants' confidence and encourage them to attend other local events.

Travelling to the Spring School together and noticing the places we had visited together was also significant. I could see their recognition of Kelvingrove Museum and the park, I could see they were starting to develop a better sense of where these places were in relation to each other, and that they were starting to orient themselves and our work within the physical ecology in a way that was far more meaningful than looking at a map in a classroom.

The bus

Negotiating the bus journey to and from the class proved to be a significant challenge and formed an important part of the learning within the pilot study as it enabled learners to practise skills that would help them in their daily lives. I supported this process for the initial sessions by accompanying them on the bus to the University, checking the bus number and seeing them onto the bus at the end of the first session. I then gradually reduced this assistance to ensure a balance between support and creating dependency. Learning to use the bus, including recognising the bus number, timetables, tickets, the location of the bus stop, are major barriers for those newly arrived not only in terms of language but also cultural differences such as maps, buying a ticket and paying. Support at this stage proved to be vital, as were the travel tokens provided by the BRC as the participants were not yet receiving benefits and would have struggled to cover the bus fare (£4.60 for an all-day ticket). Without the travel tokens, it is doubtful the participants would have been able to attend.

Working with the participants in real-life situations and physically being on the bus with them allowed us to use language in an authentic, practical way. It allowed me to understand first-hand how they coped in these situations, and this informed the content of the learning sessions by ensuring a synergy between the topics they asked to cover and my own observations of how best to support them. It took the learning beyond language into more practical life skills, and it enabled me to bring the outside into the classroom, mirroring these real-world situations within our classroom practice. These skills were put to immediate use when we stepped back out of the classroom to the bus stop and waited for the bus. As such, the bus stop became a significant place within our project: we began our journey on our first day together at the bus stop on Bath Street in the city centre; we ended our first session by waiting together in the cold, dark evening at the bus stop outside the School of Education on Eldon Street; and we said goodbye back at the same bus stop when we finished the project on a drizzly afternoon in June.

Saying goodbye to this place

Session 14: Our last session, Tuesday 18th June

After the last session, I called, texted and sent WhatsApp messages to everyone via their preferred medium of communication to arrange a final meeting. I explained that we would go through the transcripts and key findings to conclude the project. We agreed to celebrate our work together by visiting the Hunterian Museum, which meant meeting on a Tuesday as the Hunterian is closed on a Monday.

My fieldnotes below capture this last session:

After we have finished checking the transcripts, I check that everyone still wants to go to the Hunterian and the cloisters and to see the old part of the University. Yasmine isn't feeling well and decides to go home but Semira, Rushani and Lakmini are keen to go.

I give everyone information for ESOL classes in the local area and the interpreters assist me with working out which classes might work best for each of them. Yasmine is moving to London next week to join other family and tells me she is sad to leave, that she has enjoyed our sessions and that if she could stay, she would definitely like to continue.

It is the end of the school term too. Everyone asks if we can continue again and it's hard for me to say that we have to finish this week. We have extended the project twice now from the initial 7 sessions to 14, double the original 'plan'. I take this as the most significant indicator of the success of our ecological, multilingual approach.

Lakmini is now studying ESOL at college and will continue after the summer. Rushani tells me she has more confidence because of our project, that she will go to a community ESOL class now and that she did not feel confident enough to do this before. I show her the details of one class close to her home and Lakmini agrees to support her mother to go. I reiterate that they have my contact details and to let me know if they need any further support at any time and that I will help them.

Semira will go to a local ESOL class in a community centre where she has started to attend a cooking class.

We leave our classroom together for the last time. We walk along University Avenue together towards the old part of the University. I don't think they have been up here before and I point out the beautiful architecture and the library which look very different from the School of Education. They all look very impressed as we walk through the gate. The flowers are in bloom in the well-kept flowerbeds and they stop to take photos. Rushani tells us she likes the flowers, that they are beautiful. We walk through into the impressive cloisters and stop for a moment to take in the beautiful view of the quadrangle. It reminds me of Oxford, where I grew up, and I mentally connect this view to my own home and wonder what associations this scene might conjure up for Lakmini, Rushani and Semira.

I say to them 'this is your university. Maybe you could come here again to study?' Lakmini has just turned 18 and I hope she will consider this. As we walk Rushani and Lakmini chat together and I wish I could do this with Semira. There is an acceptance between us that we cannot share so much verbally but we have become comfortable with being together even if we can't talk as much as we would like.

We walk through the quadrangle and out of the other side to look out at the beautiful view across the city. I point out Kelvingrove Museum and they are surprised by its closeness and nod in recognition. We stop for a few minutes to take photos. It's June but it's another damp day and we're *all still wearing our coats, I've now changed mine for a lighter rain jacket but they are still in thick winter coats.*

There is a sense of being part of something, of connection and belonging and our time in this place feels like a mini graduation. We take a selfie together in the quadrangle and Lakmini shows me a better way to take a photo with just one hand. We laugh that she knows how to use my phone better than I do.

We go up the steps into the Hunterian Museum. It's very hard to explain in any detail when we still only share a few words but again I have a sense of simply introducing them to where this place is, that it is free to come in and that you can just walk in. It's hard to explain the exhibitions as I'm not that familiar with some of the objects, even harder in Tamil and Tigrinya.

5pm and the museum closes. We leave together and walk back down the hill.

We arrive back at the bus stop on Eldon Street where our story began five months ago. We hug each other warmly; 'keep in touch' I say – 'text, WhatsApp', showing my phone, 'you have my number' they nod and say 'yes' they all text me often so I feel confident this might continue. We say goodbye and thank each other in Tigrinya and Tamil, in the words they have taught me. We smile and look into each other's eyes. Still so much we cannot say to each other using verbal language.

It starts to drizzle again and there is symmetry with how we began this project. This ecology of place. This ecology of the relationships we have built over the last five months. People pass us on either side and we stand still in our small group for a few moments, holding on to this last moment together. We have shared something in this group and we are connected to each other by these experiences. We say goodbye at the bus stop for the last time and hug each other warmly. I walk away up the steps and instinctively turn halfway up to check they are ok as I have become used to doing over the past five months. Lakmini and Rushani are chatting and walking away closely together as mother and daughter. Semira stops, looks at me and smiles, then waves me goodbye as the bus pulls in.

I am proud of them. I am proud of them for trusting me and for believing in themselves and each other in so many 'moments of unknowingness'. I am proud of what they have achieved in these sessions and of what we have shared. It's hard to say goodbye and to know that I won't be there to check in with them each week.

(Fieldnotes, Session 14)

Conclusions

In this chapter, I have discussed the significance and agency of place within an 'ecologising' of language learning. I have contrasted definitions of 'context' and 'place' within an ecological framework and explained how I settled on an understanding of place drawn from human geography as having most relevance for our work. This chapter highlighted the need to incorporate orientation-style activities in an authentic way to connect to place in a meaningful way within this period of settling into a host community. The findings illustrate the need for the agency of place, as defined in human geography, to be taken into account and reflected within initial language classes for reunited families within their first tentative weeks adjusting to new lives in the host community.

Just as I discuss in the next chapter the importance of connecting known language to new language through multilingual learning methods, so too can ideas of identity, memory and embodied understandings of place be connected to language learning through an ecological approach as I have explored in this chapter. The importance of the porosity between our classroom-based learning and our learning outside in the local community was clear. In the following chapter, I discuss the symmetry of these connections within the third ecology, the ecology of language and 'languaging', before drawing the three ecologies together in Chapter 9.

8 Ecology 3: Language and 'Languaging'

> You and me, we're the same. You struggle with Tigrinya and I struggle with English
> Semira, Interview 1

Introduction

In this chapter, I consider the third ecology, language and 'languaging'. This discussion builds on the previous two chapters which explored the ecologies of relationships and place. I discuss how translanguaging and working multilingually formed an essential foundation for our project, and I consider the key themes of our collaborative, multilingual, co-learning relationship and how these constructs went hand in hand with our orientation-style language learning. I present the findings in the participants' own words, as the interview data clearly evidenced why an ecological and multilingual approach was an ethical necessity in this context. I make a case for looking towards an 'ecologising' of language learning as situated practice to meet the needs of New Scots by exploring the impact of taking a multilingual, translanguaging 'stance'.

This chapter is organised in three sections: first, I consider the place of repertoire and collective language ecology within the context of our translanguaging work; second, I explore the practical benefits of our multilingual approach; third, I discuss the impact beyond pedagogy.

An Ecological Pedagogy: The Significance of Repertoire and Collective Language Ecologies

The concepts of individual linguistic repertoire and collective language ecology were central to our work. Building on the discussion on language ecologies and translanguaging in Chapter 2, we began our work from a heteroglossic ideology rather than simply using other languages to scaffold our learning by code-switching. Working in this way highlighted the mutuality of translanguaging as a research paradigm in its own right and brought focus to the 'trans' of translanguaging as communication across languages and cultures.

The concept of linguistic repertoire is particularly relevant to this research, as the participants began the project at the very beginning of learning English. If we consider each of the participants' repertoires and their unique composition of linguistic knowledge, at this stage, English represented only a very small part of their linguistic repertoires, perhaps 5%. The remaining 95% consisted of mainly their home language and other known languages. García and Kleifgen (2010) argue that for bilingual children, using only English means they are only being tested on 50% of their skills, which highlights the significance of this inequality for social justice. Had we worked monolingually using English alone, we would at best be accessing and acknowledging 5% of the participants' linguistic repertoire. Other linguistic knowledge would have been rendered obsolete as having no relevance to our work. As such, working multilingually was a practical and ethical necessity.

Accepting the concept of linguistic repertoire has practical implications for pedagogy, as it impacts how languages are taught by incorporating strategies for building on language which learners already know. As each person's repertoire expands to incorporate new language as it is learnt, these strategies are also part of developing a more empowering multilingual identity, which is especially relevant during the period of profound change of settling into a host community. These concepts were fundamental to our work and necessary within an understanding of pedagogy which includes the 'practice architectures' that underpin the CPAR approach. As Simpson (2020) points out, using only English in the classroom is a long-established and often unexamined norm in English language teaching. Moving away from this unexamined norm, and instead combining our individual repertoires to form our collective language ecology, gave our group a full range of linguistic features on which to build and also made our linguistic identities visible.

Drawing on the concepts of repertoire and language ecology also allowed our learning to become more representative of the way that languages are used within our increasingly globalised world and 'superdiverse' (Vertovec, 2007) communities. In everyday communication, we know that multilinguals 'shuttle between languages' (Canagarajah, 2011a: 401). However, as discussed in Chapter 2, although translanguaging happens naturally as everyday communication, these multilingual practices do not naturally translate into meaningful classroom practice without effort and deliberate pedagogical actions. The findings presented in this chapter relate to both the practical benefits of adopting a multilingual, translanguaging 'stance' or 'disposition', and a deeper discussion about the impact of translanguaging, which is underpinned by the discussions on identity, social justice and linguistic dominance under 'Impact Beyond Pedagogy'.

Creating an Ecological, Translanguaging Space

In Chapter 2, I contrasted Li's (2017) understanding of the 'languaging' within translanguaging with the more commonly referenced origins of the term in the Welsh context. Phipps (2011: 365) explains that her understanding of 'languaging' emerged from 'the process of struggling to find a way of articulating the full, embodied and engaged interaction with the world that comes when we put the languages we are learning into action'. Languaging is 'a life skill' which is inextricably connected with living in society, it develops and 'changes constantly as that experience evolves' (Phipps & Gonzalez, 2004: 3). Li's (2017) definition is key to how I understood translanguaging within our ecological pedagogy, as it incorporated the 'engaged interaction' (Phipps, 2011: 365) in the world with the 'living in society' that Phipps and Gonzalez (2004: 3) refer to, as a feature of interconnectedness between languages, the physical place and our need for effective intercultural communication.

Had we not taken a deliberate pedagogical decision to incorporate translanguaging strategies, the participants would still have translanguaged to communicate with family members. It would not have been possible or natural to use English to do this. This is a particularly important consideration when working with reunited families and given the affective functions which home languages serve (Ticheloven *et al.*, 2019). The difference between this kind of 'natural' translanguaging and our project is that, in the latter, active use of home languages was encouraged, valued and made highly visible as a deliberate pedagogical choice.

In Chapter 2, I established that language ecology is not a separate or fixed pedagogy for teaching and learning, but rather it is an approach and a way of thinking. The same can be said of translanguaging. We sought to create:

> a translanguaging space … created by and for translanguaging practices, and a space where language users break down the ideologically laden dichotomies between the macro and the micro, the societal and the individual, and the social and the psychological through interaction (Li, 2017: 9):

Our translanguaging incorporated a constant renegotiating of identities and linguistic repertoire, which extended into the development of intercultural repertoires as part of our holistic, ecological approach. In the following section, I explore how these concepts were embedded in our work in a practical way.

Incorporating Translanguaging Strategies and Stances

Pedagogy emerging from content and context

> *'It was helpful to cover topics for everyday life like getting the bus, food, shopping, money, introductions' (Key finding)*

In keeping with an ecological approach, our multilingual pedagogy emerged from the 'everyday' topics outlined in Chapter 6 and the intercultural work which took place outside the classroom. The emergent design gave space for fluidity, allowing language and activities to flow from the context as a deliberate methodological and ontological choice. This was a firm decision grounded in an ethical conviction that I could not plan without the participants. As García (2020: xix) notes, researchers who are committed to social transformation 'cannot determine what communities want in terms of knowledge, understanding, language and literacy experiences. This must be done in and with communities'. The need for this openness also resonated with my experience working with ESOL learners in community settings where tutors will try to tailor the content to learners' needs and interests where possible.

My fieldnotes from Session 13 give an example of how we embedded the porosity between the internal and external context by bringing the outside into the classroom to work on the real-world task of shopping.

We move around the room to create a shop, I give everyone a shopping bag and we go shopping together – it's very calm and focused and everyone enjoys choosing what to buy. We take our time to personalise this: 'I would like …', 'Can I have …?', 'how much is? …'. This topic also connects with the topic of money which we have been working on, using 'money' I have bought from the pound shop to work on denominations, numbers and paying for items.

(Fieldnotes, Session 13)

We personalise this activity further through a discussion on where everyone goes shopping, and we discuss the merits of different supermarkets: 'close to home, cheap, fresh, good choice'. Participants discuss in their own languages with their family members and report back to the group. These activities build useful vocabulary, enhance the metalinguistic awareness outlined later in this chapter, and also serve as useful orientation to discuss which shops are best in the local area. This provides an opportunity to gain valuable local knowledge which can be put to immediate use following their request to cover 'everyday topics' and 'basic information.' Learning in this way also supported our co-learning relationship as the participants valued each other's knowledge on this important topic.

Building confidence and independence through multilingual learning from 'day one'

'Using my own language in class helped me at the beginning of learning English'
(Key finding)
'Using my own language supported my learning'
(Key finding)

As part of the CPAR spiral, we drew on learning from the pilot to develop our own multilingual pedagogy for our own ecology by adopting a translanguaging 'stance' (Simpson, 2020: 52) to embed 'multilingualism at grassroots level' (Simpson, 2020: 55). Horner *et al.* (2011: 311) describe a similar 'translingual disposition' as a general openness 'toward language and language difference'. Such translingual dispositions are created through a combination of complex sociocultural factors and therefore cannot be explained in a 'preconceived and uniform manner' (Lee & Jenks, 2016: 317).

This 'stance' or 'disposition' included encouraging the use of learners' own languages as much as possible by using strategies presented in the CUNY-NYSIEB guide (Celic & Seltzer, 2011) and increasing the visibility of other languages throughout each session, as detailed in Chapters 2 and 5. Doing so showed our commitment to the prioritising of other languages and the connections to the participants' existing knowledge and skills.

Our work evidenced a clear need for gentle, multilingual orientationstyle language learning from 'day one' to accompany the understanding of 'integration' as the process of settling into the physical ecology outlined in the previous chapter. The participants told me that this gentle starting point helped to build their confidence and independence. Rushani illustrated the impact of this increased confidence when she told me in the final interview that she had gained enough confidence through the project to be able to move on to a community ESOL class when our project ended. Rushani also confirmed that she was able to practise the language we had learnt in class to help her in her daily life and told me: 'I'm using what we learn in class in my daily life, it's very practical – using the bus, shopping, food, going to the doctor, the places we've been to'. Knowing that she had already successfully tried out this language in our highly supported sessions helped to quickly increase her independence, as she could use this language immediately to complete essential tasks in her daily life.

During the interviews, participants told me how important learning English was in their lives, and how the ability to speak English gave them power and control. Semira told me: 'the most important thing is to learn the language because in this country we can't communicate if we don't have the language. This class is really useful for us'. Semira added: 'this is all useful today – learning the names for food, for everyday items and cultural things'.

Everyone was keen to participate in the activities and it seemed that our learning was enhanced by using their own languages. Rushani told me: 'Tamil and English together is better' and that 'we prefer to have Tamil as well in the class because if you just use English, we don't understand what you're speaking so we are not able to follow you, it's better if you use Tamil'.

Participants found that using their own languages felt comfortable and had practical benefits. Semira told me: 'from the beginning the class is good. It's helping me like a dictionary between Tigrinya and English', adding that she liked 'the approach and the way you teach'. Rushani also told me: 'yes, it's comfortable for us to use our language, it's useful for us to use Tamil in the class because that helps us to learn quickly, what are you telling us in English. It is useful for us to know the exact definition'.

Semira also found including Tigrinya helpful from a practical point of view but kept in mind her goal of improving her English: 'It's very useful to explain things in our language. At the same time if you spend too much time with people from your country in your language ... but it's very good for explanation. It's really good to use my language and English here. It depends on the situation'.

Yasmine told me that including Farsi was 'very important' for her and Semira felt that using Tigrinya in class had helped her 'a lot'. In interview 3, all participants agreed that the inclusion of their home languages was particularly important at this early stage of learning English and this view was supported by my own observations.

Mapping single lexical items across languages to enhance metalinguistic awareness

We incorporated learners' own languages in simple ways to enhance metalinguistic awareness and make the learning accessible at this early stage. This included establishing learners' interests and building multilingual activities around the topics they suggested. Food and cooking were a topic of universal interest and one that we agreed would help in their daily lives. We revisited this topic several times to review and consolidate our learning, as it gave us plenty of material to work with. Through this topic, we developed strategies of comparing languages which worked well and we returned to these for other topics.

We began by introducing vocabulary for individual food items using images, relating each item back to learners' own languages and drawing on ideas about the usefulness of making comparisons between languages within the CUNY-NYSIEB guide (Celic & Seltzer, 2011). We found that actively contrasting languages supported vocabulary development and metalinguistic awareness, and also enhanced language learning (Rauch et al., 2012).

When working on food, we made a note of vocabulary in all the languages present, sorting pictures into piles of 'I like' and 'I don't like'. Subsequent sessions allowed scope for working on shopping, money and prices through roleplays, with the children taking the role of 'shopkeeper'. Connecting vocabulary in English to lexical items in learners' own languages helped to provide clarity and make the learning inclusive. To support these activities, I created simple worksheets with images of each item and space for the participants to record vocabulary in both English and their own language. As these worksheets were based on images, they were also suitable for the children in the group and supported the intergenerational aspect of our work.

At first, I questioned the use of worksheets as I wanted to ensure the sessions were fun and interactive rather than having everyone sit and write. However, I noticed that participants naturally made notes in class in their own languages, and I wanted to support this way of learning and creating a record. This strategy supported their natural translanguaging practices, and I took their lead in this. Creating the worksheets was simple to do, and it formalised this strategy and supported the intention of making their languages visible in every activity.

Participants told me that having a written record meant they could take their learning away with them and, as they were working with their family members, they could also practise together at home, which further supported the intergenerational aspect of the work. Identifying the equivalent word for each item and recording it in a structured way also slowed the pace to suit everyone in the group. In the interviews, I asked if this was helpful. Semira told me: 'Yes, it's kind of like a dictionary' and Rushani agreed that 'it's very practical'. Incorporating all languages took participants a few sessions to get used to. When we managed to get something right in each other's language, everyone was pleased. Although progress was slow, setting up activities in this way from the start laid a solid foundation for subsequent sessions and established a pattern of working which learners seemed to enjoy and feel comfortable with. This again reiterated the importance of familiarity and routine in our work.

Figure 8.1 Multilingual body poster created by the participants

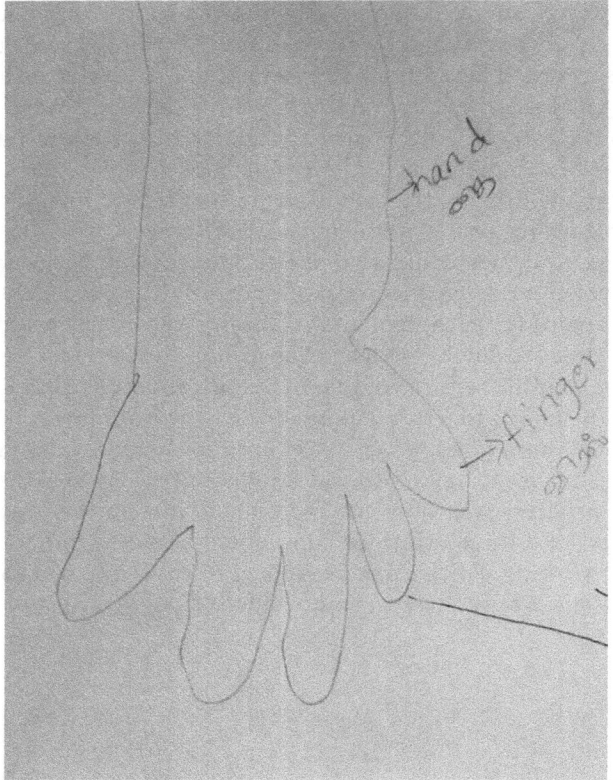

Figure 8.1 *Continued.*

My fieldnotes from Session 7 provide an example of how we worked multilingually on the participants chosen topic of health:

We make a multilingual body poster with the children drawing a body and everyone leaning in to label it in their own languages (see Figure 8.1). It feels like a good way for children to be involved with activities they can easily do and to have specific outcomes for each age group.

After our break we use the body poster to work on ailments. We point to each part of the body and ask, 'what's the matter?' To answer: 'I have a headache', 'my leg hurts'. At the end of the session, we consolidate our learning through reviewing these themes and seeing how much we can remember in each other's languages. Everyone seems happy and engaged.

(Fieldnotes, Session 7)

In the final interview, all the participants said they felt our translanguaging had helped them to make connections between English and their own languages. Of the seven ways García and Li (2014b) identify that translanguaging can be used to leverage students' learning in the classroom (Chapter 2), I found the last five of these to be most relevant for us: (3) to deepen understandings and develop new knowledge and critical thinking; (4) to encourage cross-linguistic transfer and metalinguistic awareness; (5) to promote cross-linguistic flexibility for competent language use; (6) to encourage identity investment; and (7) to disrupt linguistic hierarchies and social structures.

'Even though it's difficult, because you told me in Tigrinya I understand'

'Using my own language in class helps me to learn' (Key finding)

By the end of the pilot, the participants and I had established that they found it helpful to use their own languages for accuracy, and I also came to rely on this to check when participants had understood. In other teaching practice, such comprehension checking may happen through concept-checking questions, which would have been difficult with so little shared verbal language. I found that if participants were able to give me an equivalent word in their own language then they had understood. If they did not know what the word was in their own language, I knew I had lost them, and that further clarification was needed. This evidenced that home languages are always the foundation for comprehension, and that we learn new language through language we already know.

My fieldnotes below provide an example of how we worked between languages to scaffold the learning of new lexical items as we moved from the initial topic of 'food' into 'shopping for food'.

Torrential rain today again just as our session was due to start. Semira arrived early again without her daughter. As it was just Semira and I at the start of the session we started to review last week's work on food vocabulary and shopping, working back and forth between Tigrinya and English as we have become used to doing together. I have prepared flashcards with images of food and we take turns to pick up a card from the pile on the table between us and practise the word in each other's language and ask 'how much is the..?'. Semira picks up a card and tells me 'bread', 'ባኒ bani'. 'Bani'? I repeat, looking to Semira for confirmation, she nods. I pick another card and try to remember each item in Tigrinya. I tell her the word in English, she repeats it, then tells me in Tigrinya, I repeat this and we both make a note. Semira's face lights up when we use Tigrinya together. It's just her and I for the first 30 minutes and we both enjoy this time together. It's easier for me to focus on one language at a time, it gives symmetry working with just Tigrinya and English and it feels that we are making good progress this way. We have been working together like this at the start of most sessions for the past five months, our relationship is cemented through these wider pedagogical interactions which take place before the others arrive.

(Fieldnotes, Session 13)

My fieldnotes illustrate how comparing languages helped to ensure accuracy and build confidence. Semira had already told me how using Tigrinya helped her comprehension and accuracy at the end of the pilot and she confirmed this again in the final interview: 'Of course, it helped me to learn using my own language because sometimes when the word is difficult and I don't know what you mean exactly but when you explain to me in Tigrinya, I understand it fully'.

It almost seemed that this was an unnecessary question and that perhaps the participants questioned why I would ask them this. Wasn't it obvious? 'Of course, it helped me!' Semira continued: 'Yes, it helped me a lot. Thank you so much because it's so nice when you try to help us in our own language … we go home with some words and we understand. Since I started here you helped me a lot and even though it's difficult because you told me in Tigrinya I understand'.

Yasmine also told me that technology helped to support our multilingual classroom practices: 'using my own language has helped me a lot to understand because I didn't understand some words and I use the dictionary to find out what it is so I can say that definitely using my own language has helped a lot.'

Semira told me in the final interview: 'Any word when you translate in Tigrinya, some of them are really difficult to find out exactly what this means especially in the class when I'm speaking Tigrinya and nobody else knows that so it's quite difficult to explain to them what I'm speaking'. Our conversation continued:

Semira: You helped us in own languages even though we're equal unknown in Tigrinya and English and even if we forget about the word you try to help us with the computer and it really helps.

Sarah: In terms of this class is there anything you can do now that you couldn't do when we started?

Semira: As I told you before I never knew a word of English before so I couldn't say to you "I could do this or this" even though it's helped me. I can tell you that I started to be able to write my name and my country name. I started with a couple of words. As I've said a couple of times, it's been a pleasure. You've really, really helped us. You've made it easy. The way you're teaching us is good. You've tried to help us, and your way of teaching is good and it helped me a lot for myself.

Yasmine: I really enjoyed your classes and I believe it was very helpful and I really appreciate all your help and efforts that you put into this class for us. I really loved to attend the classes. I'm not sure if I'm going to move away but if I'm in Glasgow I want to continue this. Thank you, I appreciate you. Thank you so much for creating such a great class for us.

Acknowledging participants' existing linguistic knowledge and skills also enables us to reassure learners they are not starting at the very beginning of language learning, and that the languages they already know have value and significance. As Kramsch (2008: 392) notes, 'the meaning of a new piece of knowledge will emerge not from the syllabus but from the connections the learner will make with his/her own prior knowledge and experience'. Phipps (2019b: 42–43) also recognises how 'language learning and meaning making come together from the knowledge of this context and language which swirls and forms and falls around what is already known, and the desire to understand'. These connections were fundamental to our ecological approach and go far beyond practical scaffolding as they supported the participants to further develop their multilingual and intercultural identities. Participants felt their confidence increased by making these connections with their existing knowledge, and their feedback evidenced how strongly this strategy supported their learning.

The place of technology

The smart screen proved a valuable tool to quickly check between languages or provide an image for which we could each give a word in our own language in order to build our linguistic repertoires. Checking if the participants knew the word for the image on the screen in their own language helped to check comprehension and to let me know that everyone understood.

Where possible, I followed the participants' lead on how they used technology to support their learning. Yasmine used her phone during the learning sessions and had an app to translate full sentences from Farsi into English. She told me that she relies on this outside class, so to be able to use this strategy in the class was natural and helpful for her and connected her translanguaging practices in her daily life to our work together. When we visited Kelvingrove Museum, she also used her phone to ask me questions about the exhibits in Farsi, and I followed her lead with this.

Online translation tools were also useful when relaying messages to participants. During the confusing weeks when we tried to expand the group, several of the new participants texted me in Farsi and Arabic. I managed to respond in their languages by using online translation tools and this seemed to work for very simple messages about times and days. Ticheloven *et al.* (2019) recognise the important role technology can play in supporting current multilingual practices and this was mirrored in our work.

Giving up linguistic control: Learning to facilitate translanguaging in languages I do not know

it is one thing for a monolingual teacher to encourage students to take risks, and quite another for a teacher to model what taking these risks might look like
Flores & García, 2014: 253

My linguistic incompetence and lack of knowledge of Tamil, Tigrinya and Farsi became a defining feature of our interactions, and it cemented the foundation of the ecology of our relationship, which I explored in Chapter 6, because it impacted the balance of power in our work. One of the main questions I encountered in conversation with other teachers concerned how we can use a multilingual approach if we do not speak the same languages as the learners. This was also a recurrent theme in the interview data from Germany and Wales, explored in Chapter 4.

As ESOL classes in Scotland are typically diverse and multilingual (Schellekens, 2008), this is a key issue to address for teachers to become confident using translanguaging regardless of how many different languages are spoken in class and regardless of their knowledge of these languages. During the project, it was necessary for me to teach using Tamil, Tigrinya, Farsi and Arabic when I do not know more than a few words in each of these languages and, with a few adjustments, I found this to be possible, productive, rewarding and enjoyable. As García and Li (2014b: 94) recognise, 'a teacher who uses translanguaging as pedagogy participates as learner'. The success of this strategy necessitated an intentionality to take a decolonising, translingual stance and to become a learner within the group. I facilitated and guided the sessions but relied on the participants' input in their own languages and on their working with family members to complete tasks. As I could not always understand what was being said, this gave me less control, and although it felt strange at the start, we all adapted and committed to this way of working. Participants had a more equal and active role within the learning process as a result; it shifted the balance of power away from English and away from me.

These multilingual practices drew on the participants' full linguistic resources and all of my own as I related each word back to Tamil, Tigrinya and Farsi using online dictionaries and images on the screen. I relied on the participants to let me know if the definitions were correct. I needed to know a few key words in each language from the very beginning, and preparing a few basic phrases and flashcards helped me facilitate the initial sessions. Despite feeling that my knowledge of Tamil, Tigrinya and Arabic was severely lacking, this placed us all on a more equal footing as we tried to communicate in bits and pieces of each other's languages. I asked participants how they felt about this and Rushani told me: 'it's comfortable for us.'

García and Li (2014b) suggest that teachers should not view a lack of knowledge of learners' languages as a barrier, noting that teachers need to be willing to give more power to learners and allow them to take control of their learning to create a collaborative learning environment. García and Li (2014b: 112) suggest learners support each other and the teacher tries to meet them halfway: 'the teacher makes an effort to make herself understood using Spanish, and the students try to make themselves understood using English. In doing so more English is being added to the linguistic repertoire of the students, and more Spanish to that of the teacher'. Using these strategies put the 'two-way' process of New Scots into practice in a genuine sense, taking it beyond policy and into language learning as a meaningful, collaborative process. Translanguaging also helps learners to develop their voice as they learn to 'privilege interaction and collaborative dialogue over form' (García & Li, 2014b: 112).

This is a crucial difference between a translanguaging stance and other forms of pedagogy. I was 'in' this research as much as the participants. My ability (or lack thereof) to pick up their languages was stripped bare and highly visible in our sessions. I was not in control, not leading. In the second interview, Semira told me again that she noticed this 'struggle', by telling me: 'You struggle with Tigrinya just like me struggling with English!'

Semira had observed that I was 'struggling' with Tigrinya from the very beginning. This was honest and accurate, and I valued her openness and the fact that she did not question or falter in describing my attempts in this way. She told me this with a smile. Yes, I was struggling too. We all knew this, we could all see this. But Semira told me I was also learning 'little by little', and we accepted that this slow progress for all of us, me included, was something to be acknowledged and celebrated. I provided a direct example of how much time it takes to learn a language, that it is natural to need repetition and reminders to be able to retain new language.

The Spring School poem entitled 'Learning a Language is Hard Work' sums up our efforts perfectly. It is hard work, it is a 'struggle'. It takes time, patience and perseverance. By learning together with this visible symmetry, we provided a safe space in which to try out these new ways of learning together, supported by the collaborative relationship of trust outlined in Chapter 6.

This section has explored the practical benefits of our ecological, multilingual approach in the participants' own words. These benefits included increased accuracy and confidence, learning which was directly connected to and useful in their daily lives, increased independence, and an improved balance of power in our work. In the following section, I consider the impact of our work beyond these practical benefits.

Impact Beyond Pedagogy

Languaging beyond or besides words

Our translanguaging practices created an openness for each of us to try to communicate in each other's languages. We had accepted that these attempts would not be perfect; as Semira had identified, these attempts were a 'struggle', they were 'hard work'. The openness created by this willingness to meet each other halfway was important. My fieldnotes from Session 13 set the scene for this languaging work and illustrate the impact of having established a translanguaging space in which we were all free to communicate in whatever linguistic resources we chose in the moment.

> After a few text messages from Lakmini, Rushani and Yasmine explaining the delays with buses due to the stormy weather, the others arrive. They are soaked, yet again but we laugh, put on the kettle and take some time to peel off wet coats and 'arrive' in this space, to settle Yasmine's daughter and discuss how the rain in June is slightly warmer than the rain in February in Glasgow. This learning of language, our languaging, is always contextualised within this physical ecology of Glasgow, as they battle against the elements and the delays with the buses to make it to our sessions. I have great respect for their commitment to our project. Our languaging is also foregrounded within the ecology of our relationship and the familiarity we now have with each other – to be late, to come in and put the kettle on.
>
> Yasmine points at the window and asks me in Farsi to shut it because she is cold. There is an acceptance that she can ask me in Farsi and I wonder if she had felt that she could only use English in this space whether she would have asked at all? Or would she have sat there feeling cold, unsure of how to ask in English? These small actions, this increase in visibility and openness gives us alternative ways of communicating. It is my responsibility to understand her request in Farsi, not her responsibility to ask me in English. This is two-way, mutual integration.
>
> Yasmine pulls out her phone to translate her request but it is not necessary – we have languaged our way around the issue, I am quickly on my feet and the window is shut. I ask Yasmine to tell me her request in Farsi and I note it down so I know for next time, I write 'can you shut the window please?' and 'I'm cold' on the board in English. We check the equivalent in Tigrinya and Tamil and use body language to show 'brrrr … I'm cold'. The content of our learning has emerged from the physical ecology because it surrounds us. Once this new language is practised and everyone is comfortable we move back to our topic of shopping.
>
> (Fieldnotes, Session 13)

My fieldnotes illustrate the importance of the openness created by taking a multilingual, translanguaging 'stance' and how this created opportunities and an acceptance for us all to speak in whatever language came to us in the moment. This excerpt also shows how our language emerged from the embodied and situated 'semiotic activity' which Van Lier (2002) describes. As Van Lier (2002) notes, such interaction includes words, but these words only function along with gesture, eye contact and reference to the physical surroundings. Our languaging here is ecological. It is messy, imperfect and partial with gaps filled through non-verbal language to communicate what is necessary in the moment. We operate as 'languagers' (Phipps, 2009) here.

Our languaging allows for the transience of communicating in each moment, to call Yasmine's daughter back in the park (Chapter 6) when there was no time to check in a dictionary, and by Yasmine asking me to shut the window today. There is no need for perfect grammatical sentences but there is a very real, urgent and unavoidable need to communicate in the moment and to 'language' together. Yasmine did not ask me in Farsi because I know Farsi well, but rather because our project has created openness for her use her own language. The communicative burden is shared. We use whatever linguistic resources we have – Tamil, English, Farsi or Tigrinya, and the multimodal and embodied ways of communicating 'beyond – or *beside/s* words' (Thurlow, 2016: 503).

Our languaging is also shown later in the same session:

> At break time Yasmine's daughter takes Semira's seat as she makes coffee. Semira smiles and pretends to tell her off in Tigrinya. Yasmine's daughter answers in Farsi and I answer in English. This has started to feel normal to us and although we can't understand the exact words which Yasmine's daughter has said in Farsi or the Tigrinya which Semira uses, we all understand the intonation, the smiles and the body language as Semira wags her finger and shakes her head in mock disapproval.

(Fieldnotes, Session 13)

Embedding decoloniality and solidarity through linguistic incompetence

> You struggle with Tigrinya just like me struggling with English.
> Semira, Interview 2

The fact that my attempts to use Tigrinya, Tamil and Farsi were very limited did not seem to matter to the participants. This meant using other languages in a very different way from my own previous experiences. When I taught in Germany, I could explain English grammar in detail through German. This was not how it was in our sessions. I could not explain grammar or vocabulary in their languages; over the course of the project I managed to retain a few greetings and some simple vocabulary at most. I remained incompetent in their languages (especially Tamil, which I found particularly difficult). Tigrinya started to make sense to me, the characters reminded me of Japanese 'kana'. The simple, clear script seemed logical to me, I liked the pronunciation, and when Semira told me how to say a word, I could repeat it back to her with reasonable success. I also started to make some progress with Farsi. Unfortunately, Tamil remained incredibly difficult to me, unlike any other language I know with its long, complicated words, difficult pronunciation, and script which seemed almost incomprehensible to me. I had to ask Rushani and Lakmini for repetition many times. In one session, Lakmini repeated for me in rapid-fire and laughed shyly when I pronounced a word wrong for the fourth time. Frustrated with myself, I continued with our session while making a note on my pad. I told them and showed them: 'my homework – next time'.

Before the next session, I checked the dictionary and practised the words they had told me, determined to show I could manage at least a few words in Tamil. At the start of the next session, I told Lakmini I had done my homework and pronounced the Tamil words as well as I could. She told me 'yes'! and laughed and clapped at my efforts. Just as their investment in the project was clear, so too was mine. I had taken this home to learn in an effort to get this right because it mattered to me too.

This symmetry and my 'struggle' with their languages was evident from day one. Semira told me at the first interview: 'you and me, we're the same. You struggle with Tigrinya and I struggle with English'. She also gently encouraged me by telling me: 'Sarah, Tigrinya, little by little by little'. This showed her understanding, encouragement and kindness towards me and highlighted the mutuality of our language learning. Despite our vastly different reasons for learning each other's language, the symmetry between our learning experiences was evident to Semira.

Our work required the willingness to show and embrace this 'struggle', and I was reminded of Butler's (2005: 136) 'moments of unknowingness' when 'our willingness to become undone to experience language as wound or lack in relation to others constitutes our chance of becoming human'. My willingness to become 'undone' in front of the group provided solidarity and a firm foundation for the relationships I described in Chapter 6. For the participants to have more power I had to accept less, and this visibility was fundamental to building our decolonising relationship.

Phipps (2013a) notes how 'linguistic incompetence' is a powerful tool to express solidarity by using a non-dominant language in an unexpected context, bringing particular benefits when working with people experiencing 'pressure or pain' in the context of seeking asylum. Phipps' views were supported by my own findings. Both Rushani and Lakmini told me several times that they found the use of Tamil in the class helpful, and that my efforts to use Tamil were appreciated and seen as important. Rushani also told me: 'it's comfortable for us to use our language'.

By actively using learners' languages and acknowledging their significance, we provide 'linguistic hospitality' as a necessary 'mediation between host and guest languages' (Kearney, 2019: 1), supporting the 'two-way' integration process and counteracting some of the effects of the 'hostile environment' outlined in Chapter 1. Kearney (2019: 1) describes 'linguistic hospitality' as a middle road 'where one honors both host and guest languages equally, while resisting the take-over of one by the other'. Embedding 'linguistic hospitality' meant our learning environment was based on human connections, and reflected the ways that participants used languages outside the classroom enabling us to 'bring the outside in' (Roberts & Baynham, 2006). This is not assimilation in linguistic terms, it is meeting each other halfway with effort on both sides. The impact of linguistic hospitality was reflected in the key finding: *'Using my language in class made me feel welcome and comfortable'.*

Voice and audibility

> to have a voice and not be heard is to experience pain
> Baynham, 2020: 15

Within ESOL teaching, there is strong commitment to increase learner 'voice' and ensure learning is 'learner centred'. It is important to consider what this really means and how these concepts can be maximised in the classroom. As García (2020: xix) notes, the parameters for making learner voice heard are often set by the 'white monolingual listening subject'. Baynham (2020) notes the need for increased 'audibility', citing Roy (2004) who argues that 'there is no such thing as the "voiceless". There are only the deliberately silenced or the preferably unheard' (cited in Tyler, 2006: 199). Our work showed that listening also needs to be decolonised to improve audibility, and that embedding multilingual approaches are an effective step towards this.

The significance of listening well is also present within the feminist ethics of care outlined in Chapter 6. Noddings (2012) notes how listening well is important both emotionally and intellectually, and that receptive listening is not only part of learning but also at the heart of caring for others. Effective listening is vital as it is also linked to the potential of the language classroom for social justice (Levine, 2020). The multilingual audibility we intended to embed through our translanguaging stance was essential because, as Baynham (2020) recognises, such audibility and being heard is essential for speaking to become action.

I considered the participants' voices within our work and the impact of other people speaking on their behalf. In some cases, this was a daughter speaking for her mother during the learning sessions, a husband speaking for his wife on the phone, or an interpreter translating the participants' words. I found stepping back improved both visibility and audibility for other languages. Creese (2020) describes such a space as 'polyphony', comprised of all the different voices, and notes the need for careful differentiation between each of them.

The Spring School themes of 'labour and resting', which are based on Karine Polwart's (2019) beautiful song, 'Labouring and Resting', from her 'Wind Resistance' album, come back to mind as a refrain for this work:

stepping up
falling back
labouring and resting

Within our collaboration, this 'communitas', the need for stepping up was just as important as the need for falling back, to allow others to step up in multilingual audibility and for their voices be heard. The receptive listening that Noddings (2012) describes was significant. Participants told me what they wanted from the sessions, where they wanted to go, and how they felt about our sessions. I quietly stepped back and listened.

The ecology of our relationship created a space in which participants felt comfortable to speak and to be heard in Farsi, Tamil and Tigrinya. Participants consistently initiated interaction with me in their languages and this became more established over the course of our time working together. In my listening, a space was created for them to speak first, for example when Semira entered the classroom late in Session 9 (Chapter 6) and Yasmine shouted 'SIT'! to invite Semira to take the seat next to her. I could have spoken but I held back to leave the space for Yasmine to step up and speak instead, to be the host.

The impact of this 'audibility' was seen in the way Semira interacted with me in the sessions, arriving early and initiating conversation in Tigrinya, and the way she participated in the interviews (Chapter 6). Working with interpreters gave participants a medium through which to express their ideas more fully in their own languages, which I felt contributed to audibility.

Baynham (2020) notes how translanguaging pedagogy can be a powerful 'speaking back' to monolingual and separate bilingual norms. My Spring School fieldnotes record my observations of their introductions to the full room: *'they are here to be heard. To be seen'*. Our ways of working together can be understood as such a 'speaking back' (Baynham, 2020) to monoglossic ideology, which is often defined by the 'native speaker' who establishes the classroom as an English-only space. A space in which Lakmini felt her language was 'bad' and 'not allowed' (see 'Other languages are bad there: Attitudes to refugee languages in English-only settings').

Without this openness and stepping back from me, Semira may not have told me she had noticed the church on the way back from Kelvingrove (Chapter 7). Yasmine may not have asked me in Farsi to shut the window. Our comfortable, multilingual relationship had provided an audible space to enable their voices to be heard in Tigrinya and Farsi. This audibility intersects with the balance of power in our work and our decolonising approach to the research. In Semira's words, which have stayed with me so strongly throughout the project and the writing of this book: 'you and me we're the same …'.

As García (2020: xix) notes, translanguaging is a way 'to enable language-minoritized communities who have been marginalized in schools and society to finally see (and hear) themselves as they are, as bilinguals who have a right to their own language practices'. The small changes outlined here created opportunities for improved voice and audibility at a local level to affect wider change which permeates from the bottom up, the local to the global.

García (2020: xxi) cites Audre Lorde (1984) to highlight how essential it is for participants to be part of enacting this change: 'the masters tools will never dismantle the master's house. They may allow us to temporarily to beat him at his own game, but they will never enable us to bring about genuine change'. García (2020) notes that this is not necessarily about building 'peaceful intercultural relationships', but about disrupting false images of life on both sides and changing the practice architectures on which current pedagogies are constructed. This process of knowledge construction goes beyond language and pedagogy:

> For us to live together in ways that prosper one another we need to be able to listen, and speak, interculturally and in ways that do not see language as a barrier (Phipps, 2007: 167)

Sharing our 'languaging': The Spring School

In the previous chapter, I explored how we connected the Spring School workshop with the physical ecology. In this section, I take a deeper look at the 'languaging' which took place in planning and delivering the workshop, alongside the significance of the themes of the poem 'Learning a Language is Hard Work'.

In Chapter 7, I shared my fieldnotes from the Spring School and explored how I was worried that the participants might not feel confident introducing themselves at the workshop. I was stunned and delighted when they each jumped up to shout their introductions to the group. Here, I pick up my fieldnotes after these introductions to analyse the parts of the workshop which highlight our ways of multilingual working and how we brought these into the physical ecology of the workshop space:

I ask everyone to move around the room to identify as many languages as they can from the 20 words we have stuck on the walls. Semira, Rushani and Lakmini do this too. Semira is pleased to recognise Tigrinya and Amharic and tells me 'Eritrea language'. I have tried to give them the advantage here so they know as many of the languages as the other workshop participants if not more. I have included many different scripts alongside Tigrinya, Tamil and Farsi.

We move on to the languages café activity and I ask Semira, Lakmini and Rushani to take their place at each of the tables and hope this will not be too daunting. As with the introductions, I am careful to check they are comfortable doing this. We have prepared simple prompt cards (see Figure 8.2) to support this task and I put these on each table for Lakmini, Rushani and Semira: How are you? What's your name? Where are you from? It's great to see Semira, Lakmini and Rushani working at each of their tables with the workshop participants supporting them. The prompt cards are helpful to guide the activity. There is another Tigrinya speaker who sits with Semira and also helps.

After the languages café we move on to work on the poem and I explain how we have created this together based on the key themes from our learning sessions. Lakmini looks shy as she realises that her work, her handwriting, will be given out to everyone. I notice this and ask her if it's ok. She says 'ok' and looks proud. We read the poem together and

Figure 8.2 Prompt cards from the Spring School

pronounce the lines in Tigrinya, Farsi and Tamil and then we invite the workshop participants to add their own languages to the poem.

Lakmini and Rushani need to leave after the workshop so I take them to the bus stop, give them directions and travel tokens and offer to go with them but they say it's not necessary. Rushani tells me she is happy. I wait with them until the bus arrives and wave them off. Semira says she wants to stay at the event, so she sits in for the next session and chats to the other Tigrinya speaker.

(Fieldnotes, Spring School)

There is pride in these acts of linguistic identity in presenting our multilingual work to an external audience. For someone walking into the room,

Figure 8.2 *Continued.*

it was not clear who was leading the workshop, who was a participant, a refugee, a teacher, a university professor, a student. The labels 'non-native speaker', 'asylum seeker', 'refugee' were irrelevant. All of us co-existed in the workshop space as 'human beings in language' (García, 2020), as 'languagers' who 'move in the world in a way that allows the risk of stepping out of one's habitual ways of speaking and attempt to develop different, more relational ways of interacting' (Phipps, 2011: 365). These more relational ways of interacting by languaging recognise the limits of verbal language and allow for broader multimodal repertoires of communication.

We were learning from each other as workshop participants and *listening* to Semira, Rushani and Lakmini as they taught us their languages. The workshop became a decolonising space in which to be heard. The languaging of a few basic phrases and nothing more apart from the space in which to listen and to be heard. A decolonising audibility.

Our classroom translanguaging had established these ways of working as a foundation, and it felt natural by extension to work this way within the wider community. Rushani, Semira and Lakmini took ownership of this session using the languages present within the physical ecology of Glasgow as a superdiverse city, connecting the local with the global. As Moore *et al*. (2020: 2) note, translanguaging 'reflects the multiplicity, fluidity, mobility, locality and globality of the resources deployed by individuals for engaging in the complex meaning-making processes'. The following week, Semira fed back to me that she thought the Spring School was 'great, it was nice' and 'I was happy to share what we're doing'. I was pleased this was such a positive experience for all of us.

'Using my own language in class gives me power'

It's quite good when you are able to teach me in my own language, it gave me power. It empowered me. I thought "Oh, she's able to teach me by my own language so why not?" I will learn English. It empowered me to learn and to come each time.

Semira, Interview 2

The impact of my giving up linguistic control was reflected in the theme of empowerment in our findings. Semira's powerful words strongly underline how well this approach suited her. She was generous in saying I was 'able' to teach her in her own language, as we both knew how limited my Tigrinya was; however, the simple willingness to give a word in Tigrinya alongside English was enough for Semira to feel 'empowered to learn'.

Our multilingual practices directly addressed the unequal power relations on which investment is based by opposing the 'subordinate student identities' which Norton (2013) warns can be created through typical teacher/student power relations, in turn impacting on motivation. Working multilingually and reducing the status of English supported the development of a 'more empowering identity' in the manner which Canagarajah (2011b: 20) describes, allowing us to 'rethink our conceptions of the immigrant students we encounter in our classrooms' (Norton, 2013: 190). The themes of power and identity were consolidated through the key finding: *'Using my own language in class gives me power'*.

Semira's role as co-collaborator was highlighted during the interviews when I asked if she thought my Tigrinya was improving; she told me: 'you're doing ok' and continued that she thought it would get better 'one day'. I noticed that Semira did not find it necessary to flatter me. She was honest about my attempts at Tigrinya yet also encouraging. This also reflected the sense of balance in our relationship, as she acknowledged I was also learning. Despite our vastly different opportunities to access education, she could see how it was equally difficult for me to learn Tamil, Tigrinya and Farsi as it was for her to learn English, and this boosted her confidence with coming to our learning sessions. This style of learning suited her; she *invested* in our way of working together, and found confidence in her role as co-collaborator and as my Tigrinya teacher.

'Other languages are bad there': Attitudes to refugee languages in 'English-only' settings

'Two-way integration is recognised in our class' (Key finding)

During the interviews, I explained the aims of the New Scots Strategy (Scottish Government, 2018) and asked the participants if they could see mutual integration as a 'two-way' process and 'integration from day one' within the project. Semira and Yasmine confirmed they could see this was part of the project and added this to our key findings.

At the start of the project, only Yasmine had experience of learning in an ESOL class in Scotland. Partway through the main study, Lakmini also started studying at college. As Semira, Lakmini and Rushani had not attended other ESOL classes at the start of the project, they seemed to accept our translanguaging practices. As this was their first experience of attending a language class in Scotland, they had nothing to compare it to. The situation for Yasmine was different as she had already studied ESOL at college and was continuing to study. When she joined the project after the pilot, she checked with me repeatedly when I asked to use Farsi in class as this contrasted with the way she was used to learning English. This took her a few sessions to get used to.

In the final interview, both Lakmini and Yasmine reflected on their experiences in our sessions and the differences with their college ESOL classes. Lakmini told me: 'Here we feel comfortable to speak among ourselves in our language we can understand. There we're not allowed to speak in Tamil, the language is English, and we have to talk in English. Other languages are bad there'.

This was a strong statement from Lakmini, who had just turned 18, and one I found hard to hear, having worked as part of the ESOL community for many years. This was her impression of how learners' languages were viewed within her ESOL class. Not only were they not built into classroom practice as a resource and as recognised as part of learner identity, but she felt the use of Tamil, her own language, was 'bad' and 'not allowed' in her class.

Lakmini's comment calls into question monolingual pedagogy and the message that excluding learners' home languages gives. It has implications for how learners perceive the value of their language and the role of language in identity reconstruction, particularly within the crucial first weeks of settling into a new country. Feeling your language is 'bad' and 'not allowed' points more towards linguistic assimilation than the more progressive 'two-way process' laid out in policies such as New Scots and learning in 2+ language policy for heritage languages in schools.

Such a view is also damaging in terms of the bigger picture when we consider the already powerful position that English holds within the global linguistic hierarchy. The 'pecking order' of languages is painfully clear within Lakmini's observations as English, in her experience, has 'the sharpest beak' (Phillipson & Skutnabb-Kangas, 1996: 429). As Simpson (2020) notes, monolingualism in the ESOL classroom is often unquestioned and unexamined, but it does not make sense to teach people to be more multilingual by using solely monolingual methods. In the current under-resourced ESOL system, learners often have very limited class hours, which contributes to teachers feeling they need to provide as much time as possible for learners to use the target language. This research showed that veering away from an English only approach did not reduce the participants' development of English or disadvantage them by reducing the time spent focusing exclusively on the target language. In fact, the participants highlighted how our translanguaging strategies enabled them to make connections between languages which supported their learning.

In addition, participants told me they felt their languages were 'valued and recognised' within our sessions, and that these strategies gave them power. Working multilingually should not be a case of 'allowing' participants to use their own languages, but rather embedded within a holistic approach which is necessarily ecological and built collaboratively.

Conclusions

In this chapter, I have discussed the third ecology: language and 'languaging'. The research findings presented in this chapter support a case for multilingual working as an ethical necessity within the first weeks of acclimatising to the physical ecology of the host community, in our case Glasgow. I have explored the practical benefits of making connections between languages, which included increased accuracy, improved confidence and independence, and the development of strategies including the use of technology to support translanguaging outside of our sessions. I have discussed how I learnt to facilitate translanguaging from a position of linguistic incompetence, and highlighted the significance of linguistic repertoire and collective language ecologies. I have also evidenced the impact beyond pedagogy of taking a translanguaging stance.

The participants' feedback, presented in this chapter in their own words, is very powerful as it clearly evidences the impact of our approach on their learning experience. The participants told me they felt 'empowered to learn', that learning multilingually built their confidence and independence and made them feel comfortable. By repositioning the place of English in our work, we were able to incorporate linguistic hospitality and work more collaboratively to bring the 'two-way' integration on which New Scots is based directly into our work.

In the following and final chapter, I draw together the three ecologies to conclude this book. I make a case for an 'ecologising' of language learning and make recommendations for how such an approach could be harnessed to benefit New Scots. I then argue for a broader interdisciplinary base within this 'ecologising' to incorporate learning from the fields of human geography and intercultural research which underpin the three ecologies I have outlined within the three discussion chapters.

9 Conclusions and Recommendations

> I thought "Oh, she's able to teach me by my own language, so why not? I will learn English." It empowered me to learn and to come each time
> Semira, Interview 2

Introduction

In this final chapter, I conclude this book by drawing together the three ecologies of relationships, place and language, and I emphasise how these intersect to form the 'ecologising' of language learning I proposed in the previous chapters. I begin by summarising the key findings and illustrating how key threads travel from the initial starting point of the policy and literature reviews through the findings and discussion chapters to the conclusions I draw here. I revisit the original lines of inquiry and discuss how these were reframed by the emergence of the three ecologies before summarising my recommendations for future research.

In this book, I have shown that an ecological, multilingual approach to language learning is effective and welcome with reunited refugee families at the point of arrival. I have shown the need for and benefits of such an approach which is grounded in ethical intercultural relationships, orientation and multilingualism. I have illustrated linguistic hospitality as two-way integration and shown that it does not matter if the teacher cannot speak the same languages as the learners, and I have provided examples of the impact beyond pedagogy of working this way.

Synthesis of Research Findings: Returning to the Lines of Inquiry

Through the process of crystallisation and by piecing the research together in the manner of bricoleur (Denzin & Lincoln, 2008), I began to understand the findings as three ecologies guided, but not restricted, by my initial lines of inquiry. This openness was fundamental to the way the research was carried out and reflected the eclecticism as method that I explored in Chapter 3. I believe the development of the three ecologies coupled with the interdisciplinary base (which I return to under 'Summary of Key Recommendations') resulted in broader, richer findings which fitted the holistic nature of the research. However, as I pieced together the findings, I realised that much of what I had explored also answered my initial questions and, in this section, I illustrate how the findings respond to these initial lines of inquiry.

1. **What can we learn from language learning support for refugees in the Welsh and German contexts, and how can this learning be applied to the Scottish context?**

The fieldwork in Wales highlighted the benefits of an informal start to language learning, mirroring the community classes led by the third sector, local authority providers and FE colleges in Glasgow discussed in Chapter 1.

The Welsh ESOL Strategy encourages tutors to include Welsh in their ESOL classes to ensure that refugees are aware that Wales is a bilingual country with two languages in use. However, the findings highlighted that the success of this approach and the extent to which Welsh is included is dependent on individual tutors and their personal attitudes towards Welsh.

ESOL learners in Wales and Scotland face similar barriers to language learning due to inadequate funding, long waiting lists and insufficient childcare provision. I hoped to find examples of translanguaging in ESOL classes in Wales that I could draw on for the teaching study in Scotland, but instead this part of the fieldwork highlighted that languages are mostly kept separate within ESOL teaching in Wales. I found the translanguaging pedagogy widely used in schools to work between Welsh and English does not transfer to language learning for refugees either in terms of incorporating learners' home languages or Welsh. The visit to the BRC in Newport highlighted that women arriving through family reunion require additional support; a finding which shaped the teaching study in Scotland by underlining the need for a gentle, intergenerational approach which was necessarily multilingual.

The findings from the fieldwork in Germany had greater relevance at structural level due to the better model of funding, which results in faster access and the absence of lengthy waiting lists identified as a barrier in Wales and Scotland. The interviews with the sector specialists underlined the rigidity of the nationally funded integration courses. The focus on accuracy and grammar was viewed as too restrictive, which contrasts the benefits of the informal starting point for language learning recognised as a strength in both Scotland and Wales. This focus on accuracy and grammar also results in learners feeling cautious to speak before they feel confident with German's complex grammar rules, a finding which highlighted the importance of 'languaging' within the fieldwork in Scotland.

The overview of my visit to the GRC language school in Frankfurt highlighted a similarly monolingual approach to Wales and Scotland. The interviews evidenced similar beliefs to those found in the UK, i.e. that it is not possible to incorporate learners' languages due to the wide range of languages in multilingual classes and teachers' lack of knowledge of the learners' languages. This confirmed a lack of understanding of the openness towards other languages contained within the translanguaging disposition and stance I introduced in Chapter 2 and returned to in Chapter 8.

Combining the findings from Wales and Germany highlighted the benefits of quick access to language learning, better funding and the importance of starting with informal classes at the point of arrival. The absence of less formal, flexible learning opportunities in Germany also supported this view.

The findings also highlighted firmly held beliefs in both contexts about the need for language separation and for teachers to know learners' languages well to be able to incorporate them into their teaching. I found a lack of knowledge of the principles of translanguaging both in terms of its practical application and the impact of such an approach (which reinforced the literature discussed in Chapter 2). These findings shaped the fieldwork in Scotland by emphasising the need for further exploration of an ecological, multilingual approach at the point of arrival as part of informal language learning support.

2. **How can we better support reunited refugee families in Scotland through an ecological and multilingual approach to language learning?**

To answer this line of inquiry, I focus on the findings that relate to *'how'* we can better support reunited refugee families with this approach.

The success of a gentle, informal, multilingual approach at this key stage of integration

In Chapter 1, I highlighted that due to insufficient funding, demand for ESOL outstrips what is available in Scotland. In Chapter 2, I highlighted the gendered nature of language learning and of integration in a more general sense. My conversations with the BRC highlighted that women arriving through family reunion have specific needs beyond the difficulties which women face more generally in terms of language learning.

Although informal provision exists in the form of the community classes delivered by the third sector, local authorities and Further Education Colleges, the participants in this research told me they did not feel confident attending even informal classes at this very early stage. One of the key findings of this research is that there is a stage which comes before the informal community classes currently on offer. This initial informal learning was enhanced by working multilingually, alongside the fact that the women could attend with their children and knew they would be meeting other women who had also recently arrived through family reunion.

By the end of the project, two of the women moved on to community ESOL classes, evidencing the confidence they had developed through this project. This important initial stage was grounded in accompaniment, orientation and showing by meeting the participants at the BRC offices, travelling with them on the bus to the University and providing practical support through orientation-style activities. This helped the participants to get to know the local area, which led to the key finding: 'It was helpful to cover topics for everyday life like getting the bus, food, shopping, money, introductions'.

The practical benefits of a multilingual approach

The participants' newness to Glasgow was also mirrored in their newness to learning English. At the start of the project, no-one knew more than a few words of English and we found the multilingual approach particularly necessary given this starting point. Had we worked solely in English, our communication would have been even more limited.

In practical terms, the participants told me using their languages together with English was simply 'better' for them at this stage. Rushani told me using Tamil helped her with accuracy because she knew 'the exact definition' and Semira told me, 'even though it's difficult, because you told me in Tigrinya I understand'. Our work evidenced that home languages are always the foundation for comprehension and that we learn new language through language we already know, which resulted in the key finding: 'using my own language helps me to learn'.

The approach also built on the participants' existing linguistic knowledge and recognised the skills and experience the women brought with them to the study. Our work drew on their capabilities and, as a result, participants told me using their own language in class built their confidence, resulting in the key finding: 'using my own language in class gives me power'. This power and confidence was further shown by their participation at the Spring School (Chapter 7) and their ability to teach small groups their own languages as part of the workshop.

Stances, dispositions and visibility

I found a commitment to a translanguaging stance and disposition of openness to other languages to be a key success. Rather than needing to be able to speak the participants' languages well, it was sufficient to create an openness to including their languages and commit to translanguaging by increasing the visibility of other languages and recognising their place in our learning. Comparing and contrasting languages was well-received, enhancing metalinguistic awareness as a result. We found that simple multilingual worksheets supported this learning and that starting each session with a phrase in Tamil, Tigrinya or Farsi worked well to set the tone for each session. We also found that technology was a helpful tool to support multilingual practices, a strategy which connected to how language is used outside the classroom.

Learning in response to the context of 'day one' of integration and orientation to place

Einar Haugen's 'language ecology' (1972) provided a foundation from which to understand two key elements on which this study is grounded: the interconnections between language and environment, and the interaction between languages in the mind. This approach necessitated openness as it explored how language responds to the context, a concept brought into the study through orientation-style activities.

Taking the learning outside the classroom was vital and helped us to build skills in taking the bus and getting to know the local area. Activities in class helped to build confidence with practical topics such as shopping, using the bus and going to the doctor. The participants confirmed the practical topics they chose helped them in their daily lives and situated the learning as orientation to the physical ecology.

I considered how the project could remain true to the definition of the 'social and natural environment' within Haugen's (1972) language ecology. After problematising understandings of 'context' and 'environment', I settled on an understanding of 'place' drawn from human geography as bearing most relevance for this work. This conceptualisation allows for the connections that people make with their environment in a human and embodied way rather than an understanding of 'context' within the system of integration. An understanding of home, drawn from human geography, was also central to our work and included a sense of belonging in parallel realities. We found ritual and familiarity connected to place and concepts of home through the acts of making coffee and tea together to be a key part of welcome within this liminal phase.

Our experiences of learning ecologically acknowledged the significance of the physical aspects that Ingold (2011) describes, and I found these compatible with Haugen's (1972) description of 'social and natural environment'. Our total sensory participation was part of our embodied experience as part of 'languaging'.

I connected the layered simultaneity in Chapter 2 with our fieldwork by the example of Semira pointing out the church to me. The process of connecting old and new, known and not yet known runs throughout the research and is mirrored within the ecology of language in Chapter 8.

Presenting our work together at the Spring School, to an unfamiliar audience, in an unfamiliar place, showed both increased confidence and trust while also illustrating the support this required. This experience highlighted the importance of this work outside the classroom rather than working solely within the niche of the classroom. Our work showed that these early stages need gentle support, grounded in orientation with space for accompaniment and showing.

3. **What significance does this approach have in terms of identity, empowerment and the dominance of English within the process of language learning?**

I have answered this line of inquiry by considering the impact beyond pedagogy of such an approach, drawing on the findings in Chapter 8. I understand this in simple terms as the question '*why* use such an approach?'

Countering monolingual approaches has broader implications and calls into question the practice architecture of the unexamined monolingual norm

The gap between policy, practice and academic literature points towards the need to counteract the dominant monolingual/social cohesion narrative through pedagogies which highlight linguistic diversity in a positive way. This means increasing knowledge of linguistic diversity and connecting the way languages are taught with the local language ecology. Phipps (2019b) notes how she speaks far too many colonial languages and questions the usefulness of them for communicating with refugees. Teaching languages commonly spoken by refugees such as Arabic, Tigrinya, Farsi and Tamil in schools in Glasgow would respond better to the local ecology and better equip people for intercultural communication in this specific context.

I found Vertovec's (2007) superdiversity fundamental to understanding the physical ecology of Glasgow and its role as a dispersal city (Chapter 1). Connecting repertoire and collective language ecologies allowed us to 'bring the outside in' (Roberts & Baynham, 2006), which is necessary because the UK is not monolingual. Scotland is officially multilingual and Glasgow, as Scotland's largest city, is superdiverse with many languages and cultures present. There is a need for language learning to catch up with our increasingly globalised world. As Simpson (2020) notes, it does not make sense that we teach people how to be more multilingual by using methods based on monolingualism.

The need for 'languaging', not grammatical perfection

In Chapter 1, I called into question the pursuit of native speaker-like competence (Auer, 2007). I found Li's (2017) understanding of the 'languaging' of translanguaging particularly relevant for this study and central to the dialogical nature of our intercultural communication outlined in Chapters 1, 7 and 8. I found it did not matter that I could not speak the participants' languages well or that during the course of our project none of us were likely to reach native speaker-like competence. It was important instead that we *languaged* together. This finding was also supported by the finding in Germany, which highlighted that refugees lack confidence to try to speak German as there is such an emphasis on the need for grammatical accuracy within the integration course.

For us there could be no waiting for perfection. We needed to communicate in whatever bits of language we had: verbal, semiotic, body language – we needed it all. Using this approach helped to build confidence. Seeing me struggle to communicate in Tigrinya, Farsi and Tamil also illustrated that we prioritised human dialogical interaction rather than striving for grammatical perfection, which would have been an unrealistic goal and demotivating at this stage. As García and Li (2014b: 112) note, translanguaging 'shows students how to privilege interaction and collaborative dialogue over form and thus develops their voice'.

The impact of decolonising

The collaborative research design was shaped by both decolonising methodology and decolonising teaching pedagogy, drawing on Phipps' (2019b) 'decolonising multilingualism' manifesto. I found the collaborative approach and ethical intercultural relationships, both in terms of the CPAR methodology and the position of English, to be welcomed by the participants. My decisions to implement this approach counteracted the narrative of one nation/one language and how this is essential for social cohesion, fitting also with the translanguaging approach in Chapter 2 and the collaborative approach of New Scots. Participants showed their investment in this way of working as they weighed up the difficult journey against the benefits of coming to our sessions. Semira told me, 'we're hoping to learn more that's why we have to do that. I come because this is helping me'. This investment was further evidenced by their participation in the interviews and the long, considered responses they gave.

The discussion on translanguaging in Chapter 2 recognises the positive impact of taking a multilingual approach. I mirror this positive impact in the research findings in Chapter 8, which highlight the improved balance of power in the classroom, the implications for social justice and the opportunity to place learners at the centre of their own learning, echoing the priorities of New Scots in recognising refugees' own skills.

The findings in Chapter 6, which focus on the relationships within the project, were particularly relevant to this line of inquiry as they evidence the positive impact of our mutual, respectful co-learning relationships. I noted the importance of the principles of feminist ethics of care, taking comfort in Noddings' (2012) 'latitudinal knowledge' by stating my commitment to this openness as part of an ethical responsibility to the participants. My own position in the research was shaped by drawing on Butler's (2005) 'account of oneself' and understanding the reciprocity of these relationships.

In highlighting the balance of power created through the decolonising and translanguaging approach, I illustrated how quickly this built comfort and increased our familiarity with each other. I drew on the embedded mutual consideration and wellbeing which García and Li (2014b) note as integral to a co-learning relationship to illustrate the impact of this, showing also the importance of ritual and familiarity in building these relationships.

The importance of recognising liminality and fragility and the impact on relationships and identity reconstruction

The fragility of our relationship within the early weeks of the project necessitated high levels of emotional labour, nurture and trust. I illustrated how invested the participants were in the research and emphasised the significance of the wider pedagogical interactions in evidencing investment, such as Semira often arriving early and helping me to set up.

The gender dimension to our work meant we found common ground as women and mothers of primary school-aged children, and I returned again to Butler's (2005) 'account of oneself' to ground this discussion in Chapter 6. My linguistic incompetence combined with the collaborative approach had a significant impact and led to the key finding: 'using my own language in class gives me power'.

I found that traditional social structures appeared to be suspended within this liminal phase of creating a new identity in a host community. By understanding the project as a liminal space and drawing on an understanding of 'communitas' (Turner, 1969), I recognised this created openness for new dynamics to become established. This disruption further contributed to the decolonising of our work as it shifted the balance of power in favour of the participants.

The impact of linguistic incompetence as solidarity and mutuality

My own position in the research was fundamentally shaped by participating as learner (García & Li, 2014b), which brought a sense of vulnerability to my own role. The impact of facilitating translanguaging in languages I do not know is at the heart of this research and underpins the relationships I explored in Chapter 6. Semira identified my attempts at Tigrinya as a 'struggle'; the significance of her telling me this highlighted both how firmly she believed it and her increased confidence to make these observations directly to me. Despite my struggle, she felt I was 'able' to teach her in Tigrinya and this was enough to make her feel 'empowered to learn' and to come each week. She also told me that my Tigrinya was improving 'little by little', which showed her understanding and encouragement towards me and also the acceptance that it would take time for all of us to learn each other's languages. The findings clearly show that my lack of knowledge of their languages was not a barrier. In fact, it was a strength of our project.

My participating as learner enabled solidarity and mutuality. It brought symmetry into our language learning in a way that was both genuine and visible. It validated the place of their languages, reducing both the position of English and my power and control, illustrating genuine linguistic hospitality as part of the two-way integration laid out in New Scots. Semira told me she could see we were 'equal unknown', that we were 'the same' and that my struggle to learn Tigrinya was 'just like' her efforts to learn English. Linguistic hospitality was evidenced through the key finding: 'using my own language in class made me feel welcome and comfortable'.

I found the 'receptive listening' which Noddings (2012) describes as part of this relationship to be vital. The need to understand audibility as multilingual as an ethical necessity, which I found by stepping back to create space for the participants' voices to genuinely be heard, cannot be underestimated. The participants' descriptions of the impact of using their own languages in class are powerful and showed that the benefits of this approach went far beyond the practical benefits.

Intergenerational relationships

Intergenerational relationships played an important role in our work, and this was one of the original areas that the BRC identified as requiring further research at the start of the project. The mother-daughter relationships within the project provided three interesting contrasts due to the ages of the daughters: 5, 10 and 17. The two older daughters were able to work with their mothers in their own languages, which was shown to be useful and supportive. As Yasmine's daughter was only five, this was a different dynamic, which I found had greater significance of overcoming the barrier of childcare highlighted in Chapters 1 and 4. Another important finding was that the families enjoyed learning together and could practise new language together at home, enabling better home-class connections.

In Chapter 7, I highlighted the challenges the women experienced arriving in Scotland long after their husbands and the imbalance that this created in terms of their own independence. I highlighted the pressure and frustration that Yasmine and Semira felt to improve their English quickly. I recognised the impact of the husbands' support of the project, and that such support may not always be present, which is one of the barriers highlighted in the New Scots report (Scottish Government *et al.*, 2017) discussed in Chapter 1. This finding underlines the importance of this family support.

Recognising existing skills and known languages

The concept of linguistic repertoire was shown to be important both within the literature in Chapter 2 and in my own findings. It connected to identity by highlighting the learners' languages and illustrating the importance and value of them in our work. Acknowledging existing linguistic knowledge and skills also enabled the participants to find confidence because they were not starting at the very beginning and the languages they already knew had value and significance. These connections were fundamental to our approach and went far beyond practical scaffolding.

The translanguaging stance we adopted was particularly beneficial at this very early stage of language learning. For the BRC, it is usual for interpreters to support initial sessions for other services and, as a result, learners are able to communicate in their own languages at this point. This is in contrast to the approach of initial ESOL sessions which are usually solely in English.

The ecological, multilingual approach we took certainly had practical benefits; however, it is the impact beyond pedagogy that provides the strongest findings in this research and, as such, the whole book drives towards this last discussion in Chapter 8. I observed how the sessions prioritised what the participants *could* do rather than what they *could not* and even at this early stage how the use of their own languages 'enhanced interpersonal interaction' (Swain & Lapkin, 2000). It also served to bring my own vulnerability in this role to the fore.

Bringing the Ecologies Together: Connecting the Interconnected

In this book, I have problematised and explored an understanding of 'the right kind of ESOL' (Education Scotland, 2015) for women arriving in Scotland through family reunion by providing a real-world example of how an ecological, multilingual approach to language learning can be implemented. I have given the reasons why this approach is both appropriate and effective. By drawing on decolonising and collaborative approaches to both research and language learning, I have presented an approach grounded in the concepts of 'two-way' integration which I have situated as part of welcome from 'day one'.

Through the findings within the ecology of *relationships*, I evidenced the benefits of a decolonising, collaborative relationship which I brought into the CPAR spiral and connected with the constructs of translanguaging and co-learning. The research showed the importance of the ethics of care by working in a small group with increased support, which allowed us to work closely together and take our time to labour and rest. The multilingual approach was significant because it impacted the balance of power in our work, bringing a symmetry clearly recognised by the participants. The intergenerational relationships illustrated the benefits and support that come with learning with family members and how translanguaging naturally fits with this dynamic as it mirrors the way that languages are used in real life.

In terms of *place*, the findings clearly point towards the need for orientation-style activities as shown by the topics requested by the participants. They told me they found our learning 'practical' and this helped them in their daily lives. The more human understanding of place that we uncovered in our work allowed for connections with human geography and anthropology which are present within the work of getting to know a city as part of orientation to the physical ecology. The participants faced challenges with the weather due to specific factors within the cold, windswept and often very wet physical ecology of Glasgow. Our learning together outside the classroom showed the importance of the accompaniment and showing which Woitsch (2012) also recognises as significant within intercultural work.

In terms of *language*, the findings strongly point towards the benefits of a multilingual approach – an approach the participants told me they simply found 'better' both in practical terms and, as I have illustrated, brought significant benefits beyond pedagogy. This research calls for teachers and researchers to embrace decolonising pedagogy and to consider alternatives to the unexamined norm of teaching monolingually, particularly at the point of arrival at the beginning of learning English. Bringing their own languages into the learning process quickly enabled participants to connect with the local context in a meaningful way. The findings clearly show that it did not matter than I did not know the participants' languages, a finding supported by Simpson (2020) who also notes that teachers do not need to know much of the learners' languages for translanguaging to work well.

The three ecologies of relationships, place and language combine to form a more human understanding of language learning as mutual integration. The ecologies of place, relationships and language are porous, their boundaries are blurred by definition due to the interconnectedness of each dimension and to the approach as a whole. The combined approach is fundamentally shaped by the physical context, the liminal phase of arrival and orientation coupled with collaborative, decolonising intercultural relationships and grounded in linguistic hospitality.

The exploration and problematising of the definition of 'integration' is central to the development of the three ecologies outlined within this book. It calls for more joined up thinking to connect the ideas on multilingual approaches laid out in academic literature with teaching and learning, with a specific focus on the needs of reunited families.

Summary of Key Recommendations

Integration from day one needs support for mutual language learning from day one

Put simply, integration from day one means language classes must be available from day one. In the case of reunited families, this requires specialist support complemented by a softer understanding of the human side of integration based on multilingual learning at the point of arrival. A better system of sustainable, secure funding is needed to enable more multilingual support in the initial first weeks as family members join their partners and contend with the imbalance created by the current system. This should include language classes which better connect policy, academic literature and practice, and provide closer consideration of the unexamined monolingual norm (Simpson, 2020).

Scotland, with its history of welcoming newcomers, and Glasgow, with its 20 years of welcoming dispersed asylum seekers and strong, well-recognised third sector networks, are ideally placed to embrace the translanguaging stance outlined within this book. This could be put into practice by drawing on the experiences I have outlined, the work of CUNY-NYSIEB in the USA and, closer to home, the TLANG project I highlight in Chapter 2. Bringing this learning into current practice would complement existing ESOL provision and allow for further development to meet the specific needs of these families.

Although the New Scots Strategy has gained international recognition as a successful approach to refugee integration, the insufficient funding attached to the Strategy makes it difficult to achieve its aims, which risks the Strategy becoming ineffective. The findings of this research point strongly to the need for longer term funding to be attached to New Scots to allow the third sector organisations, local authorities and Further Education colleges, already recognised for their expertise in this area, greater capacity to support refugees with language learning from day one. The approach outlined here provides one way forward.

Collaboration and decoloniality

Lack of English should not be viewed as a barrier to collaborative approaches; instead, more consideration needs to be given to how teachers and researchers can facilitate more symmetrical relationships. Despite our limited shared language, we found ways to shape the study together with the support of interpreters at key points in the CPAR spiral. Fostering this collaborative relationship required a high level of emotional labour and support. Newly arrived refugee women with low levels of education are often labelled as 'vulnerable' or 'hard to reach', which in turn results in fewer opportunities for such collaborative working and in less data available to understand their needs.

There is power and agency in the acts of labour and resting explored in this book. The balance created by this stepping up and stepping back points to the success of a collaborative, decolonising approach which brought multiple benefits. By drawing on their own skills and experience, the participants were able to shape their own learning and the research as a whole, even at this early stage, putting the collaborative approach of New Scots into practice. To embed such approaches within existing language classes requires a shift within teacher training to reconsider traditional teacher/learner roles, but doing so would complement current informal community ESOL provision and increase understanding of power dynamics and their impact on learner investment.

Support intergenerational learning with a multilingual approach

The decolonising relationship and balance of power allowed space for learners to take a more active role in their own learning. Mothers learning with their children and translanguaging together built confidence at this initial stage and supported connections between home and our learning sessions. Translanguaging goes hand in hand with intergenerational work as it was natural for the family members to work together and support each other in their own languages.

Tailored support for family members who are joining their partners here could mirror other BRC support which already has a multilingual starting point. Such introductory courses would form a natural transition between the point of arrival and community ESOL classes. The appropriacy and effectiveness of a multilingual approach was evidenced by Rushani's experience as it built her confidence and, at the end of the project, she moved on to a community ESOL class. This finding shows the need for more supported learning at this initial stage, which includes bringing the learning to the learners, and real-world support with orientation-style activities, such as travelling on the bus based on the accompaniment and showing I highlighted in the previous section. It is difficult to include such activities and high levels of support within the remit of the current, underfunded system.

Embed translingual stances and multilingual approaches, regardless of whether the teacher knows the learners' languages or not

It was clear that it did not matter that I did not know the participants' languages well. It mattered that I was trying to use their languages and that their languages had a recognised place in our learning.

To bring this approach into language learning at the point of arrival requires awareness-raising and training for ESOL tutors on the principles of the translanguaging stance I have outlined. Such training would increase understanding of the impact of recognising both linguistic repertoire and the local ecology within teaching and learning.

Lessons can be drawn from EAL into ESOL to increase understanding of multilingual repertoire, bring fluidity into the language learning process, and change perceptions of the boundaries between languages and the perceived need to keep languages separate. This could bridge the gap between the 'multilingual realities' of ESOL learners' lives (Simpson & Cooke, 2017) and the classroom, and build confidence that teachers do not need to be able to speak all of the learners' languages to incorporate them within teaching and learning.

Although translanguaging mirrors the ways languages are used outside the classroom, translanguaging strategies still need to be taught, practised and developed for both teachers and learners. Practical ways of increasing visibility of other languages within the classroom include starting each session with a phrase in one of the home languages and encouraging learners to work together in their own languages. No specific teaching materials are required as we found through the successful use of existing published materials. Asking learners to make notes in their own language supported the strategy of comparing languages suggested in the CUNY-NYSIEB guide. The translanguaging stance and disposition I have outlined in this book complements the informal community classes currently in place in Glasgow and could be trialled within such provision.

Connecting local to global

CPAR and ecological approaches bring opportunities to connect the global and the local simultaneously. The global factors which shaped the women's experiences of coming to the UK through family reunion were brought into contact with the local ecology of Glasgow, highlighting an understanding of the duality of home within the liminal space of these first few weeks and acknowledging the shifting identities present within this period of transition.

An ecological approach also has wider implications beyond the local ecology. As Tsuda (1994) recognises, there are two paradigms; 'the diffusion of English paradigm' or 'the ecology of language paradigm'. English will continue to have the 'sharpest beak' (Phillipson & Skutnabb-Kangas, 1996) if we do not meaningfully take steps to give other languages the space they need.

As we are already living in increasingly superdiverse cities, making our local language ecologies visible as a key part of language learning would bring benefits of increased understanding for all members of the community and have an impact at both local and global levels. Speaking each other's languages increases understanding and counteracts discourses of othering, of 'us' and 'them', which focus on language learning being the responsibility of those who are new to the community.

The need for interdisciplinarity

Drawing on intercultural research, anthropology, human geography and feminist care ethics created a necessary openness perhaps not always afforded within restricted ESOL contexts in which practitioners are fighting to provide essential ESOL classes within the current precariously funded system.

Language permeates every area of our lives and, as such, I needed to draw on a broad interdisciplinary base to carry out this research. I now consider the inclusion of this interdisciplinarity to be a strength of the research and a finding in its own right. Through this interdisciplinary approach, the research highlights how 'latitudinal knowledge' (Noddings, 2012) from neighbouring fields can deepen understanding of broader factors that impact language learning.

An improved dialogue between practitioners and academics would benefit both sides. Future academic studies could also draw on this finding to incorporate other fields within an understanding of the 'latitudinal knowledge' which Noddings (2012) suggests as part of an interdisciplinary approach. I believe this is part of decolonising and collaboration by allowing research to follow the direction of the findings within such emergent studies.

Improve connections and information sharing between practitioners, academics and policymakers

The success of the multilingual, ecological approach highlights the need for better connections between policy, practice and academic literature. A more joined-up approach would enable practice to draw more directly on current academic thinking and, in turn, for theory to be closer informed by real-world experiences. Some steps towards this are being taken by the online *ESOL Research Forum* coordinated by James Simpson, which shares ESOL research and practice.

The ESOL Strategy and New Scots both emphasise the benefits of collaborative approaches. The importance of integration 'from day one' and of 'two-way integration' runs throughout this book and is central to an understanding of the relevance of this policy for the women who participated in this research. The emphasis on language within the refreshed New Scots Strategy highlights the importance of refugees' home languages and is not limited solely to improving English. Understanding these key recommendations formed an integral part of understanding *how* we can better support families arriving in this way. Combining academic literature with real-world practice highlighted the reasons for embracing such an approach and afforded me an understanding of multilingual alternatives. Continued and improved information sharing between academics, policymakers and practitioners would allow for more joined-up thinking, which would enable ESOL practitioners to trial new methods such as the translanguaging approach I have outlined.

An ecology of terms

The term 'New Scots' is used to refer to refugees in Scotland and is recognised as an ideological shift towards more inclusive terminology which is not marked from a place of deficit. However, within language learning, the predominantly used term remains 'non-native speaker', which epistemologically construes people as 'ever learners' (Prada & Turnbull, 2018: 10) and holds people to an unattainable monolingual standard. This deficit is embedded in ways of negotiating understanding as this is the most commonly used term.

Extending the use of 'New Scots' more consistently to language learning as a more progressive and inclusive term to replace 'non-native speaker' would be a positive step. In the US, García and Kleifgen (2010) suggest 'emergent bilingual' to counteract terms based on deficit, noting the positive impact of both learners and teachers using terms that recognise multilingualism as a resource. Scotland has already begun this ideological shift and this could become more embedded within language learning through more consistent use of the term 'New Scots'. This shift also ties in with the key findings of empowerment, confidence, investment and identity, which could be drawn further into more inclusive ways of integrating learners' identities with language learning.

Future Research Directions

This research is indicative of how an ecological, multilingual approach might work with other groups and in other settings. Transposing this approach to different ecologies would allow for further exploration of orientation in other host communities. By raising awareness of alternative multilingual approaches, I hope to initiate a dialogue on *how* and *why* translanguaging can be brought into language classes for refugees and how this can complement existing provision.

It would be useful to explore this approach with participants who shared a language beyond the family group to further explore the impact of mutual language learning on relationship building. A further extension to this research would also be to incorporate fathers or other family members within the learning sessions to enable whole families to learn together and further explore the impact of multilingual intergenerational learning.

As technology was used consistently in our work to translate and check meaning between languages, it would be useful to research this digital element further. Given that so many language classes have been delivered online during the COVID-19 pandemic, this strand of research could also incorporate online learning and technology to support multilingual practices.

The research would lead naturally into developing a peer-led model by building on the 'ecologising' of language learning developed here and drawing on existing models of peer-led work already present within refugee integration. Peer-led models such as the AVAIL project and 'Sharing Lives, Sharing Languages' (Hirsu & Bryson, 2017) have been successful, and learning from such projects could be developed for deeper collaboration between refugees and host communities. The participants' ability to teach their own languages to small groups of workshop participants at the Spring School indicates that such an approach might work well.

Concluding Remarks

I wrote the last half of my PhD thesis, which became this book, in lockdown during the COVID-19 pandemic. As I finalised these last chapters, I was acutely aware of how fortunate the participants and I had been to work together face to face, to visit local places together, and to have the simple human contact of learning together in the same room. The moments I have written about which formed such an important part of this work – Semira grabbing my arm to show me the church or touching my hand to say goodbye, sitting close to each other in a taxi, sharing coffee, delivering a workshop together, huddling around a table together to learn each other's languages – are all things we took for granted but would not have been possible a few short months later. Further research will be needed in the months and years that follow to understand more about the impact of the pandemic and the associated restrictions on language learning for refugees and integration more generally.

It was an honour to work with this group of quiet, strong women and to share this important first step into their new lives in Glasgow.

As I consider how to conclude this final chapter, I know that the right words to end this book are not mine, but rightfully they are Semira's. Her conclusion of our ecological, multilingual approach was that it 'empowered' her to learn 'and to come each time'.

What more could I, as her co-teacher and co-learner, hope for?

References

Ager, A. and Strang, A. (2004) *Indicators of Integration: Final Report*. London: Home Office, Research, Development and Statistics Directorate.
Ahmed, S. (1999) Home and away: Narratives of migration and estrangement. *International Journal of Cultural Studies* 2 (3), 329–347.
Auer, P. (2007) The monolingual bias in bilingualism research, or: Why bilingual talk is (still) a challenge for linguistics. In M. Heller (ed.) *Bilingualism: A Social Approach* (pp. 319–339). Cham: Springer.
Bailey, B. (2012) Heteroglossia. In M. Martin-Jones, A. Blackledge and A. Creese (eds) *The Routledge Handbook of Multilingualism*. Abingdon: Routledge.
Baker, C. (2011) *Foundations of Bilingual Education and Bilingualism* (5th edn). Bristol: Multilingual Matters.
Bakhtin, M.M. (2010) *The Dialogic Imagination: Four Essays* (Vol. 1). Austin: University of Texas Press.
Baynham, M. (2020) Comment on Part 1: Collaborative relationships. In E. Moore, J. Bradley and J. Simpson (eds) *Translanguaging as Transformation: The Collaborative Construction of New Linguistic Realities* (pp. 15–22). Bristol: Multilingual Matters.
BBC News (2018) UK should set date for everyone to speak English, says Casey. https://www.bbc.co.uk/news/uk-politics-43370514
Becker, A.L. (1991) Language and languaging. *Language and Communication* 11 (1–2), 33–35. https://doi.org/10.1016/0271-5309(91)90013-L
Beech, N. (2011) Liminality and the practices of identity reconstruction. *Human Relations* 64 (2), 285–302.
Beres, A.M. (2015) An overview of translanguaging: 20 years of 'giving voice to those who do not speak'. *Translation and Translanguaging in Multilingual Contexts* 1 (1), 103–118.
Blackledge, A. (2009) "As a country we do expect": The further extension of language testing regimes in the United Kingdom. *Language Assessment Quarterly* 6 (1), 6–16.
Blackledge, A. and Creese, A. (2010) *Multilingualism: A Critical Perspective*. London: Continuum.
Block, D. (2007) *Second Language Identities*. New York: Continuum.
Blommaert, J. (2005) *Discourse: A Critical Introduction*. Cambridge: Cambridge University Press.
Bourdieu, P. (1991) *Language and Symbolic Power*. Cambridge, MA: Harvard University Press.
Braun, V. and Clarke, V. (2006) Using thematic analysis in psychology. *Qualitative Research in Psychology* 3 (2), 77–101.
British Council (2017) *Language for Resilience - the Role of Language in Enhancing the Resilience of Syrian Refugees and Host Communities*. Retrieved from https://www.britishcouncil.org/sites/default/files/language_for_resilience_report.pdf
British Red Cross (2018) *Family Reunion Integration Service an Introduction*. Retrieved from https://www.redcross.org.uk/about-us/what-we-do/how-we-support-refugees/family-reunion-integration-service
British Red Cross (2020) AVAIL Project: Putting refugees and asylum seekers at the heart of services and policies that support them.

Broomfield, M. (2017) How Theresa May's 'Hostile Environment' created an underworld. *New Statesman*. Retrieved from https://www.newstatesman.com/2017/12/how-theresa-may-s-hostile-environment-created-underworld
Butler, J. (2005) *Giving An Account of Oneself*. New York: Fordham University Press.
Butler, J. and Spivak, G. (2007) *Who Sings the Nation-state?* London: Seagull Books.
Cahill, C., Sultana, F. and Pain, R. (2007) Participatory ethics: Politics, practices, institutions. *ACME: an international e-journal for critical geographies* 6 (3), 304–318.
Canagarajah, A.S. (2013) *Literacy as Translingual Practice: Between Communities and Classrooms*. New York: Routledge.
Canagarajah, S. (2011a) Codemeshing in academic writing: Identifying teachable strategies of translanguaging. *The Modern Language Journal* 95 (3), 401–417.
Canagarajah, S. (2011b) Translanguaging in the classroom: Emerging issues for research and pedagogy. *Applied Linguistics Review* 2, 1–28.
Care for Calais (2022) Is the UK asylum system tough enough? Retrieved from https://care4calais.org/the-refugee-crisis/is-britains-asylum-system-tough-enough/Peopl
Casey, L. (2016) *The Casey Review: A Review Into Opportunity and Integration* (1409849538) Retrieved from https://www.gov.uk/government/publications/the-casey-review-a-review-into-opportunity-and-integration
Celic, C. and Seltzer, K. (2011) Translanguaging: A CUNY-NYSIEB guide for educators. *CUNY-NYSIEB. New York*.
European Convention on Human Rights (1950)
Creese, A. (2020) Afterword: Starting from the other end. In E. Moore, J. Bradley and J. Simpson (eds) *Translanguaging as Transformation: The Collaborative Construction of New Linguistic Realities* (pp. 251–253). Bristol: Multilingual Matters.
Creese, A. and Blackledge, A. (2010) Translanguaging in the bilingual classroom: A pedagogy for learning and teaching? *The Modern Language Journal* 94 (1), 103–115.
Creese, A. and Blackledge, A. (2018) *The Routledge Handbook of Language and Superdiversity*. Abingdon: Routledge.
Cummins, J. (2019) The emergence of translanguaging pedagogy: A dialogue between theory and practice. *Journal of Multilingual Education Research* 9 (13), 17–36.
Cymru Cynulliad Cenedlaethol (2011) *National Assembly for Wales. Mesur y Gymraeg (Cymru) 2011/Welsh Language (Wales) Measure 2011*.
Das Bundesamt für Migration und Flüchtlinge (2018) Welcome to Germany: Information for Immigrants. Retrieved from https://www.bamf.de
Denzin, N.K. and Lincoln, Y.S. (2008) *Strategies of Qualitative Inquiry* (Vol. 2). London: Sage.
Der Spiegel (2017) Germany's Ongoing Project to Welcome Its Refugees. *Der Spiegel*.
Duff, P.A. and van Lier, L. (1997) Approaches to observation in classroom research; observation from an ecological perspective. *TESOL Quarterly* 31 (4), 783–787.
Education Scotland (2015) *Welcoming Our Learners: Scotland's ESOL Strategy 2015–2020. The English for Speakers of Other Languages (ESOL) Strategy for Adults in Scotland 2015*. Retrieved from https://www.education.gov.scot/Documents/ESOLStrategy2015to2020.pdf
Elgot, J. (2018) Theresa May's 'hostile environment' at heart of Windrush scandal. *The Guardian*. Retrieved from https://www.theguardian.com/uk-news/2018/apr/17/theresa-mays-hostile-environment-policy-at-heart-of-windrush-scandal
Eliasson, S. (2015) The birth of language ecology: Interdisciplinary influences in Einar Haugen's 'The ecology of language'. *Language Sciences* 50 (1015), 78–92.
Ellingson, L. (2009) *Engaging Crystallization in Qualitative Research: An Introduction*. London: Sage.
Financial Times (2017) How well have Germany's refugees integrated? Data reveal more asylum seekers are being sent to regions with fewer jobs per capita. Retrieved from https://www.ft.com/content/e1c069e0-872f-11e7-bf50-e1c239b45787

Flores, N. and García, O. (2014) Linguistic third spaces in education: Teachers' translanguaging across the bilingual continuum. In D. Little, C. Leung and P. van Avermaet (eds) *Managing Diversity in Education: Languages, Policies, Pedagogies* (pp. 243–256). Bristol: Multilingual Matters.

Freeman, D.L. and Cameron, L. (2008) Research methodology on language development from a complex systems perspective. *The Modern Language Journal* 92 (2), 200–213.

Freire, P. (1970) *Pedagogy of the Oppressed*. London: Penguin Books.

Freire, P. (1982) Creating alternative research methods: Learning to do it by doing it. In B. Hall, A. Gillette and R. Tandon (eds) *Creating Knowledge: A Monopoly* (pp. 29-37). Toronto: International Council for Adult Education.

Freire, P. (1996) *Pedagogy of the Oppressed* (Reviewed edn). London: Penguin Books.

Fullfact.org (2022) Asylum seekers, the UK and Europe. Retrieved from https://fullfact.org/immigration/asylum-seekers-uk-and-europe/

García-Mateus, S. and Palmer, D. (2017) Translanguaging pedagogies for positive identities in two-way dual language bilingual education. *Journal of Language, Identity and Education* 16 (4), 245–255.

García, O. (2007) Intervening discourses, representations and conceptualizations of language. In S. Makoni and A. Pennycook (eds) *Disinventing and Reconstituting Languages* (pp. xi–xv). Clevedon: Multilingual Matters.

García, O. (2020) Foreword: Co-labor and re-performances. In E. Moore, J. Bradley and J. Simpson (eds) *Translanguaging as Transformation: The Collaborative Construction of New Linguistic Realities* (xvii–xxii). Bristol: Multilingual Matters.

García, O., Johnson, S.I., Seltzer, K. and Valdés, G. (2017) *The Translanguaging Classroom: Leveraging Student Bilingualism for Learning*. Philadelphia: Caslon.

García, O. and Kleifgen, J.A. (2010) *Educating Emergent Bilinguals: Policies, Programs and Practices for English Language Learners*. New York: Teachers College Press.

García, O. and Kleyn, T. (2016) *Translanguaging with Multilingual Students: Learning from Classroom Moments*. New York: Routledge.

García, O. and Lin, A.M.Y. (2017) Translanguaging in bilingual education. In O. García, A.M.Y. Lin and S. May (eds) *Bilingual and Multilingual Education* (pp. 117–130). Cham: Springer.

García, O. and Li, W. (2014a) Translanguaging and education. In O. García and W. Li *Translanguaging: Language, Bilingualism and Education* (pp. 63–77). Basingstoke: Palgrave.

García, O. and Li, W. (2014b) *Translanguaging: Language, Bilingualism and Education*. Basingstoke: Palgrave.

Gaventa, J. and Cornwall, A. (2008) Power and knowledge. In H. Bradbury (ed.) *The Sage Handbook of Action Research: Participative Inquiry and Practice* (pp. 172–189). London: Sage.

Gelblum, B. (2017) Theresa May suppressed NINE reports proving immigration has little effect on employment or wages. *The London Economic*. Retrieved from https://www.thelondoneconomic.com/politics/theresa-may-suppressed-nine-reports-proving-immigration-has-little-effect-on-employment-or-wages/06/09/

Generations Working Together (2015) *Bringing Together Local Authorities and Intergenerational Practice in a Scottish Policy Context*.

Gilligan, C. (1993) *In a Different Voice: Psychological Theory and Women's Development*. Cambridge, MA: Harvard University Press.

Goodfellow, M. (2019) *Hostile Environment: How Immigrants Became Scapegoats*. London: Verso Books.

Gower, M. and McGuiness, T. (2020) The UK's refugee family reunion rules: A comprehensive framework? Retrieved from https://commonslibrary.parliament.uk/research-briefings/cbp-7511/

Gramling, D. (2016) *The Invention of Monolingualism*. New York: Bloomsbury.

Haeckel, E. (1866) *Generelle Morphologie der Organismen. Allgemeine Grundzüge der organischen Formen-Wissenschaft, mechanisch begründet durch die von C. Darwin reformirte Descendenz-Theorie, etc* (Vol. 2). Berlin: Druck und Verlag Georg Reimer.

Halliday, J. and Brooks, L. (2019) Johnson pledges to make all immigrants learn English. *The Guardian*. Retrieved from https://www.theguardian.com/politics/2019/jul/05/johnson-pledges-to-make-all-immigrants-learn-english

Han, C., Starkey, H. and Green, A. (2010) The politics of ESOL (English for speakers of other languages): Implications for citizenship and social justice. *International Journal of Lifelong Education* 29 (1), 63–76.

Haugen, E. (1972) *The Ecology of Language: Essays by Einar Haugen*: Stanford: Stanford University Press.

Haugen, E.L. (1979) Language ecology and the case of Faroese. In I. Rauch and G.F. Carr (eds) *Linguistic Method* (pp. 183–198). Berlin: De Gruyter Mouton.

Hirsu, L. and Bryson, E. (2017) *Sharing Lives, Sharing Languages; A Pilot Peer Education Project for New Scots' Social and Language Integration (January-June 2017) Evaluation Report*. Retrieved from https://www.scottishrefugeecouncil.org.uk/sharing-lives-sharing-languages/

Hobbs, L. (2021) *The Demonisation of Migrant Masculinities in British Politics*. https://www.e-ir.info/2021/04/20/the-demonisation-of-migrant-masculinities-in-british-politics/

Holmes, P., Fay, R., Andrews, J. and Attia, M. (2013) Researching multilingually: New theoretical and methodological directions. *International Journal of Applied Linguistics* 23 (3), 285–299.

Home Office (2020) *Family Reunion: for Refugees and Those with Humanitarian Protection*. Retrieved from https://assets.publishing.service.gov.uk/government/uploads/system/uploads/attachment_data/file/856915/family-reunion-guidance-v4.0-ext.pdf

Hornberger, N.H. and Link, H. (2012) Translanguaging and transnational literacies in multilingual classrooms: A biliteracy lens. *International Journal of Bilingual Education and Bilingualism* 15 (3), 261–278.

Horner, B., Lu, M.-Z., Royster, J.J. and Trimbur, J. (2011) Language difference in writing: Toward a translingual approach. *College English* 73 (3), 303–321.

House of Commons Library (2018) *The UK's Refugee Family Reunion Rules: Striking the Right Balance?* https://www.refworld.org/docid/58ac50564.html

Hughes, L. (2016) More Muslim women should 'learn English' to help tackle extremism. *The Telegraph*. Retrieved from https://www.telegraph.co.uk/news/uknews/terrorism-in-the-uk/12104556/David-Cameron-More-Muslim-women-should-learn-English-to-help-tackle-extremism.html

Ingold, T. (2011) *Being Alive: Essays on Movement, Knowledge and Description*. Abingdon: Routledge.

Joseph, J.E. (2004) *Language and Identity: National, Ethnic, Religious*. Basingstoke: Palgrave Macmillan.

Kale, A., Stupples, P. and Kindon, S. (2019) Feeling at home: A multisensory analysis of former refugee and host society residents' integration in Wellington, Aotearoa New Zealand. *Emotion, Space and Society* 33, 1–8.

Kearney, R. (2019) Linguistic hospitality-The risk of translation. *Research in Phenomenology* 49 (1), 1–8.

Kemmis, S., McTaggart, R. and Nixon, R. (2014) *Introducing Critical Participatory Action Research*. Cham: Springer.

Kibreab, G. (2003) Citizenship rights and repatriation of refugees. *International Migration Review* 37 (1), 24–73.

Kingsley, P. (2015) What caused the refugee crisis? You asked Google—here's the answer. *The Guardian*. Retrieved from https://www.theguardian.com/commentisfree/2015/dec/09/what-caused-the-refugee-crisis-google

Kramsch, C. (2002) Introduction: How can we tell the dancer from the dance. In C. Kramsch (ed.) *Language Acquisition and Language Socialization: Ecological Perspectives* (pp. 1–30). London: Bloomsbury.

Kramsch, C. (2008) Ecological perspectives on foreign language education. *Language Teaching* 41 (3), 389.
Kramsch, C., Levine, G.S. and Phipps, A. (2010) *Critical and Intercultural Theory and Language Pedagogy*. Boston: Heinle.
Kramsch, C. and Vork Steffensen, S. (2008) *Ecological Perspectives on Second Language Acquisition and Socialization*. Boston, MA: Springer US.
Kramsch, C. and Whiteside, A. (2008) Language ecology in multilingual settings. Towards a theory of symbolic competence. *Applied Linguistics* 29 (4), 645–671.
Kramsch, C.J. (2009) *The Multilingual Subject: What Foreign Language Learners Say About their Experience and why it Matters*. Oxford: Oxford University Press.
Kroll, J.F. and Bialystok, E. (2013) Understanding the consequences of bilingualism for language processing and cognition. *Journal of Cognitive Psychology* 25 (5), 497–514.
Law, J. (2004) *After Method: Mess in Social Science Research*. Abingdon: Routledge.
Lee, J.W. and Jenks, C. (2016) Doing translingual dispositions. *College Composition and Communication* 68 (2), 317–344.
Leonard, R.L. (2014) Multilingual writing as rhetorical attunement. *College English* 76 (3), 227–247.
Levine, G.S. (2020) *A Human Ecological Language Pedagogy*. Hoboken, NJ: Wiley.
Lewis, G., Jones, B. and Baker, C. (2012) Translanguaging: Developing its conceptualisation and contextualisation. *Educational Research and Evaluation* 18 (7), 655–670.
Li, W. (2013) Conceptual and methodological issues in bilingualism and multilingualism research. In T.K. Bhatia and W.C. Ritchie (eds) *The Handbook of Bilingualism and Multilingualism* (pp. 26–51). Oxford: Blackwell.
Li, W. (2017) Translanguaging as a practical theory of language. *Applied Linguistics* 39 (1), 9–30.
Little, D.G. (1991) *Learner Autonomy: Definitions, Issues and Problems*. Dublin: Authentik Language Learning Resources.
Lorde, A. (1984) The master's tools will never dismantle the master's house. In A. Lorde *Sister Outsider: Essays and Speeches* (pp. 10–14). Berkeley, CA: Ten Speed Press.
MacKinnon, C. (2015) *Glasgow's ESOL Providers English for Speakers of Other Languages (ESOL) in Glasgow: Research to Help Increase Engagement*. Retrieved from http://www.glasgowslearning.org.uk/documents/2426 Last accessed 08/02/2019.
MacSwan, J. (2017) A multilingual perspective on translanguaging. *American Educational Research Journal* 54 (1), 167–201.
Makoni, S. and Pennycook, A. (2007) *Disinventing and Reconstituting Languages*. Clevedon: Multilingual Matters.
Marsden, R. and Harris, C.V. (2015) *"We Started Life Again": Integration Experiences of Refugee Families Reuniting in Glasgow*. London: British Red Cross.
McDonald-Wilmsen, B. and Gifford, S.M. (2009) *Refugee Resettlement, Family Separation and Australia's Humanitarian Programme*. Geneva: UNHCR.
Meer, N., Peace, T. and Hill, E. (2018) *The Governance and Local Integration of Migrants and Europe's Refugees*. https://www.glimer.eu/wp-content/uploads/2018/08/Combined-Report.pdf
Meer, N., Peace, T. and Hill, E. (2019) *English Language Education for Asylum Seekers and Refugees in Scotland: Provision and Governance*. https://www.glimer.eu/wp-content/uploads/2019/09/Scotland_Language1.pdf
Meissner, F. and Vertovec, S. (2015) Comparing super-diversity. *Ethnic and Racial Studies* 38 (4), 541–555.
Meyer, J.H. and Land, R. (2005) Threshold concepts and troublesome knowledge (2): Epistemological considerations and a conceptual framework for teaching and learning. *Higher Education* 49 (3), 373–388.
Migration for Development and Equality (2022) Migration for Development and Equality. Retrieved from https://www.mideq.org/en/about-us/

Migration Scotland (2019) Asylum Seekers. Retrieved from http://www.migrationscotland.org.uk/migration-information/migration-statistics/asylum-seekers

Moles, K. (2008) A walk in thirdspace: Place, methods and walking. *Sociological Research Online* 13 (4), 31–39.

Moore, E., Bradley, J. and Simpson, J. (2020) *Translanguaging as Transformation: The Collaborative Construction of New Linguistic Realities*. Bristol: Multilingual Matters.

Morrice, L., Tip, L.K., Collyer, M. and Brown, R. (2019) 'You can't have a good integration when you don't have a good communication': English-language learning among resettled refugees in England. *Journal of Refugee Studies* 34 (1), 681–699.

Noddings, N. (2012) The caring relation in teaching. *Oxford Review of Education* 38 (6), 771–781.

Norton, B. (2013) *Identity and Language Learning: Extending the Conversation* (2nd edn). Bristol: Multilingual Matters.

Norwegian Refugee Council (2023) These 10 countries receive the most refugees. https://www.nrc.no/perspectives/2020/the-10-countries-that-receive-the-most-refugees/

Ortega y Gasset, J. (1957) *Man and People* (translated by W.R. Trask). New York: W.W. Norton and Company.

Otheguy, R., García, O. and Reid, W. (2015) Clarifying translanguaging and deconstructing named languages: A perspective from linguistics. *Applied Linguistics Review* 6 (3), 281–307.

Pavlenko, A. and Blackledge, A. (2004) *Negotiation of Identities in Multilingual Contexts*. Clevedon: Multilingual Matters.

Peat, J. (2018) Theresa May: "We can deport first and hear appeals later". *The London Economic*. Retrieved from https://www.thelondoneconomic.com/news/theresa-may-we-can-deport-first-and-hear-appeals-later/19/04/

Pennycook, A. and Otsuji, E. (2014) Metrolingual multitasking and spatial repertoires: 'Pizza mo two minutes coming'. *Journal of Sociolinguistics* 18 (2), 161–184.

Phillipson, R. and Skutnabb-Kangas, T. (1996) English only worldwide or language ecology? *TESOL Quarterly* 30 (3), 429–452.

Phipps, A. (2007) *Learning the Arts of Linguistic Survival: Languaging, Tourism, Life*. Clevedon: Channel View Publications.

Phipps, A. (2008) Was bleibt? After class and after culture: Intercultural German Life. In R.A. Schulz and E. Tschirner (eds) *Communicating Across Borders: Developing Intercultural Competence in German as a Foreign Language* (pp. 217–241). Munich: Iudicium Verlag.

Phipps, A. (2009) Tourism and languaging. In T. Jamal and M. Robinson (eds) *The Sage Handbook of Tourism Studies* (pp. 658–671). London: SAGE.

Phipps, A. (2011) Travelling languages? Land, languaging and translation. *Language and Intercultural Communication* 11 (4), 364–376.

Phipps, A. (2013a) Intercultural ethics: Questions of methods in language and intercultural communication. *Language and Intercultural Communication* 13 (1), 10–26.

Phipps, A. (2013b) Linguistic incompetence: Giving an account of researching multilingually. *International Journal of Applied Linguistics* 23 (3), 329–341.

Phipps, A. (2018) Language plenty, refugees and the post-Brexit world: New practices from Scotland. In M. Kelly (ed.) *Languages after Brexit* (pp. 95–107). Cham: Springer.

Phipps, A. (2019a) Bearing witness: The burden of individual responsibility and the rule of law. In S. Karly Kehoe, E. Alisic and J.-C. Heilinger (eds) *Responsibility for Refugee and Migrant Integration* (pp. 9–24). Berlin: De Gruyter.

Phipps, A. (2019b) *Decolonising Multilingualism: Struggles to Decreate*. Bristol: Multilingual Matters.

Phipps, A. and Fassetta, G. (2015) A critical analysis of language policy in Scotland. *European Journal of Language Policy* 7 (1), 5–27.

Phipps, A. and Gonzalez, M. (2004) *Modern Languages: Learning and Teaching in an Intercultural Field*. London: Sage.

Polwart, K. (2019) Wind Resistance. Retrieved from https://www.karinepolwart.com/home/blog/new-album-a-pocket-of-wind-resistance

Pöyhönen, S., Kokkonen, L., Tarnanen, M. and Lappalainen, M. (2020) Belonging, trust and relationships: Collaborative photography with unaccompanied minors. In E. Moore, J. Bradley and J. Simpson (eds) *Translanguaging as Transformation: The Collaborative Construction of New Linguistic Realities* (pp. 58–75). Bristol: Multilingual Matters.

Poza, L. (2017) Translanguaging: Definitions, implications and further needs in burgeoning inquiry. *Berkeley Review of Education* 6 (2).

Prada, J. and Turnbull, B. (2018) The role of translanguaging in the multilingual turn: Driving philosophical and conceptual renewal in language education. *EuroAmerican Journal of Applied Linguistics and Languages* 5 (2), 8–23.

Prince, R. (2010) David Cameron: Net immigration will be capped at tens of thousands. *The Telegraph*. Retrieved from https://www.telegraph.co.uk/news/politics/6961675/David-Cameron-net-immigration-will-be-capped-at-tens-of-thousands.html

Rauch, D.P., Naumann, J. and Jude, N. (2012) Metalinguistic awareness mediates effects of full biliteracy on third-language reading proficiency in Turkish–German bilinguals. *International Journal of Bilingualism* 16 (4), 402–418.

Refugee Action (2016) *Let Refugees Learn: Challenges and Opportunities to Improve Language Provision to Refugees in England*. Retrieved from https://www.refugee-action.org.uk/resource/report-let-refugees-learn

Refugee Action (2022) Facts about refugees. Retrieved from https://www.refugee-action.org.uk/about/facts-about-refugees/

Refugee Council (2022) Helping refugees in the UK. Retrieved from https://www.refugeecouncil.org.uk/helping-refugees-in-the-uk/

Richardson, L. and St Pierre, E. (2018) Writing: A method of inquiry. In N.K. Denzin and Y.S. Lincoln (eds) *The SAGE Handbook of Qualitative Research*. London: SAGE.

Roberts, C. and Baynham, M. (2006) Introduction to the special issue: Research in adult ESOL. *Linguistics and Education* 17 (1), 1–5.

Rutherford, W.E. (1987) The meaning of grammatical consciousness-raising. *World Englishes* 6 (3), 209–216.

Sample, E. (2007) State practice and the family unity of African refugees. *Forced Migration Review* 28 (July), 50–52.

Scaife, H. (2018) *Welsh Government Integrated Impact Assessment: Welsh Language Impact Assessment*. Retrieved from Wales: https://gov.wales/sites/default/files/publications/2018-12/welsh-government-integrated-impact-assessment.pdf

Schatzki, T.R. (2002) *The Site of the Social: A Philosophical Account of the Constitution of Social Life and Change*. University Park, PA: Penn State Press.

Schellekens, P. (2008) *The Oxford ESOL Handbook* (Vol. 62). Oxford: Oxford University Press.

Scottish Government (2014) *Adult Learning in Scotland. Statement of Ambition*. Retrieved from https://www.education.gov.scot/Documents/adult-learning-statement.pdf

Scottish Government (2018) *New Scots Refugee Integration Strategy*. Retrieved from https://www.gov.scot/publications/new-scots-refugee-integration-strategy-2018-2022/

Scottish Government, Convention of Scottish Local Authoritiesand Scottish Refugee Council (2017) *New Scots: Integrating Refugees in Scotland's Communities: 2014– 2017: Final Report* (9781786526960) Retrieved from https://www.gov.scot/publications/new-scots-integrating-refugees-scotlands-communities-2014-2017-final-report-9781786526960/

Scottish Government and Education Scotland (2015) *Welcoming Our Learners: Scotland's ESOL Strategy 2015 – 2020*. Retrieved from https://www.education.gov.scot/Documents/ESOLStrategy2015to2020.pdf

Shuttleworth, S.R. (2018) Moving Language: The Language Geographies of Refugees and Asylum-Seekers in Glasgow. Unpublished PhD thesis, University of Glasgow.

Simpson, J. (2016) English for speakers of other languages: language education and migration. In G. Hall (ed.) *The Routledge Handbook of English Language Teaching* (pp. 177–190). Abingdon: Routledge.
Simpson, J. (2020) Translanguaging in ESOL: Competing positions and collaborative relationships. In E. Moore, J. Bradley and J. Simpson (eds) *Translanguaging as Transformation: The Collaborative Construction of New Linguistic Realities* (pp. 41–57). Bristol: Multilingual Matters.
Simpson, J. and Cooke, M. (2017) Recognising multilingual realities in ESOL: The NATECLA National Conference 2017 Keynote. *Language Issues: The ESOL Journal* 28, 4–11.
Skutnabb-Kangas, T. (1995) Multilingualism and the education of minority children. In O. García and C. Baker (eds) *Policy and Practice in Bilingual Education: A Reader Extending the Foundations* (pp. 40–56). Clevedon: Multilingual Matters.
Smith, L.T. (1999) *Decolonizing Methodologies: Research and Indigenous Peoples*. London: Zed Books Limited.
Smith, L.T. (2013) *Decolonizing Methodologies: Research and Indigenous Peoples* (2nd edn). London: Zed Books Ltd.
Staver, A. (2008) *Family Reunification: A Right for Forced Migrants?* Oxford: Refugee Studies Centre.
Stoudt, B.G. and Torre, M.E. (2014) *The Morris Justice Project: Participatory Action Research*. London: SAGE Publications.
Swain, M. (2006) Languaging, agency and collaboration in advanced second language proficiency. In H. Byrnes (ed.) *Advanced Language Learning: The Contribution of Halliday and Vygotsky* (pp. 95–108). London: Continuum.
Swain, M. and Lapkin, S. (2000) Task-based second language learning: The uses of the first language. *Language Teaching Research* 4 (3), 251–274.
Thurlow, C. (2016) Queering critical discourse studies or/and performing 'post-class' ideologies. *Critical Discourse Studies* 13 (5), 485–514.
Ticheloven, A., Blom, E., Leseman, P. and McMonagle, S. (2019) Translanguaging challenges in multilingual classrooms: Scholar, teacher and student perspectives. *International Journal of Multilingualism* 18 (3), 494–514. https://doi.org/10.1080/14 790718.2019.1686002
Tsuda, Y. (1994) The diffusion of English: Its impact on culture and communication. *Keio Communication Review* 16 (1) 49–61.
Tudor, I. (2003) Learning to live with complexity: Towards an ecological perspective on language teaching. *System* 31 (1), 1–12.
Turner, V. (1969) Liminality and communitas. In V. Turner (ed.) *The Ritual Process: Structure and Anti-Structure* (pp. 94–130). London: Routledge.
Tyler, I. (2006) 'Welcome to Britain' the cultural politics of asylum. *European Journal of Cultural Studies* 9 (2), 185–202.
Immigration and Asylum Act 1999 (1999) https://www.legislation.gov.uk/ukpga/1999/33/contents
Immigration Act 2014 (2014) https://www.legislation.gov.uk/ukpga/2014/22/contents/enacted
Immigration Act 2016 (2016) https://www.legislation.gov.uk/ukpga/2016/19/contents/enacted
UN General Assembly (1948) Universal declaration of human rights. *UN General Assembly* 302 (2), 14–25.
UN General Assembly (1951) Convention relating to the status of refugees. *United Nations, Treaty Series* 189 (1), 137.
van Lier, L. (2002) An ecological-semiotic perspective on language and linguistics. In C. Kramsch (ed.) *Language Acquisition and Language Socialization: Ecological Perspectives* (pp. 140–164). London: Continuum.

van Lier, L. (2004a) The Ecology of Language Learning. Paper presented at the Conference proceedings UC Language Consortium Conference on Theoretical and Pedagogical Perspectives, March 26–28.

van Lier, L. (2004b) The semiotics and ecology of language learning. *Utbildning and Demokrati* 13 (3), 79–103.

van Lier, L. (2006) *The Ecology and Semiotics of Language Learning: A Sociocultural Perspective* (Vol. 3). Cham: Springer Science and Business Media.

van Lier, L. (2010) The ecology of language learning: Practice to theory, theory to practice. *Procedia-Social and Behavioral Sciences* 3, 2–6.

Vertovec, S. (2007) Super-diversity and its implications. *Ethnic and Racial Studies* 30 (6), 1024–1054.

Vertovec, S. (2013) *Anthropology of Migration and Multiculturalism: New Directions*. New York: Routledge.

Voegelin, C.F. and Voegelin, F.M. (1964) Languages of the world: Native America Fascicle One. *Anthropological Linguistics* 6 (6), 1–149.

Vote Leave (2016) http://www.voteleavetakecontrol.org/briefing_control.html.

Watt, N. and Mulholland, H. (2011) Immigrants who fail to integrate have created 'discomfort', says Cameron. *The Guardian*. Retrieved from https://www.theguardian.com/politics/2011/apr/14/immigrants-fail-integrate-discomfort-cameron

Welsh Government (2019a) *English for Speakers of Other Languages (ESOL) Policy for Wales*. Retrieved from https://gov.wales/sites/default/files/publications/2018-11/english-for-speakers-of-other-languages-esol-policy-for-wales.pdf

Welsh Government (2019b) *Nation of Sanctuary – Refugee and Asylum Seeker Plan*. https://www.gov.wales/sites/default/files/publications/2019-03/nation-of-sanctuary-refugee-and-asylum-seeker-plan_0.pdf

White, J. and Hendry, L. (2011) *Family Reunion for Refugees in the UK Understanding Support Needs*. London: British Red Cross.

Williams, C. (1994) An evaluation of learning and teaching methods in the context of bilingual secondary education. Unpublished doctoral thesis, University of Wales, Bangor.

Woitsch, U. (2012) Walking Through the Intercultural Field. An Ethnographic Study on Intercultural Language Learning as a Spatial-embodied Practice. Unpublished PhD thesis, University of Glasgow.

Yuval-Davis, N. (2011) Power, intersectionality and the politics of belonging. FREIA (Feminist Research Center in Aalborg), Aalborg University. https://www.brunel.ac.uk/research/Documents/N.YuvalDavisintersectionality.pdf

Yuval-Davis, N., Wemyss, G. and Cassidy, K. (2019) *Bordering*. Chichester: John Wiley and Sons.

Index

Ager, A. and Strang, A. 22, 25, 33, 172
audibility 138, 193–195, 197

Baker, C. 45, 46
Baynham, M. 193, 194
Becker, A. xix, 48, 140
bilingualism 24, 45, 47, 49, 79
Blackledge, A. 41, 51, 52, 134, 136
Blommaert, J. 38–39, 51–52, 53
Bundesamt für Migration und Flüchtlinge (BAMF) 82, 85, 89, 93
Butler, J. 61–62, 101, 127, 137, 153, 163, 192, 208

Canagarajah, S. 45, 48, 49, 50, 52, 62, 136, 140, 164, 178
code-switching 47, 89, 94, 113, 177
co-learning relationship 65, 107, 114–115, 132, 133, 136, 141, 147, 171, 177, 180, 207, 208, 211
communitas 9, 141, 158, 193
Creese, A. 21, 42, 47, 49, 193
crystallisation 67, 123, 201
CPAR 55, 60–61, 65, 97, 101, 121–122, 156, 159, 180, 207, 212, 214

decolonising methodology 57–58, 68, 101, 122, 128, 132, 207–208
decolonising multilingualism 8, 41, 42–45, 207–208
dispersal
  Scotland 21, 22
  Wales 69, 71

EAL 24
eclecticism (as method) 8, 59–60, 201
embodiment, embody 139, 151, 157, 159, 160–161, 164, 176, 179, 190, 191, 205
emergent bilingual 53, 216

emotional labour 9, 115, 131, 137–141, 148, 167, 208, 212
empowerment, empower 2, 50, 52, 54, 55, 56, 57, 60, 98, 169, 170, 178, 198, 200, 201, 206, 209, 216, 217
ESOL Strategy (Scotland) 22, 26–29, 33, 34, 215
ESOL Strategy (Wales) 71, 72, 73, 202

family reunion 1, 8, 13, 18, 27, 29–33, 34, 54, 55, 84, 98, 99, 120, 148, 154, 202, 203, 204, 210, 214
feminist ethics of care 66–67, 132, 137–141, 148, 153, 158, 211
Freire, P. 97, 118, 127
funding 23, 24, 26, 27, 29, 32, 34, 72, 75, 76, 85, 89, 93, 202, 203, 212

García, O. 39, 53, 178, 180, 187, 193, 194, 197, 216
García, O. and Li, W. 1, 45, 46, 47, 49, 50, 65, 107, 114, 128, 132, 133, 136, 137, 147, 184, 188, 189, 207, 208
Gramling, D. 41, 43

Haugen, E. 36–38, 41, 45, 82, 150, 152, 160, 205
hostile environment 2, 3, 8, 13, 17–19, 23, 30, 34, 70, 192
human geography 9, 59, 60, 118, 150, 151, 152–153, 157, 176, 200, 205, 211, 215

identity 8, 9, 20, 36, 38, 39, 44, 48, 49, 51–54, 55, 56, 58, 62, 64, 67, 112, 115, 118, 134, 136, 152, 153, 158, 163, 164, 176, 178, 185, 196, 198, 199, 206, 208, 210, 216

idiolect 46–47
Ingold, T. 160, 205
integration course, German 9, 82, 83, 85–86, 88, 89, 90, 91, 93, 94, 202, 207
intergenerational learning 9, 65–66, 93, 99, 144–146, 213, 216
intergenerational relationships 9, 116, 128, 143–146, 209–210, 211
interpreters 67
interdisciplinarity 8, 37, 59, 60, 150, 200, 202, 215
investment 9, 49, 51–52, 101, 115, 116, 199, 122, 128, 130, 132–137, 146, 153, 154, 156, 157, 185, 192, 198, 207, 208, 213, 216

Kramsch, C. 37, 38, 40, 43, 44, 150, 158, 161, 163, 187

language biography 62, 137
language separation 8, 45, 46, 94, 203
latitudinal knowledge 60, 208, 215
layered simultaneity 38–39, 161–164, 205
Levine, G. 40, 117, 132, 164, 193
Li, W. 41, 48, 179, 206
liminality 9, 52, 62, 63–64, 117, 141, 152–153, 158, 208
linguistic dominance (of English) 8, 41, 42–45, 56, 94, 178, 206
linguistic hospitality 2, 4, 6, 119, 192, 200, 201, 209, 211
linguistic incompetence 58, 62, 63, 94, 114, 135, 137, 187, 191–192, 200, 208–209
linguistic repertoire 2, 6–7, 37, 45, 46, 48, 50, 62, 65, 80, 82, 113, 114, 118, 134, 177–178, 188, 187, 200, 210, 214

Makoni, S. and Pennycook, A. 41, 46, 52
metalinguistic awareness 49, 50, 180, 182–185, 205
monolingualism 36, 41–42, 43, 44, 45, 199, 206
multilingualism xvii, 1, 7, 8, 19, 20, 24, 34, 36, 41–45, 51, 58, 78, 79, 180, 201, 207, 216
multilingual turn 44

New Scots Refugee Integration Strategy 8, 22–26, 27, 28, 33, 34, 35, 50, 57, 70, 71, 92, 115, 116, 152, 156, 189, 198, 199, 200, 207, 209, 210, 212, 213, 215
Noddings, N. 60, 127, 132, 138, 141, 193, 208, 209, 215
Norton, B. 9, 51–53, 58, 101, 115, 119, 132, 133, 136, 156, 198

Otheguy, R. 44, 45, 46, 47, 49, 51

Phillipson, R. and Skutnabb-Kangas, T. 43, 199, 214
Phipps, A. xvii–xviii, 1, 6, 8, 13, 28, 43, 51, 57, 58, 61, 62, 64, 83, 127, 138, 139, 151, 152, 179, 187, 190, 192, 195, 197, 206, 207
praxis xviii, 6, 8, 97, 118, 119, 120

receptive listening 138, 193, 209
research design 8, 54, 55, 56–57, 68, 207
researching multilingually xvii, 1, 6, 42, 54, 62–63, 136

sharing lives, sharing languages 25, 217
Simpson, J. 20, 41, 44, 52, 54, 133, 178, 180, 181, 199, 206, 211, 212, 215
Simpson, J. and Cooke, M. 48, 133, 214
social cohesion 19–21, 24, 41, 206, 207
social justice 42–45, 50, 118, 132, 178, 193, 207
Shuttleworth, S. 118, 152, 157, 158
Skutnabb-Kangas, T. 41
super-diversity 41–42 , 206

technology 186, 187, 205, 217
translanguaging 1, 7, 8, 9, 10, 36, 37, 38, 43, 44, 45–52, 54, 55, 57, 58, 65, 69, 70, 76, 89, 90, 94, 101, 104, 109, 112, 113, 118, 119, 120, 124, 129, 132, 135, 146, 172, 177, 178, 183, 184, 187–192, 197, 199, 200, 202, 203, 204, 207, 208, 210, 211, 213, 214, 216
in practice 49–50
in Wales 78–80, 81, 82
origins and definitions 45–48
strategies and stances 179–180
within an ecological framework 48–49

Thurlow, C. xiii, 59, 127, 191
Turner, V. 63–64, 141, 158, 208
two-way integration 22, 24, 51, 192, 200, 201, 209, 210, 215

Van Lier, L. 38, 39, 40, 51, 53, 124, 136, 150, 158, 163, 172, 190
Vertovec, S. 42, 49, 178, 206

voice 27, 50, 53, 136, 138, 189, 207, 209
voice and audibility 193–195

Welsh Nation of Sanctuary Plan 70–72, 92
Williams, C. 45, 46, 49, 50

Yuval-Davis, N. 19, 66, 141

For Product Safety Concerns and Information please contact our EU Authorised Representative:

Easy Access System Europe

Mustamäe tee 50

10621 Tallinn

Estonia

gpsr.requests@easproject.com